About the co-author

Debbie Ritchie holds a degree in Education from Wollongong University, and has taught full-time since 1978. In 2001 she gained a Diploma in Professional Children's Writing through the Australian College of Journalism. Following this, she began writing short fiction for the Department of Education's *NSW School Magazine*. Debbie has taught creative writing classes within programs for Gifted and Talented students in the Southern Highlands, with some of her students going on to win major writing awards.

Debbie and Donna Carson share birth dates – 31 March 1957 – and have been close, personal friends for over 25 years.

A true story of betrayal and survival

JUDAS KISSES

DONNA CARSON
WITH DEBBIE RITCHIE

Hardie Grant Books

Published in Australia in 2007 by
Hardie Grant Books
85 High Street
Prahran, Victoria 3181, Australia
www.hardiegrant.com.au

Grateful acknowledgement is made to the following for permission to
reprint previously published material:
Universal Music Publishing: Excerpt from 'Sadie the Cleaning Lady', words and music by
Raymond Gilmore/David White/John Madara © Champion Music Corp/Double Diamond
Music adm. by Universal Music Publishing Pty. Ltd. All rights reserved. International
copyright secured. Reprinted with permission.
Alfred Publishing: Excerpt from 'Diamonds Are Forever', words and music by John
Barry/Don Black © 1971 United Artists Music Ltd, for Australia and New Zealand: Alfred
Publishing (Australia) Pty Ltd. All rights reserved. International copyright secured.
Journalist and author Sandra Lee: Excerpt from 'Courage Prevails, Justice Fails', *Daily
Telegraph* © Sandra Lee, 1996.

National Library of Australia Cataloguing-in-Publication data:

Ritchie, Debbie, 1957– .
    Judas kisses : a true story of betrayal and survival.
    ISBN 13: 978 1 74066 435 6.
    ISBN 10: 1 74066 435 3.
    1. Carson, Donna, 1957– . 2. Abused women – Australia –
    Biography. 3. Burns and scalds – Patients – Australia –
    Biography. 4. Custody of children – Australia. I. Carson,
    Donna 1957– . II. Title.
362.8292092

Cover and text design by Sandy Cull, gogoGingko
Cover photograph by Geoff Tull Photography
Typesetting by Kirby Jones
Printed and bound in Australia by Griffin Press

10 9 8 7 6 5 4 3

Dedicated to those who haven't survived.

Donna Carson

For my parents, Tom and Inge Mullette.

So sorry you missed it.

Debbie Ritchie

DIAMOND: An exceptionally hard precious stone made of crystallised carbon formed under immense and continuous pressure. Diamonds must be cut from the rough and reshaped before their true beauty is revealed.

Prologue

'These violent delights have violent ends,' wrote William Shakespeare.

My violent delight came to stay in the summer of 1994. The end came just a few months later, and left me confined to a hospital bed, swaying between life and death for the next six months. During this time I was lost in a haze of flashbacks, painful medical procedures and mind-numbing drugs, but as that endless winter turned into spring, there were times when I would surface, when I was able to think back on my small, plain life and wonder, how did it come to this?

In searching for answers, I was forced to consider many things, in particular the double-edged sword of romance, its promise of pleasure, of warmth and belonging, but also its hidden snares. For me, Shakespeare's words from *Romeo and Juliet*, that timeless tale of love and tragedy, encapsulate the few short months leading up to my time in hospital, when life as I knew it began to disintegrate.

Before that, I'd led an ordinary sort of existence in a little town outside Dubbo, in western New South Wales. Geurie is surrounded by the vast, flat plains of wheat, sheep and cattle country, and capped by wide blue skies. In the afternoons, noisy clouds of white cockatoos would erupt over the heated landscape. The locals were a mix of tough, down-to-earth farmhands and small business owners, as well as office workers and government employees who, like me, travelled to nearby Dubbo or Wellington for work. Like most country towns, Geurie had its share of 'characters' – mostly old folk who'd been there forever – people such as Garnett Mawbey, originally from nearby Breelong and famous for his real-life role in *The Chant of Jimmy Blacksmith*. He was the tiny child who, in 1899, had hidden beneath a bed while Jimmy Governor, his brother Joe and friend Jackie Underwood went on their vengeful spree through the Mawbey homestead, hacking or clubbing to death the rest of the occupants.

Sitting in the town's main pub, the Mitchell Inn, listening to the locals tell their stories was just one form of entertainment in Geurie. There were barbecues and cricket matches, and dances and fundraising nights at the local bowling club. But underneath all the laughter and good-natured banter, there was a shifting, restless feeling, fuelled by alcohol, idleness and heat.

I wouldn't say I was an especially happy person back then, but I always tried to make the best of things. I threw myself into the life of the town and my teaching career at Orana Heights Public School in Dubbo. I loved the kids I taught and more than anything I loved my own two sons, Coe and Bodean. But I couldn't escape the fact that my marriage was unhappy; after many years my husband's love affair with the drink began to transcend his love for me.

When Brian left, I yearned more than ever for romance. I was desperate for some sort of Hollywood hero to arrive on my doorstep and sweep me off my feet, look after me, make me feel whole again.

'Be careful what you wish for,' the old saying goes.

Enter my violent delight.

Garry was a handsome, dark-haired farm labourer, tanned and muscled, with an easy smile and a chivalrous yet vulnerable way about him. This was not the first time I'd been involved with him. He was several years younger than me, but I felt I deserved a bit of fun and excitement after the tiring years of being both my family's breadwinner and caregiver.

I didn't look too bad for 36 – in the mirror I still saw that blue-eyed, long-legged 21-year-old who'd arrived in town a decade and a half before. Perhaps I had a few extra freckles from the blazing central western sun, and maybe the odd wrinkle or two, but I thought Garry and I looked good together, like we belonged with each other.

From the start he did everything that Brian had avoided and had left me to do: mowing the lawn and fixing things around the house; and spending time with the boys, playing with my toddler Bodean, or kicking the ball around the yard with 12-year-old Coe. He even took us on outings and shopping excursions, showering us with presents.

In January 1994, Garry moved into our modest cream-brick bungalow and what had begun as a tentative rekindling of our once covert relationship soon turned into a passionate affair.

Betrayal can come from anyone – friends, loved ones, neighbours – I know that now. I don't think everyone's treacherous and can name countless good and honest people who never gave up on me and whose love and faith got me through my darkest days. But it's a sad fact: betrayal is like treason. Sometimes the people who are meant to be on your side shaft you instead.

The worst part about being betrayed? You don't see it coming.

Take the afternoon it all started, back in April 1994. I was at home, supposedly the safest place there is, but that day I was the victim of the Trojan horse tactic. There had been early warning signs, of course – there was a sullen side to Garry which, desperate to preserve my dream, I did my best to ignore. Not long after he moved in, Garry's moodiness would develop into angry outbursts and fits of jealous rage, often followed by tears of remorse when he realised he'd gone too far. His weeping always softened me. And secretly I worried that maybe he was right: maybe it was my fault he got so mad.

I wasn't totally blind though. A few weeks before Easter, when the pushing started, I decided to take a stand: over the holiday weekend I would talk to Garry about his behaviour. But on that still autumn evening, when I said he couldn't take the car, it was too late for talk. I was worried he'd have an accident: the old bomb was unregistered – no lights, hardly any brakes – and, to make matters worse, he'd been drinking. The brick-red Corolla was out of petrol, so he was using a plastic container to siphon some from my Ford Escort into the Corolla's tank.

I remember the rest of that day in snapshots – a rapid series of freeze-frames barrelling through my head ...

I'm next to Garry, in the carport. I see my hand, reaching out to take the container from him. He goes ballistic. Spittle flies from his open mouth.

'You stupid fucking cunt what the fucking hell do you think you're doing bitch fucking bitch?'

He starts pushing me around. He's wiry but farm-fit. He gets up a rhythm: grab shove grab shove. He rips the front of my ropey crocheted top. He rips the sleeves. He tears it away in handfuls. It's coming off in tatters.

I'm lurching all over the place, flopping back and forth like a rag doll between the rusting Corolla and the side of the house. My head slams against the pale bricks. I feel a trickle of blood. I'm clinging to the petrol container, trying to stay upright. A voice inside my head is screaming: If he gets you on the ground you're a goner. You've had it. He'll kill you.

The container is yanked from my hand. It swings in Garry's grasp. There's petrol everywhere. It's spilt down the wall, across the steps, over the dirt floor of the carport. It's all over our hands.

Coe is standing in the kitchen in shorts and a T-shirt. His terrified face swims behind the glass sliding door as he stares into the carport. My blond toddler is clinging to Coe's leg, his apple cheeks stained with tears. He tips back his head and begins to wail.

My heel catches on the step. I stumble backwards. I twist my face towards the glass. The door slides open, just a crack.

I yell out to Coe, 'Stay inside and lock the door!'

Garry is startled and I scramble upright. In seconds, he starts again. I must fight back. I bunch my fists, jab at his chest. I grab handfuls of his hair. He's too strong. Eventually he pummels me sideways. I stagger out towards open space.

He has the container.

I cop the petrol. A stinking chemical wave smacks me in the face. It's in my hair. It's all down the front of me, all over my chest. My jeans are saturated. My bra is saturated. I can taste the oily fuel on my lips, feel it drip from the end of my nose. My eyes are stinging. I scrub at them with my knuckles.

I hear a click. Silence. Another click. I force my eyes open.

There's a gigantic hand, right up in my face. Poking out above the curve of his fingers is the silver tip of a lighter. His thumb rests on the top. I alter my focus from his thumb to his face. His blue eyes are crazy, his wet lips twisted, his teeth bared like an animal's. A sheen of sweat glistens over the black stubble around his mouth.

I'm running in kitten heels, jeans and black, lacy bra. My top is gone. My hair, soaked with petrol, springs around my bare shoulders. I'm out the other side of the carport now and careering into the ragged backyard of my half-acre block. In the fading light I pelt through the overgrown grass and past the Hills Hoist. A lone cotton shirt hangs limply from the line.

I head towards the sagging fence at the bottom of the yard. I look over my shoulder to see if Garry's following and, as I turn, there's a tumbling, whooshing sound, a sudden roaring suck of wind followed by an ear-splitting crack as the air explodes, bright orange in my wake. I see a furious golden trail of flames behind me. I'm alight. I begin to scream.

Coe is at the back door. His voice tunnels through the noise and confusion. It's my lifeline. 'Roll, Mum! Roll!'

I throw myself on the ground near a cluster of newly planted saplings and begin to roll, trying to smother the flames. Ten times, 20 times, 30 times. Backwards and forwards I go.

I try to beat myself out but it's useless. Everything is on fire. My hands are on fire. My chest is on fire. My hair, my legs. I'm engulfed in a searing, white agony, as though I'm being dragged over razor wire. My skin blisters and peels. It's curling away, disintegrating in sheets. I can smell it.

Now I'm still, exhausted and caught in a thick plume of smoke. I lie on my right side and stare through the grey air at the back fence. This is it, I think. I did my best to save myself, but my best wasn't good enough.

I know Coe is nearby. I want to see my boy. As I go, I want to fix his face in my mind. I heave myself over and look up and across. The lights of the house are on, the windows pale yellow in the encroaching dusk. Coe is standing on the back porch outside the laundry. He's in silhouette. Behind him shines a blinding aura.

With his image fixed, I squeeze my eyes shut. I'm waiting for the pain to stop. I'm waiting for heaven. A strange calm slips over me. I'm almost free.

It's April Fool's Day and, even more ironically, Good Friday, that sacrosanct day of mourning on the Christian calendar. In the garden of Gethsemane, Judas Iscariot has already betrayed Jesus, pressing his lips to the cheek of Christ in a sign to the waiting soldiers. Judas kisses. If you look, they're everywhere.

It's around 5.30 in the afternoon. Tea is cooking. The washing is on. The kids' Easter eggs, symbols of new life, are safely hidden on top of the cupboard. I lie facing the house, curled up in the foetal position, unconscious.

When I wake, I'm sure I'm dead. With a flutter of anticipation I open my eyes. I'm curious to see what heaven looks like. Through the long blades of grass, I see instead my own backyard. I'm still here. I know my injuries must be horrendous. I know I'm in for the fight of my life. To put it bluntly, I know I'm in hell.

There are people around.

'My children. Hang on to them until my mother gets here,' I croak. I struggle to explain what happened and who did this to me.

Water is spraying from the hose. It's so cool. It feels good. I ask for more.

I look down and see my bleached midriff, my exposed breasts. My bra has burnt away. The underwire has melted into my skin. I tell my neighbour to cover me, but she won't listen. I'm embarrassed. I'm getting angry. Finally she snatches the shirt from the clothesline and covers me with it.

There are flashing lights, the wail of sirens. Someone is tugging at my fingers. They're taking my rings.

After all that, they're stealing my jewellery.

Life

One

I wasn't always Donna Carson. I was born Donna Lee Leonard on 31 March 1957 under Aries, the fire sign. Although I'd never thought of fire as particularly symbolic, let alone indicative of my personality, after that Good Friday in 1994 it became a potent symbol of misguided and destructive love. When I looked back over my life, I realised fire had in fact made a number of small but ominous appearances, the first being at my sister Kathryn's wedding when I was 12.

If God was preparing to send me a warning about the dangers of hasty relationships, I was oblivious. After all, like most of my friends, I was a romance addict, brought up on *Golden Years of Hollywood* love sagas. Well before Kathryn's big day, I became caught up in the excitement of the preparations: a whirlwind of activity dampened only by a persistent anxiety that I would somehow mess things up for the bride-to-be. Sissy's fury at my lack of breasts didn't help my confidence, let alone my fragile self-esteem.

'I'm not having a flat-chested bridesmaid,' she declared. 'Get yourself a bra and we can stuff it with tissues.'

My beautiful sister was the star of our small family. I inherited the strawberry-blond hair, lanky body, pale skin and freckles from my father's Irish ancestry, but Sissy was fine-boned and striking, with a perfect waist, perfect hips and, of course, a small but perfect bosom. Mum's father was Aboriginal, part of the Collis clan, originally from around the lower Botany/ Yarra Bay area of Sydney, and Sissy was blessed with Mum's olive skin, thick, dark hair and deep-set eyes.

I thought she was exotic. I adored her and wanted to be just like her. If I could achieve this, then everyone would love me the way they loved her. She was expected to do something with her life, whereas I was 'the girl next door' who would no doubt go to work in the local boot factory where my mother still toiled from seven-thirty to four, five days a week.

Kathryn was only 18 when she got married. Despite the prophecies of greatness, she'd left Sydney Girls' High at the end of fourth form, got a job in a bank and moved out of home to flat with a girlfriend. Now she was determined to marry Eric, a fellow bank clerk, as soon as possible, nagging my parents to sign the necessary papers that would allow the ceremony to proceed. In my mind, her pending marriage to a pint-sized Elvis Presley look-alike, complete with sidelevers and flares, gave her more status than any sort of career or stardom.

The conversation about my chest took place in the sparsely furnished but spotless lounge room of our two-storey semi in Sydney's Redfern. Sissy had dropped in after work and the neighbourhood teatime smells – corned beef and cabbage, fried sausages and baked lamb cooked in dripping – were wafting through the back door. From where I stood I could see past Sissy and out the window onto the street: a landscape of red-brick flats with a few straggly shrubs and ragged patches of lawn, and, behind these, a wall of high-rises, touted as a vision of the future and the answer to Sydney's housing problems. As dusk fell, the blue-collar workers arrived home, sweaty and exhausted after another long day. This last leg of their journey was on foot, but they would have travelled most of the way on public transport, jammed into the green and cream buses, or the old red rattlers that shuffled through Redfern railway station.

Soon I'd hear the creak of our metal gate and see Mum's familiar figure, weary in her thick nylon stockings, sensible shoes and faded cotton dress, with a cardigan slung over one arm and her white, vinyl work bag hanging from the other. Our corner of Redfern was a community of battlers, and my parents were no exception. In those days, we looked out for one another; we were in the same boat.

As soon as Mum walked through the door, lowering her bag onto the bare floorboards with a sigh, Sissy started up again. I stood still, in front of the window, while they appraised my top half. Looking down at my bare feet, gangly in my green and red South Sydney jumper and no-name jeans and still clutching a pair of wire-cutters, I wondered just what I'd done to deserve all this criticism. I was grubby from adjusting the wires on the rabbit hutch in the backyard – as Dad had instructed me over the previous weekend – but instead of being thanked for coming home from school to peel potatoes, sweep the floor then work in the backyard until nightfall, I was being talked about like some second-rate addition to the family that everyone had to make the best of. Great, I was going to have pretend breasts for the wedding. It seemed I couldn't get anything right, not even my chest measurement.

Sissy snatched up my bridesmaid's outfit from the back of the vinyl lounge and held it in front of me. She pointed to the two small puckers in the filmy white bodice, which was encrusted with tiny pink glass beads to match the skirt.

'If we don't put something in there, it'll look ridiculous!' she said, glaring at me.

✺

The next day Mum and I traipsed into town on what I felt was surely the most embarrassing mission of my short life. We headed up Elizabeth Street and past Redfern Oval, the home ground of the South Sydney Rugby League club. The Rabbitohs were our winning team and in those days many of the players lived locally; even when I wasn't there to see the game in person, I could follow their progress from the roars and moans of the crowd, which filtered across the rooftops to our house.

Before long we reached Central Station, passing its slender clock tower and the network of urban pathways in and out of the city. Further on was Hyde Park, a green oasis of giant fig trees, wide manicured stretches of grass and the famous Archibald Fountain. I loved anything to do with art, and never grew tired of admiring the bronze statuary: Diana the Huntress, Theseus and the Minotaur, Jason and the Golden Fleece, and Apollo, standing tall against the skyline in front of the fanning sprays of water. We sat down on a bench and Mum handed me a parcel of stale bread from her straw shopping bag. I threw crumbs to the pigeons, aiming several pieces at a smaller bird, tattered and lame, hanging back from the flapping, squabbling throng.

Rolling her eyes, Mum dug into her bag and passed me a Granny Smith apple. 'No doubt about you, Don. Can't turn your back on the weaklings. Next thing you'll be bringing the bloody thing home in your pocket to join the rest of the strays.'

'You're the same, Mum. You just hide it better.' I tossed a large crust right at the injured pigeon's feet. It was true, I was a sucker for the underdog, and at home our menagerie of rescued animals was testimony to the fact.

Mum grunted and stood up, her face flat and expressionless. Straightening her skirt and picking up her bag, she nodded in the direction of the shops. 'Best be going, love. Eat your apple on the way.'

The reason for our visit to town was getting depressingly closer with every step. I trailed after Mum to the edge of the park and back down into Elizabeth Street, merging with the thin crowd of Saturday shoppers. It was a dull morning made greyer by the shadow of the buildings, the cement and tar underfoot and my increasingly glum mood.

Mum led me through the double glass doors of the David Jones department store, a place we rarely visited, except to occasionally window shop. Pausing in the marble foyer among the perfume and make-up, I yearned for the luxury of having money in my pocket: I would've loved to wander by the glass counters buying bubble bath or lipstick, leather gloves or pearl earrings; whatever new and pretty things took my fancy. With a disloyal pang, I felt the growing, familiar desire to escape my upbringing. It didn't really matter though – today there would be no opportunity for strolling through the ground floor's delicious scented aisles for even a look. It was straight up the wooden escalators and into the lingerie department.

A giant, perfumed redhead in a black skirt and white blouse and, naturally enough, sporting a pair of magnificent breasts, immediately swooped and asked if we needed any help. Mum took her to one side and the two women had a hushed conversation.

Turning to me, the saleswoman then said, 'Into the change room, dear, and take your top off. We'll measure you up.'

Once inside the cubicle, I unbuttoned my blouse and stood in frozen embarrassment in my singlet and skirt. Mum had followed me in to make sure it all went smoothly.

'Stand up straight, Don,' she said, taking my shirt and folding it over her arm. 'Don't hunch.'

Around went the tape measure. The saleswoman frowned. 'There's absolutely nothing there. No point working out cup size. She wouldn't even be an A. Does she really need one?'

Mum was uncomfortable, but she looked the woman in the eye. 'Our Kathryn's getting married and, like I said, we want Donna here to have a bit of chest, for the bridesmaid's outfit. Something with a bit of room, so we can pad it.'

The saleswoman looked disapproving but held her tongue. After all, a sale was a sale.

'Just something plain,' Mum added as the saleswoman swept off in a gust of floral scent.

In a moment she was back with a tangle of white and skin-coloured undergarments. 'Take the singlet off, dear,' she said.

I looked at Mum pleadingly.

'Hurry up, love, do as the lady says.'

I didn't dare disobey. In my family, and in that era, you did as you were told, no arguments, otherwise you could expect the proverbial clip around the ear. I took a breath and tugged the singlet over my head, wanting the floor of that little dressing room to swallow me up in one big gulp.

The saleswoman helped me into the first bra, white and lacy, pushed my tangled ponytail to one side to hook the back up, ratcheted down the shoulder straps and gave the front a tug. I sneaked a look in the full-length mirror. If that pale, skinny creature in the glass was meant to reflect womanhood, God help us all. I looked away and caught Mum examining the price tag that dangled from one strap.

'Haven't you got anything cheaper? This one's a bit pricey.'

Nobody was mentioning anything pricey about Kathryn's wedding. Buy Donna a bra though, and make sure it's the cheapest one you can find. And plain. Let's not forget that.

The white lacy number was whipped off and another slipped on and adjusted.

'Stand still,' said Mum as I shuffled.

The two women appraised the baggy cups.

'She won't get away with anything bigger, unless you want to make it obvious it's padded,' said the saleswoman.

'All right.' Mum nodded. 'It looks quite well made, and the price is right. We'll take it.'

The next weekend our house was filled with the chaos and laughter of family and friends eagerly anticipating the impending nuptials. Aunty Dassie's young daughter, Linda, and Sissy's friend, Julie, arrived early. My cousin was to be the flower girl, and Julie, the matron of honour. Unfortunately, I'd had little sleep the night before: Sissy had stayed over, sleeping in her old bed and relegating me to the trundle mattress, made up on the floor beside her. I'd spent the night tossing and turning, my hair tightly wound around several rows of prickly, lumpy curlers. I was coming down with another bout of tonsillitis, but the excitement in the air overrode my aching head and sore throat and I was determined not to let anything ruin the wedding ceremony.

Dad had spent hours the previous weekend polishing his Valiant station wagon, and that morning he parked it on the lawn to give it a final clean and vacuum. Car ownership in 1960s Redfern was a rarity, but Dad loved cars, and it was our one luxury. Once the bonnet was dry, I watched from an upstairs window as he and Mum decorated it with a thick cream ribbon. The usual ragged bunch of neighbourhood kids had appeared by this stage, hoping they could pile in the back and join us on one of our regular sightseeing jaunts. Most weekends, Dad starting his car had a similar effect to the Pied Piper playing his flute. Boys and girls would come streaming out of their houses and we'd set off with a full tank of petrol and a basket of sandwiches, fruit, cordial and coffee for the North Shore or the Eastern Suburbs to see how the other half lived. We were never jealous, we just felt that somewhere along the line, someone's hard work, and perhaps a bit of luck, had paid off.

We also visited parks and beaches, travelled to the Blue Mountains and Jenolan Caves, to Orange to see snow, and Dural to go blackberry picking. Mum would make blackberry pies, big and small, for packed lunches the next week. As an adult, long-distance driving never worried me. It was a form of entertainment I learned from my dad.

Today, however, the Valiant was to be used for a different purpose.

'No outing today, kids,' said Mum. 'Our Kathryn's getting married. Get off home now. Maybe next week.'

Mum passed the adopted girl from up the road a handful of ribbon scraps. She stuffed them in her shorts pocket before the group finally ambled off, no doubt planning a game of backyard cricket, hopscotch down on Kettle Street, or jacks with the knuckles saved from lamb roasts. I wished I could join them. Dressing up for the wedding had a certain allure, but I much preferred climbing trees or swinging our makeshift cricket bats.

But Sissy was running today's show. 'Can someone help me fix my hair?' she sang out from Mum and Dad's bedroom.

I left my spot at the window, popped a throat lozenge in my mouth and stuck my head around the corner of my parents' room. Still in her dressing gown, Sissy was sitting at the mirror in front of a clutter of jars, bottles, brushes and lipsticks, her head bulging with pink and blue plastic curlers. She smelled of roses.

'I'll do it,' I offered, already in my bridesmaid's outfit complete with tissues shoved down the front.

Sissy scowled at me. 'Not you. You go and check on Linda. And get Julie to pin your hair up, like we did it the other night. She's good at that sort of thing. Mum can do mine. Fix your face too.'

Aye, aye, Captain. I scuttled off to do as I was told, my pink skirt rustling around my ankles.

Later, after Julie had fixed my hair into an elaborate twist of ribbons and cascading curls, and helped me with my make-up, I took a last look in my bedroom mirror. Already in her flower-girl outfit, Linda perched on the side of the red chenille bedspread and watched.

'You don't look like you, Donna,' she said. 'You look beautiful.'

I had to agree, on both counts. I wasn't used to seeing myself with powder covering my freckles, my hair up and a delicate dress on, and I was pleased with what I saw. I actually felt pretty. Satisfied, I stood up and smoothed my skirt, then held out a hand to my cousin.

'Come on, Linda, we've got one more thing to do, but you have to promise not to tell.' I put my finger to my lips. For several weeks now, I'd been planning to keep mementos of my sister's wedding day and then present them to her some time down the track, maybe on the couple's first anniversary, or after the birth of their first child.

As Linda and I passed the bathroom, Johnny Farnham squeaked from a tiny transistor radio in my parents' room where Sissy was still getting ready:

Worked her fingers to the bone
For the lad she had at home
Providing at the same time for her daughter ...

The music lent an upbeat backdrop to the chatter and giggles all around us. Dad had changed into his morning suit and was combing his wavy, ginger hair in the mirror above the hand basin while Mum brushed the back of his coat with her hand. He held the comb in front of his face like a microphone and, with a toothy grin, began to sway and sing along to the words, his voice smooth and perfectly in tune:

Scrub your floors, do your chores, dear old Sadie
Looks as though you'll always be a cleaning lady ...

My dad was an innovative man, and his ability to think laterally made a deep impression on me. He did the best he could with very little, whether it was turning an inner tube into a makeshift toboggan at the snow, or making a billycart out of bits and pieces of junk from his shed. Ingenuity aside, I knew my parents were often tired, stressed and worried about money, so I loved celebrations when they could relax, because the rest of the family could do the same.

While the women chided Dad to quit his singing and get out of the bathroom, Linda and I began collecting my treasures: a stray curler and a scrap of silky pink hair-ribbon dropped in the hallway, a lipstick-stained tissue discarded among Sissy's jars and bottles and a tiny white rosebud from one of the bouquets. I tucked these items away in a decorated shoebox beneath my bed, planning to gather more bits and pieces at the ceremony and the reception.

The former was held at St Matthews, an Anglican church in Botany. My family were Catholic, but not devout; their childhood faith was almost entirely flogged out of them by the nuns. The church had been Eric's choice, and what Eric wanted, Kathryn now wanted too.

We waited nervously on the footpath as Dad and Sissy whispered to each other. I watched, trying to ignore the pain of my red-raw throat, as Sissy reached up to adjust the white carnation in Dad's jacket lapel. A group of khaki-clad boy scouts milled around the front steps, shuffling into a haphazard guard of honour. Eric was a scout master and he'd organised this touch especially for his bride.

Approaching the entranceway, I could hear the rustle and murmur of the congregation rising as the organ music swelled to fill the small church. I stepped slowly down the nave clutching my pink and white posy, with Linda in front carrying her tiny basket of blooms and Julie several steps behind. Fortunately all eyes were on the entrance.

As I neared the altar I managed to sneak a sideways glance at the guests. I didn't recognise too many of Eric's lot but, on the bride's side, all our close friends and family seemed to be here: Grandpop Leonard, stiff and formal in his usual three-piece mission-brown suit and tie; Aunty Dassie, dressed in a powder-blue twin set with matching hat; and my mum next to her in a similar, pale green ensemble. Even from this angle, I could see both women were dabbing at their eyes with their lace hankies.

Uncle Ronnie, in his stovepipe trousers and well-worn jacket, stood next to my aunty. He was an affable sort of bloke, as famous for his rice custard as for his gambling and drinking. Alongside him were their four scrubbed boys, in an untidy, restless line. One of them, Jeffrey, began to wave as Sissy moved past, and Uncle Ronnie bent to whisper something in his ear.

Behind them was our family friend, the pedantic Uncle Jack, obsessed with gadgets and now taking up several spaces with his giant camera bag, so large we used to say he could put wheels on the thing and drive it. He was the official photographer and was leaning out like some big-beaked bird, clutching the contraption to his face to snap Sissy as she made her way down the nave on Dad's arm.

My throat was still throbbing and, without warning, I began to feel dizzy. The red carpet swam in front of me and panic lurched in my chest. I could feel myself breaking out in a sweat. Keep going, I willed myself, looking up at the midday sun streaming through the stained-glass window behind the altar. Let me be all right, God. Don't let me faint. Don't let me mess this up. My earlier excitement had vanished and I was suddenly petrified I was going to do something really stupid.

By the time Sissy and Dad reached the altar, I had sidled over to one of the front pews, clinging on to its wooden back, my hands clammy inside my white gloves. I could hear the wedding vows being exchanged in front of me, and I tried to distract myself by breathing deeply and focusing on the words the minister was saying.

'Will you love, honour, comfort her from this day forward, forsaking all others . . .'

As the minutes ticked by, I was dimly aware that Eric and Sissy were kissing. It was over. I'd made it. Thank you, God. Although I'd managed to stay upright through the ceremony, I knew that I had to get outside and into the fresh air in a hurry. It took forever, waiting for the papers to be signed, then moving back past the smiling congregation to the entrance. I was aware I was staggering, but I'd got this far and I was determined to keep going. I'm nearly there. Just let me get to the door.

Finally I made it outside into the watery sunlight. But I wasn't out of the woods yet. Now we were being marshalled for photographs. With a mumbled 'sorry' I pushed past the rest of the wedding party, through those wretched boy scouts and into a blizzard of confetti. I stumbled over to the side of the steps, spots flickering before my eyes.

I heard Dad's muffled voice somewhere behind me. It sounded like he was speaking from the other end of a long tunnel.

'Are you all right, love?'

My legs folded and he caught me as I fell. My dad was a hard man, sometimes a frightening man, but he was also fiercely protective. I'm lucky he was there for me that day.

※

The reception house was packed by the time we arrived. Most of the guests were seated, and the large formal dining area, with its acres of starched linen and silver cutlery, was abuzz with light-hearted conversation and the clinking of glasses. Tom Jones and Frank Sinatra crooned in the background as waiters circled with prawn cocktails and bowls of beef consommé.

The photo session following the ceremony had been delayed after my fainting attack but, by the time I found my way to the official table and swallowed a couple of Aspros, I began to feel relatively normal, aside from my sore throat.

My new brother-in-law bent over me solicitously and asked if I was okay. 'Must be the worst feeling in the world, to get that crook in the middle of a wedding.' He squeezed my shoulder.

I breathed in the smell of his Old Spice aftershave and turned, opening my mouth to reply.

'She's fine now,' Dad cut in with a grin. 'Underneath all them ribbons and curls my Cupcake's pretty tough, aren't you, love? She was determined to get through the wedding, though she can be a bit of a coward when it comes to pain.' He looked at me with a larrikin twinkle in his eye. I knew what was coming next. 'Remember your foot, Don?'

I smiled weakly as Dad related the tale to Eric. One afternoon, while playing cricket with the gang, I cut my foot and so went home for a bandaid. Mum took one look at my foot and went as white as our bleached cotton sheets. I was bundled into the family car and taken straight to the doctor. In the surgery, he tried to jab a needle into the sole of my foot to deaden the pain in preparation for stitching, but my feet were so tough from constantly going barefoot that the first needle broke. Mum and Dad, as well as the doctor, all leaned on me as I struggled to escape, and a second needle was jabbed into the centre of the wound. I'm sure my phobia of needles stems from this childhood incident.

I continued smiling at Dad as he finished the story. I knew he told it with fondness, even though it made me sound cowardly. Apart from that phobia, I was actually a stoic kid, boyish and resilient. My childhood was spent trying to be the son Dad never had, going with him to the Speedway at the Showground or the wrestling at Sydney Stadium, where we'd be held in thrall by the likes of Killer Kowalski, Big Chief Little Wolf and Mario Milano. I'd hang around Dad at home too, learning how to fix and build things.

Whether outside being a tomboy or inside helping Mum clean and cook, I had determination. Giving in was unheard of in our family. Like many in our community, we were a die-hard lot and, as Mum was fond of saying, self-pity was a luxury we couldn't afford. After all, there were always others worse off than us.

My family's high spirits continued through the meal and the speeches. Mum and Dad rarely drank, but they were enjoying a glass or two now. More importantly, they both liked Eric, and felt confident he'd look after their precious older daughter, despite their initial misgivings that they were just too young to contemplate marriage.

I'd been secretly surprised at the positive turnaround in Dad's attitude. A couple of years earlier, Sissy had invited an army bloke home. Dressed in full uniform, he'd drawn Dad aside and asked if he could date my 14-year-old sister. Dad went ballistic.

'Who the hell are you? I don't know you from a bar of soap and you're asking if you can go out with my daughter!'

Soon the pair were embroiled in a heated argument; Sissy's would-be beau jabbing at the air with his folded beret as they traded insults. His authority challenged, Dad grew even more furious.

Anger was a common enough emotion in our household and from a young age I became adept at reading people's moods from a distance and altering my behaviour accordingly. I would tiptoe around, do my chores and make sure I didn't rock the boat. So this particular evening, I made myself invisible, my usual survival tactic in these circumstances. I do remember Sissy fled the house in tears. As for the young soldier, we never laid eyes on him again.

As the dessert plates were cleared from our table, I salvaged Mum's name card for my sister's memory box and wrapped it in a paper napkin along with the wishbone I'd saved from my main meal. I'd miss Sissy. Although she'd left home a while ago, the wedding underscored the fact that she had left forever. I thought back on our relationship: the good parts, the not so good. As a young girl, Sissy had been my protector but by the time she'd reached her teens I felt like the pesky younger sister, her constant shadow both after school and on weekends.

'Take your little sister with you,' Mum would say when Sissy tried to sneak off to the local pool at Prince Alfred Park to hang with her friends and flirt with the boys. Tagging along served a dual purpose: I was her unwitting chaperone and she provided free babysitting for Mum and Dad.

'Keep away from me,' she'd growl, making me walk several yards behind her on our way to the pool. 'And don't come near me when we get there. I'll be with my friends and I don't want you hanging about.'

Despite her bossy ways, I enjoyed our early morning training sessions, swimming lap after lap to the strains of 'Winchester Cathedral', with Sissy the graceful, talented freestyler, and me, the kid stuck on a kickboard for two years, too scared to put my head in the water. I also remembered riding our homemade skateboards that Dad had fashioned from a pair of skates Sissy had outgrown. We'd take the boards to a nearby hill and speed down the footpath, sending out loud clicketty-clacks as the metal wheels bumped in rhythm over the pavement seams. Like clockwork, one particular neighbour's angry face would appear at the window overlooking the street. The sash would fly up and she'd stick her head out, shouting, 'You bloody kids! Piss off home to your own place and make that bloody noise!' It was so predictable. We'd get her going every time.

I sighed as the waiter took my ice-cream-smeared dish.

Uncle Jack was fussing around with his camera gear again. The piped music had finished and the staff were hovering, anxious to move the luncheon to a close so they could begin setting up for the next function. Sissy and Eric were happy to oblige as Uncle Jack waved them over to stand in front of the three-tiered wedding cake. It was so beautiful: a pristine, snow-white tower of icing nestled in a wreath of creamy roses and flanked by a pair of silver candelabra. Uncle Jack hunched in front of the newlyweds, fiddling with his dials and knobs while Mum and I stood off to the side watching the happy scene.

'Wish he'd just take the damned picture,' Mum whispered, rolling her eyes and shuffling from one foot to the other. 'I ate too much, and this girdle's killing me. Just want to get home, get it off and stick me feet up.'

'Step back just a little,' Uncle Jack urged, peering at the happy couple alternately through the lens and then over the top of the camera. 'A little more. Back a little more.'

Still smiling, the couple moved back until they were leaning against the table. In a split second, the flame from one of the candles caught Sissy's net veil and within moments the orange tongues of fire were all around her head like a flaming halo. There was a gasp from the guests as Eric grabbed the burning veil with his bare hands, reefed it from Sissy's head, and threw it on the floor to stomp on it. Mum and Dad dashed over and, in a rare show of open affection, Mum put her arms around Sissy as she burst into tears.

※

My sister's marriage lasted less than a year and, a few months after they separated, I found that memory box, still in its hiding place beneath my bed. The rosebud I'd forgotten to press was shrivelled and brown, the name card smeared with grease, and the lipstick tissue had lost its bright kiss shape. I crept downstairs that night and tipped the shoebox and its faded contents into our garbage bin.

Later, as I lay propped up in bed, my curtains open to the twinkling cityscape beyond, I shut my eyes and listened to the familiar neighbourhood sounds: brakes screeching out on the street, our dog's incessant barking from the backyard below, my Dad's angry rap on the window and, a moment later, my parents' raised voices from the lounge room downstairs.

I thought about romance and love, my sister's ruined marriage, and my parents, still bickering as they trudged upstairs to bed. Weren't Mum and Dad once blissfully in love? And if they were, what had happened? Maybe this love business was all a big lie, something that got its hooks into us early in life before we knew any better. I remembered my primary school years, not so long ago, when Australia was in the grip of Beatlemania. We'd swooned over magazine and newspaper photographs, watching the Fab Four's grainy black and white faces on our TV screens and listening endlessly to their music. Perhaps, even back then, we were already victims of the romantic love trap.

Surely there were happy couples out there, people who were meant to be together, like Spencer Tracy and Katherine Hepburn, Humphrey Bogart and Lauren Bacall. I wanted it to be true, for my own sake if not for the rest of the world, but somewhere in the back of my mind, an unpleasant idea lingered. What if love didn't conquer all? What if it were a disappointment, a cruel trick?

After a moment I opened my eyes and leaned over to snap off my bedside light, pushing away these depressing thoughts. I was an optimist after all; of course it was possible to find lasting love and happiness.

Two

Almost a decade after Kathryn's first marriage, my own wedding took place. I met Brian Blakemore while completing a diploma in teaching in the stately country town of Bathurst, some 200 kilometres west of Sydney. Our courtship began in 1976 – the year that Swedish band ABBA had rocketed to fame, *Alvin Purple* was attracting moviegoers around the country, and colour televisions were the new 'must haves' for middle-class Australians. The Whitlam Government had been dismissed the previous November and Malcolm Fraser was our new prime minister. A faded bumper sticker, 'SHAME FRASER SHAME', clung tenaciously to my best friend Debbie's 1970 Toyota Corona. The Corona was our only means of transport to and from lectures, parties, college dances and socialising at Bathurst's Oxford Hotel, or 'the Ox' as we affectionately knew it.

I met big, blond and affable Brian at the Ox. He was a bricklayer and was there most afternoons in his crusty work gear, sitting down one end of the smoky little bar with a sloppy collection of drinking buddies, downing schooners of Old and puffing away on his smokes. 'Here she is!' he'd call, as Deb and I walked in. Apparently he was smitten with me from the moment he first saw me.

Brian was a big talker and there was nothing he hadn't done or didn't know about. And the money he earned! Sometimes several hundred a week, according to him. Here was someone who seemed to know what he was doing and where he was going and, most importantly, who'd love and protect me. Here was a real man, unlike those boyish college students, and it wasn't long before he'd snared me, hook, line and sinker.

When I finished college I was appointed to a school in the large country town of Dubbo, in the central west of New South Wales, the first in my family to become a 'professional'. Never a natural A student, my persistence to get out of Redfern and escape my destiny as a factory worker had finally paid off. The struggle was over now. I'd been one of those kids who couldn't wait to get to school, and now I was the teacher.

Brian's parents lived in nearby Geurie, a nondescript little hamlet with a general store, a post office and a pub. There was a tumbledown servo and a railway station too and, nearby, a cluster of wheat silos which towered over the dust, the flies and the heat, shimmering in the unforgiving sunshine. Brian and I moved in with Mr and Mrs Blakemore until we could afford to buy some land of our own. Brian's dad was also a bricklayer, and Mrs Blakemore his labourer, and they generously offered to help us build our first home.

I'd made it: I had a loving relationship and a good job, Brian had plenty of work and we were engaged to be married. Owning our own home seemed only a heartbeat away. How rosy the future looked. There was, however, one small problem. Brian was an easy-going bloke, with no airs or graces, but he liked a drink and, by the time we moved to Geurie, that 'like' had turned to 'love'. I confided my concerns to his mother.

'Ooh Donna, he just needs to be given some more responsibility,' she told me in her lilting Irish accent. 'He's young. If he were somebody's husband it'd be different. What can you expect from a bachelor?'

I was brought up to listen to my elders, to respect what they had to say. And so I fell into the age-old trap of thinking I could change my fiancé into a different man. I don't think I ever considered breaking up with him. He was too much a part of my life. He needed me. And perhaps I was lucky to have him.

◈

We set the wedding date for December 1978 and, naturally, for several weeks beforehand there was much discussion about its organisation.

The idea of getting married in a church had been quickly dismissed, along with my visions of a traditional white dress and bridal veil.

'You can't be in white after being in a relationship with a man,' Mrs Blakemore told me, shaking her head. 'Only virgins wear white.'

Determined to do the best I could within the Blakemore regulations, I arranged a garden ceremony at Butler's Falls – a beautiful stretch of parkland, dotted with magnificent eucalypts and other native flora, and wide beds of perfumed roses – just outside Dubbo. I'd bought my outfit in Dubbo and, although it wasn't the gown of my dreams, I thought it was special. I would be married in a pretty sleeveless blouse and matching skirt of silky blue-grey material printed with a pink and cream bamboo pattern. I also planned to wear white flowers in my short, curly hair and hold a small bouquet of red roses.

Brian's parents had offered their home for the reception, as long as it was 'just family'.

'I'd really like to invite a few of my friends and relations,' I said to Mrs Blakemore, sitting in her kitchen one day. 'I mean, there's my friend Debbie from college, and Aunty Dassie and Uncle Ronnie, and ...'

Mrs Blakemore waved her hands in the air. 'Ooh Donna, if you start inviting this person and that person, there's no telling where it'll stop.'

'Mum's right, love,' Brian piped up, stubbing his cigarette out in the overflowing glass ashtray. 'It'd be too much.'

'You've got your dad coming to give you away, haven't you?' Mrs Blakemore said. 'It's a shame your mum and your sister aren't speaking to him, but that can't be helped. Divorce is a nasty business. At least you'll have your dad.'

I nodded.

Discussions about the guest list led to the problem of food. Mrs Blakemore decided her daughter-in-law, Denise, could cater. 'I can't manage it myself,' she said, her body hunched over in an increasingly familiar posture of frailty. 'But Denise is a marvellous cook. She's coming up a few days before the wedding. She can organise the buffet. You'd pay her for the food, of course, and give her a bit extra for her trouble. It'd be cheaper than getting a professional caterer, and I know she could use the money. She could probably even bake you a cake.'

Denise and I had met a few times and, although we were civil towards each other, I suspected she was the favourite daughter-in-law and that I'd better keep my place. From our first meeting, I got the impression that my 'professional' qualifications made her uncomfortable, and on one occasion I'd heard her and Mrs Blakemore remark to each other that I was just a primary school teacher and what would I know about anything.

⁂

Our wedding day was hot and bright, with a characteristically huge blue sky spread over the dusty landscape. The ceremony wasn't scheduled until 6 pm, but by late afternoon, the heat still hadn't abated. Dad drove me to the gardens in his 1974 sky-blue Ford Fairlane. It was a relief to be alone with him for this brief time, although he looked hot and uncomfortable in his patterned bronze shirt and cream safari suit. Beads of sweat had formed on his forehead before we'd even left Geurie.

'I hope Brian looks after you, love,' he said, his eyes focused on the long straight ribbon of road in front of us.

'Of course he will, Dad. Anyway, I thought you liked him.'

'He's got no pretensions about him, easy to talk to and all that. Likes the grog though, doesn't he?'

'Yeah, Dad, but maybe that'll sort itself out when we get married.'

'Can't take to his relatives,' he grunted. 'Put up with that sister of his – Carol, isn't it – and her three kids all the way from Sydney to Geurie. Christ, it were a long drive.'

'The look on your face when you arrived was like thunder! I thought you were going to explode.'

'Bloody kids in the back seat jumping and bouncing and yahooing all the way. Their mother didn't chip 'em once, and didn't like it when I had a go. Anyway, they're your future relos, so good luck.'

I put a hand on his freckled arm. 'It's okay, Dad. You're here now. Just enjoy the wedding. Let's put some music on.' I sifted through the glove box to find a tape. 'Here, Shirley Bassey. How about that? Sing for me like you used to.'

Dad grinned across at me, then turned his eyes back to the road, opened his mouth and began to sing:

Diamonds are forever
Sparkling round my little finger
Unlike men, the diamonds linger
Men are mere mortals who are not worth going to your grave for ...

I smiled to myself and closed my eyes, imagining for a moment that I was a kid again, sitting in the Valiant with Mum, Dad, Kathryn and the usual assortment of neighbourhood kids on one of our long-ago weekend jaunts.

⁓

Everyone had gathered at the rose garden. I noticed that, along with her black and white spotted sundress, Carol was now wearing the white cotton shawl I'd knitted for her mother, Mrs Blakemore, the previous year. Carol looked bored, and stood with folded arms, her wavy brown hair hanging loose around her shoulders. In contrast to Carol's casual look, Denise was dressed in a tight, off-the-shoulder, emerald-green outfit, and stared at me coquettishly from under her blond fringe; all teeth and dark mascara. Next to her stood her husband Danny – Brian's brother – with his slicked-back blond hair, long, narrow sidelevers, trimmed moustache, dark shirt and wraparound sunglasses. Although I hadn't really wanted children at the wedding, a collection of Brian's nieces and nephews raced around the manicured gardens, whooping and squealing.

Mr and Mrs Blakemore stood apart from the rest, surveying the scene. Mrs Blakemore seemed unusually happy and relaxed, dressed in a fire-engine-red blouse and red, white and blue skirt. Her short, pale orange hair had been freshly done, and her sun-hardened complexion softened by make-up. Her husband was wearing cream trousers, a white, open-necked shirt, and a tan sports coat buttoned tightly over his rotund belly.

'There you are, Donna,' called Mrs Blakemore, giving Dad and me a wave as we strolled over to the group. 'We wondered where you'd got to.'

Mr Blakemore chuckled. 'Can't have you leaving Brian at the altar, can we?'

Right then and there, I wished there was some way I could. I'd made a promise though, and in my family, your word was everything. I looked over at Brian, standing beside the celebrant in a short-sleeved safari suit similar to Dad's, but in cinnamon brown, the oversized collar of his brown and white striped shirt crumpled inside the neck of his jacket. His blond mop of hair had been plastered over his forehead, and his moustache needed a trim. His big, blue eyes seemed unfocused under his shaggy eyebrows, and I wondered if he'd already had a drink.

As I walked over to him, with the flies buzzing lazily about and the small, untidy cluster of guests shuffling closer, my heart was leaden. I smiled weakly at my future husband and stretched up to straighten his collar. He looked down and gave me a sloppy grin, squeezing my hand.

'Put your smoke out, Bri,' I whispered, nodding towards the half-burnt cigarette he held between the nicotine-stained fingers of his free hand.

'Oh, yeah, sorry, babe.' He dropped the butt and ground it beneath his shoe. 'Just nerves.'

'Did you remember the ring?'

He looked at me blankly. 'Huh?'

'The ring. Did you give the ring to Danny?'

'Oh, yeah. She's right.' He turned to his brother and said loudly, 'You got the ring, didn't you, mate?'

Danny nodded as the celebrant, a thin, grey-haired man wearing black-rimmed glasses, stepped forward and cleared his throat. 'Are we ready?' he began. 'Let's get under way then, shall we?'

He read softly from a floral folder as the relatives flicked away flies, stubbed out cigarettes, snapped photos and shushed their restless children. I thought of my mum and my sister, my aunt and uncle, mates from high school, and my best friend Debbie. I longed to see their friendly faces among the other guests. I took a deep breath. *Pull yourself together. This* is meant to be the happiest day of your life. Stop feeling sorry for yourself. Try hard and the marriage will work!

As Brian slipped the small, white-gold band on my finger, the relations clapped softly and murmured their congratulations. We signed the papers on a large stump, beneath the dappled shade of a huge gum, and then posed for more photos.

The reception was held in the Blakemores' cavernous family room. It was 1970s in style, with low ceilings, cream-brick archways, and feature walls covered with fake wood panelling and geometric wallpaper in tans and creams. Orange plastic light fittings glowed from the ceiling as we lolled about on an odd assortment of furniture: aluminium folding chairs, a floral orange and brown day bed, and a dark, vinyl lounge. A record player with speakers the size of small refrigerators dominated a side table, but no music played.

There were children everywhere, dashing over the shag pile carpet, zipping and diving around the straggly array of food in an unruly mob, dipping their fingers into the bowls of macaroni and rice salad, picking over the platters of cold meats, and ignoring any half-hearted chastising from the group of smoking, drinking adults.

'You're the schoolteacher. Anybody'd think you didn't like kids,' grumbled Brian in response to my mutterings.

'I do like them, Brian. I just don't appreciate my wedding turning into some sort of out-of-control kiddies party. All we need now is a game of musical chairs, a jug of red cordial and the birthday clown.'

Denise had organised the food, including a small round chocolate cake decorated with a paper border and a white plastic wedding arch. I knew I should be grateful. Although it hadn't been the formal sit-down meal with family and friends that I'd dreamed of, I was married now. Grow up and get on with it, Donna, I thought, as we cut the cake together, a cigarette dangling from Brian's free hand.

'Watch the ash, honey,' I whispered, as he swayed beside me, glassy-eyed and grinning, already three sheets to the wind. 'You know your mum doesn't like it on her carpet.'

There was plenty of alcohol that night and by the time we were ready to leave for the nearby Wellington motel, my new husband was staggering and stumbling all over the place. I didn't have a driver's licence, so Brian drove us in his tiny work ute. It had been decorated at some stage during the evening by the kids, and was now swathed in toilet paper and paper plates left over from the buffet.

No matter what I told myself, I knew I'd made a mistake, even before the ring was on my finger. That night, sitting on the edge of a bed in a cheap motel room, with Brian passed out behind me, fully clothed, I quietly berated myself.

'Shouldn't have got married. Shouldn't have got married,' I murmured over and over, weeping into a handful of sodden tissues.

※

We continued to live with Brian's parents for a while after. Brian was bricklaying on and off and I was bringing in a regular wage teaching. We paid half the bills, splitting everything down the middle, including food, rates and utilities. We also paid board. We planned to move and soon after the wedding I borrowed money from the Teachers Credit Union to buy a block of land two doors up from my in-laws. Brian and his dad began building our new home, with me taking on brickie's labourer duties during the school holidays and weekends. In spite of our joint effort, progress was slow.

'I work all week and then you expect me to keep going on the weekend,' Brian would say when I brought up the subject. This was despite the fact that he had many free weeks in between jobs.

'Brian's right, Donna,' said Mrs Blakemore. 'He works very hard. And no one likes a nagging wife.'

It wasn't only her son's work habits that prompted my mother-in-law to dish out her own brand of homespun wisdom. Increasingly worried about Brian's drinking, I confided in her again. Of course, it was my fault.

'If you were a good enough woman he wouldn't drink so much,' she said, with a shake of her head. 'He's under a lot of pressure, you know, what with working all week and then having his own home to build.'

I resolved once more to do my best to support my husband. Surely love would conquer all.

Mr and Mrs Blakemore had gone away for a few days, and I was enjoying a brief respite from the subtle disapproval of my mother-in-law. This particular day I'd arrived home before Brian, holding my basket of work on the school bus and primly ignoring the smutty suggestions from the high school boys up the back.

'Come and sit with us, miss,' they called. 'We'll look after you.'

I was feeling good that afternoon, not only because it was the weekend but also because I'd had a major triumph at work. For several days I had politely but firmly refused to teach my class of five- and six-year-olds in our demountable classroom, which was surrounded by glaring concrete and exposed to the western sun. These kids couldn't even breathe, let alone work. When the crayons began to melt over the sides of the tins, that was it. We'd been having lessons in the shade of a large tree in the playground each afternoon for almost a week before the principal relented. That day, an airconditioner had miraculously appeared and I'd agreed to move my class back indoors.

I had a quick shower, changing out of my blouse and skirt into a T-shirt and mini, and began to prepare tea, expecting Brian to be hungry after a day of hard work. He loved chips, and I wanted to please him, so I set the biggest saucepan on Mrs Blakemore's new stovetop, filled it with cooking oil, and turned the hotplate on. A minute later I heard the rattle of Brian's ute.

Just like those romance movies I was so fond of, I met my husband with a kiss at the front door. 'How was your day?' I asked.

'I'm buggered, love,' he said, pushing his dusty hair off his cement-encrusted forehead. 'How about we go down the pub for a cold one?'

I rushed off to the bedroom to grab my handbag and run a comb through my hair while Brian waited at the front door. In those early years, I welcomed any chance to get out and about as a married couple, even though I assumed he'd soon be occupied with his mates, his beer, his smokes and his pool cue while I sat alone in the lounge or hung around in the bar.

As it happened, we met a friendly group of people: the Fergusons, the Mays, Meg and Mick Andrews and local pig farmer and barman John Heller. I'd met John before, and he reminded me of a beardless Santa, with his thinning white hair, broad grin and chubby pink cheeks. That night I had a good old chinwag with John, as well as a couple of the old-timers, Garnett Mawbey and Jackie Bartholomew. It wasn't long before Jackie was regaling us with stories of cricketing legend, Sir Donald Bradman, waxing lyrical about the determination and strength of character it required for this Australian icon to reach the pinnacle of success.

He tapped a bony finger on the counter. 'That's the trouble with young people nowadays. Everything comes too easy. Not enough fundamental fortitude. Fundamental fortitude – that's what the world's lacking.'

If fundamental fortitude were a quality that had stood me in good stead thus far, I was shortly to need a fair bit more of it. When we got home, I pushed the front door open, switched on the light and caught a glimpse of a strange grey fog inside the house. A second later we were plunged into darkness as the bulb above us exploded with a loud pop, and glass tinkled onto the tiles.

'What the hell …?' I murmured, stepping carefully into the pitch-black entranceway, my heels crunching over broken glass. Clouds of smoke billowed around us. As the acrid stench hit me, I felt suddenly sick, not only from the smell but also from the realisation of what I'd done.

'It was the chipper,' I said, covering my face with my hands. 'Shit. I left the chipper on.'

Brian looked at me wordlessly, frozen in the doorway.

Coughing, I groped my way into the stinking interior. My eyes were already streaming and I fumbled around in my bag for a hanky, pressing the cotton square to my nose and mouth for a makeshift mask.

'I don't think anything's burning, Bri,' I gasped as I made my way back out to the doorstep. 'The house was all shut up, so maybe the oxygen ran out.'

'You'd know, wouldn't you, being the schoolteacher?'

Under the circumstances, I decided to ignore his dig. 'There's a torch in the ute, honey,' I said, trying to control my shaking. 'How about you go and get it. I can't see two inches in front of me in there.'

The damage was worse than I'd expected. As Brian ran the beam of light over the ceiling, floor and walls in the kitchen and lounge room, I saw everything was coated in a layer of black soot. The curtains were also covered in ash, along with the shag pile carpet and every stick of furniture. Exploring further we found that even the bedding was filthy. The kitchen was gutted. On the ruined stovetop sat the charred and twisted remains of the pot.

We began opening windows, switching on the cooled lights and dragging out rags and buckets to begin cleaning. But it was hopeless. The soot had impregnated every square inch of the house and our scrubbing only spread the dirt from one spot to another. Hours later, we'd made little headway, the pair of us resembling chimney sweeps, covered in ash from head to toe. Finally we showered and crawled into bed in the early hours of the morning. At least we'd have a few days to work on the clean-up before the Blakemores returned home.

Could I be that lucky? Of course not. The next morning, while on my hands and knees scrubbing, there was a knock at the door. I froze and looked aghast at Brian as he appeared from the other end of the house. Dear God, don't let that be them. Please don't let it be them.

It seemed this time God wasn't going to grant me my wish.

When I saw the look on Mrs Blakemore's pinched and ashen face, I wanted to die. She drifted through the house, her mouth hanging open in shock, her eyes roaming the charcoaled interior. As she reached the kitchen she burst into tears.

'Oooh Jeff! Look at me kitchen! Look at me brand new kitchen!'

Mr Blakemore, stalwart as usual, came up behind her and put his arm around her crumpled form. 'Now, Annie, it'll be all right.'

'I'm sorry! I did it,' I blurted out, also in tears. 'I was careless. I left the chipper on. It was all my fault.'

Brian moved to his parents, nodding agreement. 'I had nothing to do with it. I didn't know she'd left it on. If I'd known, I would have reminded her to turn it off.'

'Ooh, you're nothing but an irresponsible, unthinking young woman,' Mrs Blakemore sobbed. 'After all we've done for you, you repay us by doing this.' She began pointing erratically around the incinerated kitchen. 'Look what Donna's done, Jeff!'

'Calm down, Annie,' said Mr Blakemore.

But Mrs Blakemore would not be silenced. 'We can't leave you for a minute. You're not to be trusted! As soon as we go away, look what happens. It's a terrible, terrible thing you've done!'

Brian was nodding again, and just in case his mother hadn't got the message the first time, he repeated his previous words. 'I had nothing to do with it.'

This particular fire story did have a happy ending, however. Not only were the Blakemores insured, but they put in a quote for the job of rebuilding the kitchen, and won the tender. So after all that, they got a new kitchen and a job as well. As for me, I was never allowed to forget the error of my ways.

'Don't let Donna cook the chips. Remember what happened the last time.'

And they weren't joking, either.

Halfway through 1981, drought had a stranglehold on the land and the Western Plains lay bleached and withered under the sun's fierce eye. Emaciated stock picked at the brown roadside. Hawks circled in the heated air, scanning the highway for roadkill. Dams dried up, exposing their cracked beds, and tanks sat empty as water became rare and precious. Desperate farmers scanned the acres of jewel-blue sky for signs of rain, and many had no choice but to leave the land. The suicide rate soared.

I was pregnant with our first child, hot as melted butter, round and slow and irritable. As the birth drew nearer, I was also becoming agitated about our still unfinished house. But Mrs Blakemore had counselled me that a baby would change Brian, giving him that much-needed responsibility and the feeling that he had a family of his own. Like a fool I believed her, and so moved even deeper into a trap of my own making.

I'd arranged to give birth in Sydney at the St George Hospital, which was near Mum, who was now living in a flat in Kogarah. What with the loan repayments and my reduced income while on maternity leave, Brian and I were short of money, so before the birth I implored him to at least find temporary work. As luck would have it, some flats were being built directly behind Mum's place and despite his reluctance, he soon got a job on site. Of course he took umbrage at the fact that I was sitting around all day with my feet up, sipping tea.

The night I lay writhing and moaning in the labour ward at St George Hospital, something big was happening on *Dallas* and the nurses didn't want to miss a minute. Brian wasn't much help either, urging me to 'hurry up and have the baby'.

The labour went on for hours as my son struggled to be born. *Dallas* came and went and Brian continued to pace and grumble. Nurses wandered in and out, checking on my progress. The contractions grew worse, sweeping over me in long, intense waves. Finally I was given an epidural. There was a change of shift. The pain returned, even stronger than before. The epidural was topped up. The gynaecologist, Dr Pannikote, arrived, with three students in tow. The doctor had a whispered consultation with one of the senior nurses and, after quickly examining me, began barking orders.

'This baby is in stress! It has to be born now!'

I stared up at him, suddenly terrified. 'My baby ...' I struggled to sit up.

A nurse appeared at my side and pushed me back gently. 'Lie still, dear. Doctor's taking care of things. It'll be all right.'

Down the other end of the table, Dr Pannikote had picked up a scalpel and was rapidly slicing me open – surrounded by the trio of gaping students, another nurse and Brian, peering over the top of their heads. I remember lights, lots of blood and some sort of tyre-lever contraption being used to reef the baby out from inside me. It was a boy. The cord was wrapped under his arm and around his tiny throat like a boa constrictor. He was blue. He'd swallowed faeces. I stretched my arms out, but they wouldn't let me hold him. Instead he was rushed off to intensive care while I lay with empty arms, in a sore and tired heap.

Over the next few days, I was overcome with melancholy, brought on by seesawing hormones, distress at my sick and bruised baby, painful stitches and, of course, my husband, who disappeared shortly after the birth only to reappear three days later, which lost him his job.

'It's not fair they fired me,' he said. 'They've got no right. I've just had a son.'

'You didn't bloody well give birth, you know,' said Mum.

Meanwhile, our beautiful baby Coe had begun to gain strength. Mum and Kathryn were frequent visitors, Dad came over several times and I received cards, flowers and small gifts from my family.

※

Once out of hospital, Brian, Coe and I stayed at Mum's flat for a week or two, while Mum and Kathryn helped me with the bewildering array of skills I needed to acquire as a new mother: bathing, wrapping, nappy changing, the establishing of sleep routines. But by far the most daunting task of all was breastfeeding. No matter how hard I tried, I couldn't get Coe to attach properly, and my nipples were soon cracked and red raw.

Things reached crisis point one day when Brian wanted us to visit his brother Danny and sister-in-law Denise, our wedding caterer. They were living in Greystanes, in Sydney's west, and as it was a typically humid February day, and with no airconditioning in Brian's ute, we arrived at their place in a lather of perspiration. Somehow, Coe had slept all the way and was still dozing as I carried him inside in the crook of one arm, with the overflowing baby bag dangling from my other. Brian strolled up the path ahead of me, lighting a cigarette as I followed several metres behind.

No sooner had we got there than Danny and Brian departed for a session at the club, leaving me with Denise, who was pregnant with her fifth child. I'd been told many times by Mrs Blakemore how experienced Denise was with children; the fact that she'd had her first around her 16th birthday was considered a virtue.

Being left alone with her and her two youngest boys, Kevin and Brendan, while Brian and Danny went off on a binge was one of the most unpleasant fates I could imagine. In the stinking summer heat, Denise's house was oppressive – even with the windows open and a portable fan churning away, the air was like porridge. Rivers of perspiration ran from my armpits, down either side of my body under my cotton dress. Coe's damp head resting in the crook of my arm made me even more uncomfortable as I sat on the sticky vinyl lounge. If I moved him, he might wake, and if he woke, he'd be hungry. The last thing I wanted to be subjected to was Denise scrutinising my bumbling attempts at breastfeeding.

As I sipped tepid tap-water and tried to make polite conversation through the long, hot afternoon, the inevitable happened. First there was a whimper, then a wriggle, then another whimper. I rocked Coe gently, making little shushing noises while praying he'd go back to sleep. He wouldn't be soothed though, and within minutes his insistent grizzles turned into full-blown wailing. Naturally, his hungry cries brought Denise's two young boys out from the other room where they'd been engrossed watching television.

'What's the matter with the baby?' Brendan asked his mother.

'He's hungry,' Denise replied. Then she turned to me. 'You'd better feed him.'

Feeling too unsure of myself to ask for the privacy I craved, I balanced Coe in one arm and fidgeted with the buttons on my dress. By this stage my hands were shaking and my face was on fire.

Denise turned to her two boys and said, 'Do you want to watch?'

'Yes! Yes!' they cried, clambering over the lounge, leaning on top of Coe and squashing him into me.

Denise smiled. 'You don't mind, do you, Donna?'

I longed to be as far away as possible from this woman and her wriggling, gawking children. Clumsily I managed to feed Coe, biting my lip against the pain and fury, with Kevin's and Brendan's hot little faces centimetres from my breast, twisting and turning for a better view of my sucking baby. Finally I finished the feed, struggling to do myself up and keep hold of Coe.

'He'll have wind – you'd better burp him,' Denise reminded me with another small smile. 'Or didn't they teach you that in college?'

'Thanks, I know what to do,' I replied, laying Coe awkwardly against my shoulder and giving his back a gentle rub.

Later, as I changed Coe's nappy in the other room, my anger at Brian welled up. Leaving us to spend this sweltering summer afternoon with Denise while he and Danny disappeared on one of their bloody drinking escapades was the last straw.

'I'm going to get going, Denise,' I said, placing Coe in his bassinette and gathering up the baby paraphernalia. 'Brian's been gone for hours. He said he was only going for one drink, and I'm tired of waiting.'

'You know what they're like when they get together,' said Denise, all smiles. 'You can always bunk down here. We've got spare mattresses.'

'No thanks, Denise. I want to get home to Mum's.'

I was an inexperienced driver, only just on my P plates and unused to manoeuvring through the vast tangled road system of Sydney. To make matters worse, it was peak hour and in the heat the other motorists seemed intolerant of my hesitant driving. Coe cried all the way back to Mum's, making it even harder to concentrate on what I was doing. When Mum opened her front door I burst into tears.

She held out her arms. 'Come here, love. What's the bastard done now?'

卐

On the way home to Geurie, we paid another visit, this time to my college friend, Debbie, at Kurrajong. After I'd made myself comfortable on the lounge with Coe, Deb placed apple juice and cake on the table in front of me, along with a couple of packages.

'Something for you and something for the baby,' she said, leaning over to give me a kiss on the cheek.

'More presents,' Brian commented sulkily, reaching for a cold drink. 'What have you done that's so special?'

'Given birth to your first child, for a start,' Deb said. She rolled her eyes at me and I giggled. She wasn't normally rude. Maybe Brian just brought it out in people.

'You shoulda seen all the flowers in hospital! Bit much, if you ask me.' He planted himself in a chair by the corner and reached for the newspaper. 'If this is going to be one of them girlie sessions, I'll have a read while you and your twin catch up.'

Although my family called her 'the twin', Deb and I looked nothing alike. She had the rounded face and body, pink cheeks and blond hair of her German mother. The twin comment referred to the fact that Deb and I were born on the same day. She insisted we were always destined to be soul mates, our futures brought together in some weird cosmic alignment on the night of Sunday, 31 March 1957. Maybe she was right, or maybe it was simply because, even though she was from Sydney's North Shore and I was from Redfern, we were alike in so many ways. We had the same sense of humour for a start. Like me, she always managed to see the ridiculous in the awful. At college we had also shared a certain naivety when it came to our choice of men. I was sure she'd redeem herself one day though, with a respectable marriage and a life of luxury.

'What do you think of my beautiful boy?' I asked as soon as Brian had disappeared behind the newspaper.

'He's gorgeous,' Deb said, sitting down next to me. 'But you mentioned on the phone you had some trouble.'

'Trouble! That's an understatement. Notice the size of his head? It was like giving birth to a watermelon! You know what a chicken I am when it comes to pain.'

I went on to tell Deb all the gory details and suddenly things didn't seem so bad. Pretty soon we were laughing and gossiping just like old times. I realised then just how much I missed having a friend like Deb around.

Back in Geurie, Brian soon returned to a routine of minimal work and plenty of cricket and drinking at the Mitchell Inn or the bowling club, where he'd regularly volunteer behind the bar.

'Do you think you could talk to him?' I asked my mother-in-law again one day. 'Get him to spend more time helping me with the baby?'

Mrs Blakemore shook her head. 'You can't go expecting a man to be babysitting. That's your job.'

'But I'm so tired. I'm left to do everything.'

'Other people manage. Look at Denise: she's had four kids with another on the way, and *she* never complains. And she doesn't expect Danny to be changing nappies and doing women's work.'

'If I was a stay-at-home mother, I wouldn't need Brian's help. But I work all day and I'm up all night with a baby who won't sleep. I cook. I clean. I shop. On the weekends I work on our unfinished house. I'm like a zombie!'

'Ooh, it's obvious you're not coping. Maybe you should spend some time with your mother.'

Yes, maybe I should, I thought, with a surge of anger. It was school holidays after all.

Early the next morning, as magpies warbled in the tepid dawn, I packed the car: a bag of clothes for Coe, a small hold-all for me, and the baby stuff in a jumbled mass of plastic bags. I stowed Coe in his bassinette, strapped it in on the front seat and, still smarting from my conversation with Mrs Blakemore, defiantly headed off for Sydney as the rest of the household enjoyed their lie-in.

I stayed with Mum in Kogarah for two weeks, pouring out my heart to her and my sister, Kathryn, who was newly married to John Daly, a bank official, and renovating a beautiful old house nearby. They had an auburn-haired daughter, Jennifer, who was two.

Although I dreaded losing my family's support, Mum reminded me that I'd made my bed and it was my duty to go back and lie in it. And so I reluctantly bundled Coe back into Brian's old rattletrap and wearily made my way home. However, while I was in Sydney, that small seed of defiance had taken root. I may be going back, but I would be moving out of my in-laws' house as soon as possible.

〰️

Shortly after returning to Geurie I bought a front and back door on credit, installed them myself and, with an esky, an electric frypan, a cot and a double bed, moved into the half-finished house. It wasn't long before Brian decided to join us. Later Mum visited and brought two old lounge chairs, a bar fridge, a beautiful floral oil painting and a sign for the house: 'Miracle'.

I'd picked up a bit of incidental building knowledge from Dad and I took control of much of the interior: plastering, sanding and painting, even finishing the bathroom tiling and installing kitchen cupboards. I also made curtains for every room. Finally, after months without any floor coverings, I arranged to have carpet laid. Not the plush wool pile I'd wanted, but a cheap nylon substitute. Still, it was better than the concrete slab. I also bought a brown modular lounge on hire purchase, knowing full well I was getting into more debt, but feeling I had no choice if I didn't want to continue living like a squatter in my own home.

One night, soon after these luxuries were installed, I fell into bed around 10 pm, assuming that Brian was at the pub and wouldn't be back for a good few hours yet. When he arrived home about midnight, I heard him crashing about in the kitchen getting something to eat. I drifted back to sleep only to be woken shortly after by a horribly familiar smell. I leapt out of bed and ran down the hallway in my bare feet and nightie, just in time to see Brian heave himself off the smouldering lounge and stagger around the room in drunken astonishment. The back of his head was aflame.

'You're on fire, you bloody idiot!' I yelled between coughs. 'How many times have I asked you not to lie on the lounge and smoke!'

Dashing back along the hallway, I checked on Coe, who was still asleep. The blanket across his doorway had prevented any smoke from entering his room and, as soon as I was sure he was safe, I ran to the bathroom to grab some towels.

In the lounge room, Brian had somehow managed to put himself out. He lurched forward and grabbed the smoking chair, cartwheeling it across the brand new carpet and over the freshly estapoled cork tiles to the back door. As the night air gushed in, the lounge burst into flame. Brian seized the fiery mass in his hands and threw it outside. Bits of his clothing were glowing, and the back of his head was blackened. I couldn't even imagine what state his hands would be in. I ran to the kitchen sink to wet my armful of towels, draping the sodden material over his head and plunging his hands under the running water.

Miraculously, he suffered only minor injuries from the mishap: the worst was a persistent headache, which forced him to stop drinking for a couple of weeks, although he continued to smoke. The new carpet was reduced to a nasty network of melted trails, and the cork tiles streaked with permanent black scorch marks. The curtains were also ruined, and the remaining half of the lounge was peppered with burn holes.

'That lounge was cheap shit anyway,' Brian said.

'Yeah, of course. It's all about the lounge.' Apart from that valuable fundamental fortitude, at least I still had my sense of humour.

Three

Almost everyone seemed to be off with someone else's husband, wife, boyfriend or girlfriend in Geurie. At first I'd been too naive to notice, but after spending some time in this Venus flytrap of a town, I realised that affairs were practically a part of daily life. After ten years of loyalty to Brian – enduring his drinking, his irresponsibility and his parents – I longed to be loved, nurtured and appreciated, and so I too became entangled in a secret relationship of my own. My euphoria was short-lived though when the object of my affection broke the news to me that he'd found someone else.

Needing to confide in someone, I poured out my heart in a letter to my old friend Deb, who was still living the single life in the picturesque village of Kurrajong on Sydney's outskirts.

> *... I knew it wouldn't come to anything, but I still feel used and let down. It was such a good feeling to be attractive and adored by someone. At least it gave my dull life a bit of sparkle ...*

I vowed that my self-destructive need for love must cease and resigned myself to making the best of my marriage to Brian. But no sooner had I resolved to make amends than I met someone who would change my life forever.

It was 1989, the year of the Tiananmen Square massacre in Beijing and the Exxon *Valdez* oil spill off the Alaskan coast. For me though, tucked away in a sleepy town on the other side of the globe, little had changed. Brian continued to drink while I concentrated on raising our son, running the house and working full time.

Deb had married. Brian's parents had left Geurie and were now living on the New South Wales mid-north coast, just up the road from Denise's mother and father. My mum had moved to the coast too, and was living in Laurieton with her doting new husband, Clyde. Dad had married a charming Indonesian woman named Bea. My sister Kathryn and her husband John had had a second child, Patrick, and had settled on a small property outside Wingham, unwittingly close to Mr and Mrs Blakemore.

On this particular day, Brian, Coe and I had been invited to a casual evening barbecue across the road at the Fords', our neighbours. The Ford family was an important part of my growing social network and I counted Yvonne Ford as one of my dearest neighbourhood friends. This Aussie battler with her craggy face and unruly mop of dark hair always seemed to have a knot of little ones around her wherever she went, usually her grandchildren or some of the neighbourhood kids she minded on a casual basis, including Coe. Her husband, Colin, worked at the Grain Elevator Board and they struggled financially – their home was a mishmash of second-hand furniture, mismatched crockery, threadbare floor coverings and crooked additions – but Yvonne kept the place spotless and the yard well maintained, and she was a warm and generous host.

I was especially close to one of Yvonne's daughters, Sue. I was at the birth of Sue's little girl, Kristy, and subsequently became her godmother. When Sue was given a housing commission place in Geurie, I helped her turn it into a home. Together we scrubbed and painted rooms, searched out second-hand dealers for cheap furniture, sewed curtains and weeded garden beds. Soon after, Sue met Adrian. She said he was good to her. After all, he'd drive her around and sit in the car and wait for her while she cleaned people's bins for a small fee. How chivalrous, I'd say, tongue firmly in cheek.

Sometimes when Yvonne and I took Coe and the other kids to the river for a picnic and a swim, we'd find Sue waiting for Adrian on the grass bank like a faithful dog, stranded with little Kristy and then later

Elizabeth and Dean as well. Adrian and his mates would be off fishing in the boat. Sue's social network had dwindled since she'd met Adrian, but I refused to disappear from her life even though I suspected Adrian resented me for hanging around his woman.

Brian, Coe and I arrived at the Fords' at around four in the afternoon. Brian was ahead of me in his trackpants and sweatshirt with his precious carton of stubbies, lumbering across the neatly mown grass, past the yellowing geraniums in cement tubs, the green plastic whiz bin and the empty paddling pool abandoned from the previous summer. I trailed behind with an esky of meat, salad vegetables and wine as U2's 'Desire' belted out from a portable cassette player.

The backyard was full of the sprawling Ford clan. They were a casual lot, an extended family with its share of hard-drinking, volatile men who'd give you the shirt off their back one minute and have you shaking in your shoes the next, depending on how much alcohol they had under their belt.

The Ford daughters, Sue and Sandra, were bringing wood over for the barbecue and clowning around in time to the music. I was struck by how much they looked like younger versions of their mother, with the same tangles of dark brown hair, the same worn faces, the same baggy T-shirts and stretch pants, and the same vaguely vulnerable look, although Sandra was no pushover.

Adrian was nursing Kristy, and gave me a curt nod from his battered easychair as I heaved the esky around the corner. He looked like a sulky bandicoot with his long nose, mousy brown hair and pouting lips. Mark Clynes stood up when he saw me though and immediately came to help. Like a dark, wiry pirate, he wore silver earrings: double loops hanging rakishly from his right earlobe. He grinned at me. He was charming but, like his partner Sandra, reputed to be stroppy at times.

'Here, Donna, give that to me,' he said, tugging the plastic esky from my grasp.

I let him take it, rubbing the palm of my reddened hand on the side of my jeans. 'Thanks, mate. Bri's loaded up with the beer.' I rolled my eyes. Coe, now a big, fair-haired boy of seven, ran past me with a fist full of potato chips. I called him over. 'I hope you asked before you helped yourself,' I said quietly, squatting down to put my arm around him.

'Yeah, Mum,' he said with a gappy grin. 'Yvonne said I could.'

Yvonne, Coe's beloved surrogate nanna, came over with a glass of wine for me in one hand and a stubby for herself in the other. 'He's okay, Don. You know he always does the right thing. That kid's got the best manners in town.' She lowered herself down onto a folding chair and lit up a rollie.

I sat down next to her and took a sip of my wine. 'That's what comes of having a schoolteacher for a mother. Poor child.'

'You know Garry, don't you, Don?' She nodded towards a young bloke in a red and black checked flanno, tight black jeans and black motorbike boots sitting next to her. 'Mark's brother.'

I'd first met Garry months before, when he'd blown into the Mitchell Inn one night looking for Mark. A young traveller in worn jeans and basketball boots, with a swag over one shoulder, he'd paused in the doorway to scan the bar. The locals had stared back in silence. Strange males were not usually welcome on their turf.

He'd looked familiar and, feeling sorry for him, I called out from my seat near the door. 'You'd have to be a Clynes. You look so like Mark. I know he's got a heap of brothers.'

He smiled in relief and as he stepped closer to my table, the resemblance was even more striking: both had the same full lower lip and wide grin, although, unlike Mark's chocolate-coloured eyes, Garry's were a clear light blue and his hair was shorter, a mass of curls that framed his face. His cheeks bunched up like small pink plums and I noticed he had dimples.

'G-g-g-good guess,' he'd said, blushing. 'G-g-g-Garry's my name.'

The last thing I'd expected was for this attractive young guy to have a stutter. I'd tried not to react, but had felt an immediate pang of sympathy, as though he were some poor stammering kid in my kinder class who'd needed immediate remedial input.

'If you're looking for Mark, he's just nipped out the back for a moment.' I'd told him, nodding towards the Gents. At least he'd have his older brother for moral support.

A day or two later Garry had drifted on to Dubbo, securing a job at the meatworks and becoming friends with Adrian Ross. With his brother Mark seeing Sandra, Garry gradually became entwined with the Ford household, bringing Adrian with him to socialise in Geurie on weekends.

'Garry's not working at the abs no more. He's going to do some farm work out on the property where Mark and Sandra are living.' Yvonne took a swig from her stubbie. 'Mark had a word to the manager out there.'

'That's great. You're going to live with Mark and Sandra?' I asked.

'Na, here at Yvonne's f-f-f-for the moment. But if you hear of anything else, like, it gets a b-b-bit crowded here, with people staying and all that.'

I yawned then. 'Sorry. It's not the company, guys. I was up until all hours last night doing the posters for the latest club fundraiser.'

'You do too much, love. You look bloody exhausted, and you're that thin,' said Yvonne, taking another drag on her smoke. She turned to Garry. 'This lady's got a full-time job, a husband and a kid to look after and a house to run, and she spends whatever spare time she has left being the good Samaritan, at everyone's beck and call.'

I laughed and stifled a second yawn. 'It's not quite that bad.' I stood up and stretched, draining my glass. 'I'm going to get another drink and then I might help the girls in the kitchen. You two want another beer?'

Garry jumped up and took my glass from me. 'N-n-n-no. You sit down and relax. I'll sort the drinks. P-p-p-please. Sit down.'

I laughed at his sudden and insistent outburst and held up my hand. 'Okay, okay, you win. I'm doing as I'm told. I'm sitting.'

He gave me a beatific smile before turning to saunter off towards the kitchen.

It was indeed crowded at the Fords' and it wasn't long before Garry came to board with Brian and me. We had a spare room and, as Yvonne had suggested, the extra money came in handy. Besides, he seemed like a nice enough bloke; he was obliging and liked nothing more than to hang around with Coe and me, watching videos, helping with the chores and doing odd jobs around the house and yard.

'P-p-p-put the axe down,' he'd say when he found me out the back chopping wood for the Kosi heater. 'You've got me to do that now.'

'Leave the mowing, Donna. That's a b-b-b-bloke's job.'

'Give me that sh-sh-sh-shopping. I'll take care of that.'

He had a lot of time for Coe too, kicking the football around the backyard or having tea towel–flicking competitions over the washing up. I suspected he may have had a murky past, but he avoided talking about it. Nonetheless, the tattoos – a grinning skull on his left shoulder, a small scratchy crucifix on his leg, and a scroll reading 'Rest in Peace Dad' between his two shoulder blades – threw up many questions.

When I made an unfortunate discovery in his room one afternoon, I decided Garry and I needed to talk. Brian was at the pub and Coe was asleep when I broached the subject. Sitting in an old armchair beside the fire, I was brushing Garry's sun-hardened hair as he sat in contented silence between my feet.

'I need to talk to you about something, Garry,' I began. I was in schoolteacher mode, my voice soft but firm. 'This afternoon when I was vacuuming, I found a heap of food stashed under your bed: some old fruit and a pile of stale bread.'

He turned his head around to face me. 'Yeah, s-s-s-sorry. I try not to, it's just . . .'

'Where'd you pick up that little habit anyway?'

'I dunno. Sydney, maybe. You do things, you know. To get by. At least a bit of food stashed away for later made some stuff easier.'

'What sort of stuff?' I asked, taken aback at the thought of what street kids had to do to survive. 'And what about your family?'

He shrugged and gave an embarrassed curl of the lip. 'Dad was dead, Mum put away. I went to me aunty's to live. For a bit, anyway.'

'Where'd you go then?' I asked, carefully selecting another handful of tangled curls.

'D-d-d-don't want to talk about it.'

'Okay, but quit hoarding food. We'll have mice and God knows what else before long.' Garry didn't reply, and I wondered, not for the first time, what had happened to him as an adolescent. 'You did what you had to do to survive, but life's different now. You see that big white box over there –' I nodded towards the kitchen '– it's called a fridge. Help yourself. Anytime. Just make sure you clean up afterwards.'

In time, Garry all but lost his stutter and quit his food hoarding. He continued to help around the house and yard without being asked, and anything I did for him was met with enthusiasm and appreciation.

'This looks great!' was his frequent response as I placed a home-cooked meal in front of him night after night.

When Brian made an appearance at the table, he would urge Garry to leave the dishes for me to clean up, but Garry always refused. 'No. Donna cooked, so I'll wash up. Come on, Coe. Give us a hand.'

Arriving home from work, I'd find the washing had been pegged out, or brought in and folded. Wood was chopped, the lawn kept neat, repairs made around the house. Life was becoming easier than it had been in a long time.

In return I continued to foster his independence, encouraging him to investigate a welding course at TAFE and to brush up on his driving skills in preparation for getting his licence. The day he passed his practical test he jumped out of the car and grabbed me around the waist, whirling me around in a circle. I felt light, like a silk scarf.

'Put me down, Garry!' I laughed. 'Someone might see. Think the wrong way.'

'I don't care if the whole damn town sees. Good things happen when I'm with you.'

With his new licence, Garry hopped behind the wheel of my Corolla at every opportunity – on our weekend bush drives and yabbying trips with Yvonne and the kids. 'This is where I should be, and this is where you should be,' he'd say, smiling. 'Me in the driver's seat and you taking it easy.'

As the months wore on, I didn't want to admit it to myself but I was becoming attracted to this young man, 13 years my junior. To prevent myself from falling headlong into an embarrassing Oedipal trap, I encouraged Garry to find a nice young Geurie girl. Initially my ploy worked: in February 1990 he began to date one of the local girls, and being the great romance expert, I continued to help with hints and tips from the sidelines. But despite my coaching, the relationship eventually foundered.

Meanwhile, Garry was changing. He was no longer the gaunt, stuttering kid who had first come to stay. He was becoming more and more confident, assertive, manly. And another thing was clear: my feelings were not one-sided.

'God, you look beautiful, Donna,' Garry would say, gazing across at me as I headed out the front door to a staff dinner or bowling club do, with Brian yelling, 'Hurry up, will ya!' from the carport.

'If you were mine, I'd never let you out of my sight.'

One night we were sitting together on the porch, drinking coffee and talking. The moon was full above us, the night air crisp.

'Don't know how you pair find so much to bloody talk about,' Brian called through the doorway as he left for the pub.

As the sliding door closed and Brian retreated into the night, Garry turned to me, flexing his workman's hands around the mug. 'He don't know how wonderful you are,' he murmured. 'I could listen and talk to you forever. If you belonged to me, I'd never leave you alone.' He put the mug down and leaned closer, taking hold of my hand.

I didn't pull away.

My affair with Garry was the most intense relationship I could imagine. Even holding hands was a delight. And after years of fumbling, disheartening sex with an inebriated partner, lovemaking with Garry was the full fireworks. Brian had made me feel ugly, but with Garry I was beautiful. I'd always cared about my appearance, but I took extra joy now in looking good for Garry, wearing clothes he liked to see me in and jewellery he surreptitiously bought me, jewellery that Brian never noticed.

At last I'd found my knight in shining armour. How I'd yearned for a man to make me feel cherished and desirable, to whisper to me, 'Donna, there's nothing I don't love about you. Let me look after you.'

But my euphoria was short-lived; the affair abruptly terminated when Brian came in one night and caught us snuggled up together on the lounge. He was upset and shocked that anyone could be interested in me. As I jumped up and the excuses tumbled out, he pushed me aside and strode back outside through the sliding door.

'Brian, let's talk about this!' I cried.

But Brian headed back to the pub.

Although I was ashamed, it didn't take long for me to make up my mind about what I wanted to do next.

'I love you, Garry. I'm going to leave Brian,' I said. 'I deserve to be happy.'

'You are a one-in-a-million lady,' he crooned, his arms around me. 'I'll look after you, I promise I will. I'll never treat you like Brian does.'

~

It was several days before Brian would talk to me in a civilised manner. At first he was full of snide remarks: 'You're old enough to be his mother,' and 'He's only using you. He'll dump you for a younger version,' and 'What would people think? You look ridiculous with him!'

But after I told him of my decision to make a life with Garry, he insisted that he wanted to make the marriage work, bombarding me with reasons why I should change my mind: 'We've been married for years! Are you ready to throw all that away?' and 'What about Coe? He'd miss me. How could you be so selfish?' And finally: 'I'll give up the grog if you give up Garry. I promise you, this time I will. I'll even forgive you for being unfaithful. Just don't leave me.'

Having lived with broken promise after broken promise, I was suspicious of just how much effort he was prepared to make but, after much thought, I decided to give Brian and our marriage another chance. It was with a heavy heart that I explained to Garry that he could no longer stay with us and that he'd have to move out to Mark and Sandra's place, on the property where he and his brother worked.

I finally find happiness and I have to give it up, I thought, as I lay sobbing on my bed with the door shut. That'll teach me. Although I was sad, at the same time I was riddled with guilt over what I'd done. I was making the mistake of thinking things just couldn't get any worse when, around the corner, another nasty surprise lay in wait. A few weeks after Garry gunned down the dusty highway, I found I was carrying his child.

Initially I have to admit I was elated. I'd lost Garry, but at least I had our child. Soon though, reality intervened. Although I was opposed to aborting the foetus, Brian pointed out there was no other solution.

'People would know it's his,' he said. 'We can't have that!'

He drove me to Sydney for the abortion, with me weeping all the way there and all the way back as he sat behind the wheel in stony silence. It was 16 December 1990, our 12th wedding anniversary.

§

Soon after, and with considerable determination, Brian quit drinking and for the first time in years I saw a glimmer of the man that grog had all but obliterated. Brian was finally coming good; he became helpful and responsible, trying hard to hold down a job, and finishing all the odd jobs that needed to be done around the house. He hung doors, built a shed and repaired the leaking gutters. Most importantly, he became a dad to Coe.

To cement the renewal of our relationship, Brian suggested we try to have a second child. At nine years of age, Coe was ecstatic about the prospect of a baby brother or sister. I was sensitive to the fact that he'd been an only child for so long, that he and I had operated for much of his life as a close team. I knew it would be easy for him to feel displaced and jealous. Wanting to avoid any sibling rivalry, I took care to make him as much a part of things as I could. Together we converted Coe's old room into the baby's room and then revamped the larger spare bedroom for Coe. By the time December arrived, he was fizzing with excitement over the impending birth.

Bodean Jesse Blakemore was born early on 5 December 1991 at Dubbo Base Hospital. We nearly lost him as he had Rh incompatibility and required a full blood transfusion at birth, but he was a gorgeous baby: fair-skinned with my dark blue eyes and a halo of strawberry-blond hair. My parents, Kathryn and other friends and relations all came to stay at various times over that long, lazy summer as we welcomed this joyous new arrival into our family.

I wish I could say this was the happy ending to a romance addict's struggle for love and lasting happiness. I wish that I could pull the curtains closed here, leaving the audience with a final glimpse of the blushing mother, a reformed and attentive husband by her side, slumbering baby in her arms and beaming nine-year-old at her feet, on their way to a prosperous new life. But no. After this brief hiatus, my marriage took a turn for the worse.

As soon as my pregnancy was confirmed, Brian started drinking again, and by the time I gave birth, he was in the clutches of alcoholism once more, this time worse than ever. Locals regularly approached me, asking to be reimbursed for money they'd lent Brian, saying they were sick of chasing him for it. People were reluctant to sit near him at the pub, knowing that as soon as their backs were turned he'd be polishing off their drinks. In short, he had developed into such a nuisance that most of the Geurie residents gave him a wide berth.

All this time, Garry was hanging around in the background of our lives, often over at the Fords' or drinking at the club or pub. In spite of all that had happened, Brian had maintained a friendship with him – after all, it wasn't Garry's fault that I'd had an affair with him. They were occasional drinking buddies and, over time, Garry became a regular visitor at our place once more. He was now 21.

Saturday night was my socialising night, and the one night of the week that Brian eased up on the drinking and stayed home to babysit Coe and Bodean. I had a large circle of friends and acquaintances by this stage, and enjoyed chatting to a variety of people, having a few games of pool and a brief flutter on the pokies or raffles. But by far the thing I looked forward to the most was seeing Garry, and it wasn't long before we resumed our affair. He would saunter in like a cowboy, in rolled-up shirtsleeves and tight blue jeans, his Harley Davidson belt, emblazoned with a silver eagle, sitting low on his narrow hips. As soon as he caught sight of me he'd smile like a cherub. 'Mind if I join you?' he'd ask, barely able to contain his excitement.

Although there was still much of the boyish charm about him, something in his demeanour had changed. Perhaps having to deal with Mark and Sandra's fiery relationship on a daily basis had brought out a darker side in him. I'll never know. But whenever I stopped to talk to John and his wife Shirl on my way back from the bar, or took a break in my conversation with Garry to catch up with the club president, Neil Beehag, and his wife, Ngaire, I would sense him staring hotly in my direction.

'What did they want?' he'd ask upon my return.

'They're my friends, Garry. I was just saying hello.'

'Donna is well liked. Lots of people enjoy her company,' Yvonne Ford would often chastise him.

He never seemed to listen though. 'Say hello to me instead,' he'd drawl as soon as she was out of earshot. 'I miss you. I wait all week to see you.' He'd run the toe of his boot softly over my high heels and up my leg as he gazed across the table at me.

How wonderful to have a man who adores me, I thought, mistaking his jealousy for love.

Late one Saturday evening, we'd taken the car to a local lovers' spot, under a bridge on the outskirts of town, bumping down the rough dirt track to the water's edge. It was black as pitch by the river, and only a tiny fingernail sliver of a moon hung above us in the inky sky. I got out of the car and shivered as the cool air slid like a wraith from the water. I could smell jasmine, sharp and honeyed, and although I couldn't see it now, I knew it twisted around the bridge supports in a sweet stranglehold. Garry would often pick the small white flowers and place them in my hair. He would not be doing this tonight though; he was brooding about something. He'd been silent on the short drive to the river. As we stood together on the sandy bank, my eyes gradually adjusted to the gloom. I glanced sideways at Garry and leaned out to take his hand. He snatched it back as if he'd been stung, then swung around and pushed me away.

I stumbled backwards. 'Hey, what's wrong?'

'You were playing pool with Tommy Culkin,' he said.

I laughed at Garry's accusation and at the shove, assuming this was a joke. 'But Tommy's an old man.'

'I saw the way he looked at you.'

I took a step backwards, closer to the water, and held up my hands. 'Just hang on a minute, Garry. I –'

He seized my wrists and shook me hard. I saw a flash of white teeth. 'You bitches are all the same, flirting with other men!'

My heart was pumping like I'd run a marathon. I'd never seen him like this. 'I don't understand, Garry,' I babbled, trying to tug my wrists away from his grasp. 'I'm sorry it upset you.' My voice was high with nerves, quavering all over the place. I made myself swallow.

'Shut up! Shut up! Just shut the fuck up!' He let go of my hands with a shove, but continued to glare at me from the shadows.

'Don't look at me like that, Garry. You're frightening me,' I said. 'I want to go home.'

Garry was a stuttering, apologetic mess when he saw me the next weekend up at the club.

'P-p-p-please Donna, I didn't mean it. I didn't m-m-mean to scare you. I love you so much,' he murmured in my ear as I sat at a table by the wall. 'I want to be with you all the time. It d-d-drives me crazy that I can't.'

Of course I forgave him. He looked so forlorn and, after all, he loved me so much. And maybe I shouldn't have been playing pool while Garry sat alone. Maybe it was partly my fault.

For a while, he reverted to being the perfect gentleman and soon I was wondering whether I had blown the 'episode' out of all proportion as I replayed it over and over in my head. As time went on and Garry continued to show his sweet, uncomplicated side, I was lulled into complacency. But another fire warning was not far away.

One night, Garry and I were preparing to drive back from the river, now our preferred parking spot since local police constable Matt Adderley had caught us a while back, parked on the road to Deep Creek. This particular evening, on the road back to town, we saw something glowing in the distance, a giant torch illuminating the winter dark.

'Let's go and have a look,' he suggested, pointing the car towards Geurie.

Soon we discovered the source of the strange orange light. In a paddock by the side of the road, the burning remains of a once majestic gum sparkled and crackled beneath the stars. We ducked through the wire fence to get closer. Tiny sparks spat from the smouldering tree and one or two orange flames curled around its massive base. Its upper branches were scorched and the ground below was littered with blackened debris. The enormous hollow trunk glowed like a fiery lantern.

Once through the fence, Garry, like an impetuous kid, wasted no time in rushing up to the tree. He was metres from the trunk, warming his hands by the glowing wood. I stood back, gazing up at the burning branches.

'Move back, Garry,' I said after a minute or two. 'It's dangerous to be so close. A branch could fall on you.'

He shrugged. 'Okay,' he said, stepping casually away. As he did so, there was a sickening crack above his head. I screamed out for him to run. A flaming branch crashed onto the very spot he'd been standing. It was the size of a cow and probably every bit as heavy.

'You saved me, baby,' he said, wrapping his arms around me as the fire continued to burn in front of us. 'You saved my life. I'm yours forever. I'll never let you go.'

///

One night, as we were leaving the club, Garry, without warning, suddenly whirled around, picked me up and held me against the outside wall.

'Why were you talking to John for so long?' he shouted. 'Bloody bitch. Are you fucking him too?'

Before I had time to react, John Heller burst through the front door of the club, hauling Garry away from me by his shirt collar. 'I'll break your bloody neck if you lay a hand on her,' he said, his voice low and venomous. 'You hear me? I'll break your bloody neck!'

As John continued to berate Garry, dragging him away from the entrance of the club, I took off, scrabbling in my bag for the keys as I bolted towards my car. By the time I'd made the short trip home, I was shaking uncontrollably.

'Christ, what's happened now?' asked Brian as I slammed the glass door behind me. He was spread out on the lounge watching a movie with a cluster of empty stubbies on the floor nearby. Beside the bottles, the remains of a fry-up were congealing on a plate.

I sat down at the table and put my head in my hands. 'Something's wrong with Garry. He went crazy up at the club. He really scared me. John's dealing with it.' Right on cue, there was a light tap at the door behind me and I turned to see Garry standing, white-faced, on the other side of the glass.

'I don't want him here,' I told Brian.

'Calm down, drama queen,' he said and got up to open the door.

The next minute Garry was inside. Ignoring Brian, he came straight over to where I was sitting. 'I'm s-s-s-sorry Donna, I'm real sorry. I had too much to drink ... the boss has been on my back lately ...'

'Go away, Garry.'

Brian hovered behind him. 'Here, mate, don't mind her. Sit down and have a beer with me.'

'No way, I want him out of here,' I said, crossing my arms and glaring at the pair of them.

Brian pulled a face. 'Christ, you go on sometimes.'

'I mean it. Out, Garry! And don't come back!'

'Okay, okay,' Brian said. He looked at Garry and shrugged. 'Maybe you'd better go, mate.'

'I said I'm sorry,' he whined. He paused for a second or two then turned on his heel and stormed out, banging the sliding door shut behind him. I took myself off to bed without another word, vowing never to talk to or even acknowledge him again.

I kept that promise to myself for about 18 months, despite his apologies over the phone and his frequent late-night drive-bys. Although I wouldn't speak to him, he and Brian remained drinking buddies and from time to time I'd see him at the Fords'.

'What's he doing here?' I'd ask. 'If he's staying, I'm going.'

'It's okay, I'll go,' he'd mutter, gathering his things and leaving quietly.

I was disappointed in Garry, but even Brian was changing: instead of the once easy-going inebriate I'd known, he was now showing signs of violence as well. What was going to happen next, I wondered.

Each afternoon, I'd arrive home from work with the kids, having collected Bodean from a day-care mother I'd chosen specially, but who unfortunately lived across the other side of town. The house would be a pigsty, with the remains of Brian's drunken feasting – dirty dishes, food scraps and greasy frypans – scattered across the filthy benchtop. Brian was usually nowhere to be seen, more often than not arriving home around three or four o'clock in the morning, when I'd begin the next day.

One morning just before dawn, I was woken by Brian's drunken ranting. I heard him crashing around in the kitchen, and a few minutes later he had the record player on, with Led Zeppelin blaring at ear-splitting volume. I sighed, swung my legs out of bed and strode down the hall in bare feet and an old T-shirt, shouting over the music for him to turn it off.

In a split second I found myself on the lounge room floor, my eye throbbing from the impact of Brian's fist. Constable Matt Adderley's number was already highlighted in my address book. It hadn't been the first time I'd needed to ring him about my husband.

Brian was putting on his shoes. 'Tell him not to bother coming out this time. I'm going.'

The following morning, sporting a black eye, I went to the police station to apologise to the clean-cut young constable for waking him up. He and his wife had just had a baby. I was sure that the last thing they needed was the phone ringing at all hours.

He seemed surprised by the sight of my bruised face as we stood inside his front office. 'So what are you going to do now?' he asked.

'This marriage was over a long time ago,' I said. 'I'm going to buy Brian out of his half of the house, and the kids and I are going to manage on our own.'

'Well, good luck. Life'll probably be a lot quieter.'

Two days later, on 28 March 1993, Brian returned with his brother to collect his belongings. He was moving in with Denise and Danny, now living in Parkes. And so it was that shortly before my 36th birthday, I began life as a single woman.

After Brian left, despite numerous visits from my ever-supportive family, I hit rock bottom. During the winter of 1993, I would arrive home with the two boys after dark to a cold and cheerless house. The flue had fallen apart, putting the heater out of commission, so Coe and I would strap hot-water bottles beneath our jumpers, taking turns to cuddle Bodean under a blanket in between cooking tea, pouring baths and taking care of the usual household chores. Sometimes, we'd turn the electric blanket on and the three of us would pile into the double bed to read, talk and watch television.

It was unlike me to succumb for long to this maudlin state of mind, but as 1993 dragged on, I sank deeper into an embittered state. By the time those pale shoots pushed up through the warm spring soil, I was sick with longing for someone to share the load, be there for me, fix the bloody heater, be a father to my sons, and turn our small trio into a proper family.

I began to reminisce about my early romance with Garry and how caring he'd been. Surely after spending over a year in Coventry, things could be different. And, just as the pain of childbirth blurs with time, so too had the fear I'd experienced at the hands of this paradoxical young man. As the months passed, in my mind he'd become not nearly as scary, and the rosy memories of our happier times together elbowed their way to the fore. The more I thought about it, the more it seemed to me that Garry had been truly supportive.

I drove over to see him one day, confronting him about his abusive behaviour all those months before. He had been upset, he explained. Dreadfully upset. I'd chosen Brian over him in spite of the fact that he'd loved me so much. All he'd ever wanted was to look after me and my two boys.

With the benefit of hindsight, it's now clear that I should have run a mile. But I had been brought up to trust and see the best in people. I didn't recognise the Trojan horse. In the latter half of 1993, Garry and I started seeing each other and, over time, he made himself invaluable to me again – socially, emotionally and physically.

The rekindling of the relationship began well, due in part to the fact that we were taking things slowly. He had his place. I had mine. But a few months later, in January 1994, Garry suggested he move in. The boys and I had just come back from staying with Mum and Clyde in Laurieton. Garry told me that while we were away his brother Mark and sister-in-law Sandra had asked him to move out because there wasn't space, and that he had spent the last few weeks sleeping on their laundry floor. I felt I couldn't say no. Maybe, too, it was time to 'go public', and explain things to the kids, especially Coe.

The news of my relationship with Garry was not met with the rush of disapproval I'd imagined. One or two locals even remarked that we made a lovely couple. But John Heller was not so sure.

'Be careful, Donna,' he said one afternoon outside the general store. 'He's a wild young bloke. Terrorised Wellington last year, so they say.' He tossed his head in the direction of the neighbouring town. 'Mention his name around there and they'll tell you a thing or two.'

Shirl, his wife, was standing next to him. 'John's right, Donna. Garry could be trouble.'

I liked and respected this salt-of-the-earth couple, but I became defensive.

'You know what this place is like for gossip. There's plenty of good in Garry,' I told them. 'The other week I had the shovel out and he said,

"Donna, I never want to see you working in the yard. I do the outside work, you do the inside work. And if I finish early, I'll come in and help you".'

'Yeah?' John grunted, batting a fly away from his face.

'Yeah! And you know what? He keeps his promises, unlike you-know-who. He's there for me. The kids love him. And so do I.'

Shortly after Garry moved back in, I had cause to reconsider John and Shirl's solemn words. My lover's prowling jealousy had resurfaced fairly quickly and his casual enquiries as to why I was a few minutes late soon turned into heated interrogations and ridiculous accusations. He'd hooked me. Now he wanted to control me.

'Where've you been?' he asked one night as I arrived home with Bodean on my hip and an overloaded school basket in my other hand. Garry was sitting on the sofa, arms folded. He looked at his watch. 'You're late.'

I could tell that it was going to be on if I didn't defuse the situation. 'Take Bodean, Coe. Go and run a bath for him, will you?' I set my basket down and turned to Garry. 'Don't you remember? I had to get two new tyres for the car.'

'No, I don't remember.'

I rummaged around in my basket. 'I'll show you the docket. Look.' Walking over to the sofa, I held out the crumpled receipt.

Snatching it, he spent several seconds glaring at the evidence. 'How come he's written just "Donna" on the top?'

Because that's my name, I wanted to say. I didn't dare though. Instead I wiped my clammy palms on my checked skirt and said, 'He knows me. I've been there before.'

Garry stood up and sauntered over to the fridge, still in his work singlet and old blue jeans. 'I *bet* you been there before.'

I gulped, staring at his hunched back as he leaned into the fridge to retrieve a beer. 'I haven't been up to anything, Garry. I just needed new tyres. When Dad got me the car he said I'd have to do that before next rego and so –'

'Shut the fuck up!' He slammed the fridge door and whirled around to face me. 'You're a fucking slut. You bitches are all the same. I know what you get up to behind my back.'

I hid my face in my hands and began to weep, my shoulders heaving, snot dribbling from my nose. Eventually I heard the glass door slam. He was gone. For the moment.

He didn't return that night, and I was relieved. For someone I'd loved so completely, at that moment I despised him. The following afternoon, when the boys and I got home, the washing had been brought in and folded neatly. There was a scruffy note on the kitchen table. It was written in blue biro on lined paper ripped from an old exercise book. It was an apology. It begged my forgiveness.

I did forgive him, outwardly at least. I knew though that this couldn't go on. I would have to speak to him, but would have to pick my time.

It was Friday, 18 March 1994.

God's final fire warning was exactly two weeks away.

Four

Friday, 1 April was a clear autumn day, still and warm, and I woke early. I'd turned 37 the day before. I hadn't celebrated though. My birthday had fallen on the last day of term, a whirlwind of Easter hat parades, belated parent interviews and desk clean-outs, followed by a huge after-school grocery shop with Bodean and Coe. After that, I'd dropped into the hospital to have some stitches removed from a kitchen-accident injury – I'd managed to slice my hand open while washing up.

Even if I'd wanted to celebrate, after a full-on day and several phone calls that evening from family members, I was too tired to do much except lie in front of a video with Coe, Bodean and Garry, eating homemade hotdogs.

The following morning, Garry lay beside me, snoring softly. His cheeks were flushed, his mouth slightly open. His hair fell in soft curls around his tranquil face, like Michelangelo's David. I watched him for a while, propped up on one elbow to gaze down on him as he slept. How could two such completely different people inhabit the same beautiful body? And, more importantly, were they destined to be bound forever?

My thoughts drifted as I contemplated those complex operations they performed on conjoined twins. Teams of surgeons working in shifts, snipping, slicing, stitching. Unjoining. Sometimes one twin was sacrificed to let the other live. If only it could be like that with Garry. Just hack away the stranger. Set the angel free.

I blinked and sat upright, trying to flush away these thoughts. Slowly and carefully, I swung my legs out of bed, took my dressing-gown from behind the door and slipped my feet into a pair of jewel-green slippers, a present from Garry. Not a birthday present. He hadn't actually bought me anything for my birthday yet. He'd promised to take me to Dubbo the next day to choose something special. Not the same as a surprise though, I thought wistfully, padding down the dim hallway.

It was Good Friday. An image of Christ's twisted, sinewy body hanging from the cross hovered in my mind's eye as I filled the kettle. Iron nails puncturing bleeding palms, a face in tragic repose. Stop it, I told myself sharply. Stop thinking about carved-up twins and bodies on crucifixes. Think about your birthday. Think about that.

While the kettle boiled, I slipped out the back to feed the cat. I squinted up at the high country sky overhead, blue as far as the eye could see. I closed my eyes and breathed in the air. It smelled fresh, like rainwater. I let the gory visions trickle away then, and in the still morning sunshine the world was full of promise again as a whole two weeks of holidays stretched ahead, big and beautiful, like that enormous sky. I decided then and there that not even Garry's increasingly erratic behaviour would dilute my optimism. I would deal with him later, I told myself. Not today though. Today was Donna's day.

We had an early lunch of hot chicken, oven chips and green beans. The chicken was Coe's favourite, a working mother's concoction of French onion soup powder sprinkled over drumsticks and shoved into the oven. I'd made it for him especially, as compensation for having to stay home and babysit his little brother, for which I usually gave him a small amount of pocket money. Normally he didn't mind this arrangement, but he wanted to visit his friend Lindsay. I was determined to have a few hours of birthday celebration up at the Bowling Club, and told him he'd have to see his friend later that afternoon.

After lunch, I put Bodean down for his nap and whizzed through the washing up so I could take some time getting ready. I'd been thinking about what I would wear. I didn't want to look like a kindergarten teacher, that was for sure. I'd be staying away from the side of the wardrobe that bulged with belted gingham frocks, neatly collared blouses, pleated skirts and cheerful cardigans. Instead, I chose from the other end: a pair of blue jeans, kitten heels and a black crocheted shirt over a singlet top. I painted my lips glossy red, slicked mascara through my lashes and put on some gold earrings, another present from Garry. I scrutinised myself in the mirror. You look good, I thought. No matter what Garry says, you look good for 37.

Finally, around my neck, I fastened Coe's present. It was a gold filigree heart. He hadn't forgotten. I knew he wouldn't. I fingered the heart softly. My darling sons. They loved me, and I them; nothing could take that away.

The whole town seemed to be gathered in the modest fibro clubhouse that day and everyone was in a holiday mood. There were leather-faced farmers in their checked shirts, moleskins and elastic-sided boots; the CWA set, easily recognisable by their pastel print dresses and sensible shoes; local characters like Richard Carpenter and Johnny Dewar propping up the bar, and the usual larrikins and layabouts, scrubbed up in flannos and clean jeans, primed for a day of socialising.

I didn't quite know where I fitted into this mixed bag, but I knew everyone there. Over the past 16 years I'd been invited into these people's homes, gone to their families' christenings and funerals, and attended their kids' 21st birthdays and weddings. Various friends wandered over to wish me a happy birthday, offering to buy me a drink, challenge me to a game of pool or just chat for a bit. I was lucky to belong to such a close-knit, loyal community, I thought.

This warmth and companionship, this good-natured camaraderie, was something that had slowly but surely leaked from my life. First, as the wife of one of the town's most cash-strapped drunks, I had been avoided. Then when Brian left, I'd been so busy struggling with a combination of low moods and fatigue, I couldn't find the energy or headspace for much socialising. Finally, Garry's presence had deterred even the most loyal of friends from having too much to do with me. Now, surrounded by well-wishers, I realised what I'd been missing and how suffocating Garry's love had become.

I wasn't any less frightened, though, when I saw him sitting in the corner with folded arms and scowling face, throwing another schooner down. Pretty soon I was hard at work trying to curb his rising anger.

'Come on, Garry.' I held out my hand. 'Come and have a go on the pokies with me.'

'What were you talking to her about?'

'Ngaire? Her children. Come on, my favourite machine's free.'

He gave me a dark look.

I sighed. 'Garry, we've got the day off. It's my birthday. People just want to wish me well. Now are you coming or not?'

He stood up, put his cigarettes in his shirt pocket and shoved his lighter, a red plastic disposable, in the back pocket of his jeans. 'Yeah, yeah. I'm getting a drink first. Okay with you? I won't ask you if you want one, Miss Popularity.'

'I'll be over at the machine,' I mumbled, my euphoria ebbing away. I would talk to him over the holiday break. When the time was right we'd talk.

We'd been together at the machine for half an hour; I was on the stool feeding money into the slot and Garry was pressed behind me in hard, frosty silence. My prison warder. The smoke from his cigarette curled over my shoulder and I could smell his beer-breath. I made myself focus on the machine. We'd won a bit already, and I'd managed to squirrel our original investment away in my purse, plus quite a bit more. I had at least a couple of hundred dollars tucked away, and it seemed that our run of good luck wasn't over.

The jackpot went off, sending the machine berserk. Whistles and sirens blared from the chrome robot in front of us, and its multi-coloured lights flashed like a Broadway show.

'We've won the big jackpot!' I screamed, leaping off the stool and throwing my arms around Garry. 'We've won a thousand dollars!'

'Birthday luck, eh?' He managed a small smile, but lapsed into stony silence as the Geurie locals streamed over, clapping me on the back, handing out hugs, kisses and beers, and largely ignoring Garry.

'Congratulations, Donna!'

'Birthday present, love! Well done!'

'Good on ya, mate!'

Landing a thousand dollar jackpot at the Geurie Bowling Club was like winning Lotto.

As the crowd cleared, I grabbed Garry's calloused hand and gave it a squeeze. 'This is great, isn't it?' I said, tugging him towards the bar so I could sign for the prize. 'When the money comes through we'll go into Dubbo and treat ourselves. We can get the boys some new clothes, pay some bills, and you can get some more chrome work done on your Holden –' The words tumbled out. I was like a desperate puppy at his master's feet: Come on, cheer up! I'm excited, I need you to be excited too.

But it seemed that Garry's festering mood would not yield and by the time we got to the bar, his lips were pressed into a thin, sulky line.

'Here, you sign for it, Garry,' I blurted out, handing the pen to him. Surely being in charge of the money would lighten his mood.

He didn't object, but took the biro without a word, signing his name with awkward authority. Although we'd have to wait a few days for the jackpot money, we'd already cashed in a couple of hundred. I handed a fistful of notes to Garry. 'You hang onto this, babe.' I was prepared to do just about anything to make the angry Garry disappear.

We didn't stay long after that. Coe had already rung the club to find out when we'd be back, and I needed to get home, put a load of washing on, bath Bodean and begin teatime preparations. Apart from that, I was tired of being there with Garry. I felt flat and sad. My mouth tasted sour.

Before I'd even driven out of the carpark, he started. 'You think you're just *it*, don't you? Everyone falling over you, birthday girl. You're up to something.' His voice was low and threatening.

'Nothing's going on, Garry. You're the love of my life,' I lied. 'They were just wishing me a happy birthday.' I had to speak to him, but not then. Can't reason with him now, I told myself, must talk to him over the holidays. When the time is right.

'Bullshit! I know you're having it off with someone.'

I flicked him an annoyed look as I turned onto the road. 'Christ, Garry, how many times do I have to tell you? There's no one else.'

Without warning, he began screaming like a lunatic. 'Bitch, ya bloody old slag! I know you're fucking someone, ya bloody ugly slut!' His knuckles slammed into my forearm as I tried to control the car. The palm of his other hand caught the side of my face.

My heart banged violently. 'Garry! I'm not – not – not –' I tried to speak, but the words wouldn't come out. I began to cry instead.

As we neared the house, I yanked hard on the wheel, hurling the car into the front yard and zigzagging down the side of the house as Garry continued his verbal and physical battering.

Coe was watching out the back window, although I didn't know it then. He could see the car rocking and weaving across the yard. He told me later that he could hear us. Shouting and arguing. Us? Both of us? Funny how I was lumped in as well, as though there were an equality to it.

By the time I'd brought the car to a shuddering halt in the carport behind the unregistered Corolla, my head was so fat with tears and fury that, even if I'd wanted to, I couldn't have got a single word out. I snatched the keys from the ignition and threw them into my handbag, knowing from experience that to leave them in the car would result in my vehicle being hijacked for the rest of the evening.

Once inside, I headed straight for the bedroom, slipping off Coe's gold filigree heart and placing it on the dressing table. I left on my rings, earrings and bangles. I stared at my puffy face in the mirror. Fresh tears rolled from swollen, mascara-streaked eyes. A purple bruise blossomed over one cheek. I sat down on the edge of the bed as Coe's anxious face appeared around the corner.

'What's up, Mum?' He came in and sat down beside me, putting one arm around my back.

'Just Garry being a dickhead,' I sniffed, using the back of my hand to wipe my nose.

Coe passed me a box of tissues from the dressing table. 'Here, have a tissue. You're always telling kids not to use their hands. Now you're doing it.'

'Thanks,' I muttered, trying hard to smile. I took a handful and blew my nose a few times. 'That feels better.' I leaned over and kissed him on the cheek. 'Don't worry, honey. I'll sort it out. How about you go check on Bodean and I'll start tea.'

I don't know what I'd planned to cook that evening, but I remember I had pots rattling away on the stovetop and some sort of fishy casserole in the oven for Good Friday. I fiddled about in the kitchen for a bit longer and put on a load of washing. The washing machine was in the kitchen, near the back door. All this time I could hear Garry outside, cursing and shouting and kicking the furniture around the back porch. I could hear it crashing against the back of the house.

Keep out of his way, I told myself. Make yourself invisible.

At some stage, I went back up to the other end of the house, possibly to run a bath for Bodean. Coe followed me. Suddenly Garry burst into the master bedroom. He had Bodean under one arm and threw him on the bed. Not dangerously hard, but hard enough to give him a fright.

Bodean pushed himself upright and sat wide-eyed in the middle of the bed. He was silent for perhaps three seconds. Then his little face crumpled and he began to scream.

'Look after your fucking kid, why don't ya,' Garry growled as he crashed back down the hallway. 'Keep ya fucking kid away from me.'

Soon I heard the back door slam. Although I didn't know it at the time, he'd disconnected the phone on the way out, wrapping the cord neatly around the handset before carrying it out to the old Corolla. He placed it neatly on the back seat.

When I saw Bodean wailing with fright, I became really angry. How dare he touch my baby like that!

Garry was out of control though, and fear still prickled around the edges of my temper. I knew I had to be careful. I waited several minutes, cuddling Bodean then settling him with some toys on my bed. I made my way back to the kitchen. I stood at the back door, straining to pick up Garry's outpourings over the churning washing machine. The swearing and crashing seemed to have stopped. Maybe he's gone, I thought. Probably gone to Yvonne's. The Fords were like parents to him and he often fled to them after a scene.

The washing machine was almost ready to release its rinse water by this stage. I needed to direct the outlet hose onto the back lawn to water the grass. This would give me a chance to see if Garry was still around, and was an excuse for opening the back door in the first place. I didn't want to be accused of spying.

I dragged the hose out the door and cautiously looked about. No Garry. Setting the hose down on the grass, I stopped to listen once again. Silence. I edged along the back of the house, past the whiz bin, past Coe's BMX, around the corner to the carport, without a sound.

He was there, beside the old, brick-red Corolla. He had a black petrol container in his hand. A piece of garden hose lay at his feet, next to the petrol cap.

He swivelled around to face me. 'What the fuck do you want?' His face was crimson.

'I'm just putting the hose out, Garry.'

'Bullshit. You're bloody spying.'

'What are you doing, anyway?' I had a fair idea what he was doing. I'd seen it all before.

'What the fuck does it look like I'm doing, stupid? I'm getting petrol so I can piss off.'

I stepped closer. My heart was beating wildly. My hands felt clammy. 'Fine by me. By all means go. But you're not taking the car.' I knew the Corolla would be lethal with Garry behind the wheel in this state.

But saying no was like a red rag to a bull. 'I'm taking the fucking car, bitch! I'm going!'

'If you want to go, go. Just walk. Go! But you're not taking the car!' I came right up to him then, my legs rubbery beneath me. I snatched the handle of the petrol container.

'You can't tell me what to do, slut! I'll do what I fucking well like!' Garry yanked the petrol container back as I clung on. Petrol slopped over our hands. Our deadly tug-of-war had begun.

Garry was cyclonic, batting me around with his free hand as though I were a dishrag, all the while continuing his screaming. 'Bloody fucking bitch! I'll show you! Say fucking "no" to me will ya, cunt!' He was ripping my top. He tore a chunk out as he tossed me back and forth. Handfuls of thick, crocheted material lay around us. He still had the container in one hand and I clung desperately to it, to him, to anything, trying to stay on my feet. In seconds, his pummelling disconnected me from the container. There was petrol everywhere. I flailed back and forth, trapped in the narrow alleyway between the car and the house. I stumbled then, backwards over the brick steps.

Within moments, Garry had me pinned down on the steps. I twisted my head and saw the glass door slide open, just a crack. I yelled out to Coe, telling him to stay inside and lock the door.

Coe led Bodean away from the glass and headed out the front door towards the sandpit. He shoved an armload of sand-encrusted toys in front of his brother before running back to the house.

Back in the carport, Garry had been startled by the door opening, by my yelling to Coe. For a second he released his grip. I scrambled up, which seemed to enrage him even more. I knew I had to fight back.

I grabbed a fistful of his hair, bunched my fists, swung haphazardly at his chest and face. I fought long and hard. But in the end he was too strong. I didn't know it then, but Coe was back at the door, watching from behind the glass.

Under Garry's blows I staggered sideways, towards the back of the carport. It was then I copped the petrol, straight in the face and all down my front. My eyes were stinging. I clamped them shut.

My son watched as Garry pulled the lighter from his pocket. Coe turned and ran through the house to the back door, to the hose.

By the time he'd flung the back door open, he could hear my screams. I was on fire, running blindly, a trail of flames streaming in my wake.

'Roll, Mum! Roll!'

I dropped to the ground in a burning heap and began throwing myself back and forth. I rolled many, many times, on and on, until I just couldn't roll anymore. But I needed to see my son. Like a dying fish, I forced myself to flip over one more time. Give me strength, God. Give me strength. I have to see my boy.

At this point, in a single heartbeat, I knew this was it. I was going to die. In my need for romance I'd been playing with fire. I'd been playing with it for years.

I closed my eyes and Coe ran for the hose, uncurling it, dragging it over to where I lay smouldering. He said my hair was black, but not my face. It was a strange leathery white. My cheeks were tinged with green. Wispy strands of charcoaled skin hung from my face and jawline. My eyes were tightly shut. My clothes had all but burned away but I still wore my shoes. Pointed toes and kitten heels.

My nextdoor neighbour, Trevor Dunn, had heard the screams and scaled a six-foot-high fence to reach me. He'd called for Dave Hayward, living two houses down. He'd snatched the hose while Coe ran inside to call the ambulance. And Bodean? I suspect he'd probably crept around the back, drawn by the commotion, the fire and smoke, the screaming.

Inside, Coe knew Garry had taken the phone. He ran to Bodean's toy chest and frantically dug around among the plastic blocks and soft toys. He was looking for the other phone, one of those clunky plastic handsets with the old-fashioned dial. I'd rescued it from school only weeks before, when our telephone system had been updated, as a toy for Bodean.

'You want it for a spare phone?' the technician had asked. 'You can't do that, you know.'

'No, I want it for my baby to play with, that's all.'

'Sure you do,' he'd said. 'Yeah, you can have it, but you won't be able to use it.' He'd picked up the cord hanging from the old phone and snapped off one of the connecting prongs. 'Be my guest,' he'd said, pointing to the disabled machine.

Now, Coe pulled the old phone out of the toy chest and stumbled back into the lounge room, jamming it into the socket. He grabbed the receiver and held it to his ear. Miraculously, he heard a dial tone. Whatever the phone engineer had snapped off didn't stop the phone from working. Coe's emergency call was logged at 5.25 pm. Just minutes later, two ambulances hurtled out of their station, flashing and wailing, belting along the blacktop towards Geurie.

At 5.41 pm the ambulances swept into the driveway. The place was lit up like a party. There were police, the media, local State Emergency Service volunteers and a cluster of neighbours: Trevor and Dave from next door, Yvonne Ford, her daughter Sue and Sue's husband, Adrian. I don't remember much, but I know that as my eyes fluttered open, I expected sweet heaven. Instead I saw my own backyard. I was gutted.

Yvonne's face hovered above me, right up close.

I asked her for water. I whispered urgent instructions about the boys. 'My children. Hang onto them until my mother gets here,' I told her. Then, realising I was naked, 'Cover me up, cover me. Cover me!'

Sue dressed me in a shirt from the line. Someone else draped me in a wet blanket.

More people were bending over me, murmuring. Their faces swam and stretched, like a Munch painting. Behind them I saw lights flashing.

I blinked. I knew I had to speak. 'Garry did this. Garry did this to me.'

There was a lot of smoke around and voices barking orders. Fragmented commands and questions whirled around me.

'... wet blankets ...'

'... any known allergies?'

'... your name ...'

'... morphine infusion ...'

'... the toddler ...'

Garry was sitting several metres away on the back doorstep, near the melted whiz bin. He'd put himself out. He had been burned down the side of his face and body. His hands were damaged too. I didn't know this back then. Didn't know about the shirt, the blanket, about Garry. Didn't know about the melted whiz bin. Like some horrible omen, it had melted right at the spot where Garry, Coe, Bodean and I had sprayed outlines of our hands with yellow paint before Christmas. They had been bunched together on the green plastic like an Aboriginal hand painting. Hands together, the four musketeers.

One of the ambulance officers attended Garry while the senior officer, George Harper, worked on me. My body had begun to swell, puffing up like a giant blister. My rings and bangles were ringbarking me, so George had to cut my jewellery off. He pushed a thin metal tube into my inside elbow, through the burnt flesh, plunging it deeply, accurately, into my vein. He was pumping me with fluid. Minus my outer layers of skin, I was leaking, and without fluid I would die. He said he injected morphine but I don't remember. I don't remember much. I remember being lifted onto a stretcher, though. I felt light, like a plastic bag or a wispy feather.

The ambulance swept out of Geurie at 6.08 pm. I lay unconscious, with George watching over me. I died once or twice on the way. Two people needed to work on me to bring me back. George must have hollered for the driver to pull over – to slide off the long, flat highway into the dust and gravel – and leap into the back. Just like on television, they pressed two electric paddles into my chest, and maybe someone counted: one, two, three, before jolting my heart back to life. I don't remember the heart machine, but I remember the light. I remember death. Or near-death. Heaven's gate. I've been there. It wasn't time for me to leave though. I was tossed back, and would continue to be, over and over again in the months that followed.

We screamed into emergency at about 6.30 pm. They say I was conscious, but I don't remember. Brian arrived a while later, pushing through the ring of medical staff working on me.

'What are you doing here?' I asked. 'Who's looking after the kids?'

At Dubbo Base Hospital, they slit my ballooning arms, my neck and chest. They pushed fresh blood into my cooked body – four packs of concentrated red blood cells. They filled me with pipes and tubes and wrapped me in gauze, like an oversized mummy. Intubated, ventilated, sedated. I don't remember it, but I read it in my medical records many months later: intubated, ventilated, sedated. It had quite a jaunty tone to it, I thought.

They couldn't deal with me at Dubbo Base Hospital, or with Garry. In the early hours of the morning we were loaded onto a careflight helicopter, K918, and taken to Sydney. It all happened in a haze but I know it happened – the documents recorded it but so did my subconscious. For many years after, when helicopters flew overhead I entered a panic. Somewhere deep in my brain I must've kept a tiny locked box of nightmare memories. Occasionally one would seep out and scare me witless.

We arrived at Westmead Hospital at 3.15 am and were rushed straight to intensive care, along with our bandages, tubes and drips, machines and masks. Aside from all this, we came with one more attachment. It had nothing to do with high-tech medical paraphernalia, but it flew with us in the air ambulance, embedded casually in my medical records like a cunning little virus. It was a story. A story of a double suicide pact.

Death

Five

I had suffered full-thickness burns to 65 per cent of my body: my entire face, neck, breasts, midriff, shoulders, both arms, armpits, hands, all fingers, legs and tops of feet. Muscle and fat had simply burned away. I had extensive damage to my throat, airways and lungs. My vital organs were in shock, and each was taking its turn to shut down.

The doctors at Westmead described my injuries as 'horrendous lethal burns'. There's a formula to roughly gauge your chances of surviving burns: add the patient's age to the percentage of burns. One hundred is death. My tally was 102. Survival seemed hopeless. In the Intensive Care Unit, or ICU, a Catholic priest was summoned for my anointing. The last rites.

I was barely conscious as the priest presided over my presumed departure into the next life, although I dimly remember a sliver of wafer being placed on my tongue. I couldn't see the priest, but imagined him, wrongly no doubt, in a large, unbelted tunic, with lacy hems and embroidered sleeves. I believe the ceremony normally involves a confession or an act of contrition. But I was unable to speak. If things had been different, I would have said I was sorry, so deeply sorry, for choosing the men that I had. For allowing devils and drunks into my boys' lives. For leaving my two babies now, when they needed me most.

Fragments of prayer floated around me in the darkness: '... forgive ... forgive ... trespass against us ... temptation ... evil ...' The priest's voice was sonorous as I hovered like a tiny broken bird at the threshold between life and death.

'Through this holy anointing, may the Lord in His love and mercy help you with the grace of the Holy Spirit. May the Lord who frees you from sin save you and raise you up. Amen.'

Clyde, my stepfather, had been watching the nightly news in Laurieton on the Friday when a shot of my backyard flashed on the screen. Mum was washing up and missed the bulletin, but Clyde poked his head around the corner of the kitchen. 'It was some sort of fire, they said. A couple very badly injured in the blaze. It definitely looked like Donna's yard, from what I could see.'

Mum dismissed his concerns. 'If that were Donna, don't you think we'd be the first to know about it?'

'Well, it looked like her place, that's for sure. Didn't catch where it was, but they mentioned Dubbo Hospital.'

'One backyard's pretty much the same as another, Clyde. You must have made a mistake.'

But it was no mistake. Mum was startled when the phone rang. It was very late and she and Clyde had been preparing for bed. The voice on the other end of the line was muffled, and the sounds of laughter and music in the background didn't help.

'You'll have to speak up, I can't hear you,' Mum said. 'Who is this?'

'It's Denise Blakemore. You know, Brian's sister-in-law.'

Mum frowned. What was Denise, of all people, ringing for, and late on a Friday night too?

'Haven't you heard?'

'Heard what?' Mum tried hard to concentrate, catching a string of disjointed words and phrases.

'... Donna ... badly burnt ... hospital ...'

'Speak up, love. What's that you say? Has something happened to Donna? Where is she?'

'They're waiting for the helicopter,' Denise shouted over the party noises. 'They're taking her to Westmead, but she'll be dead before she gets there.'

I cannot imagine how my mother felt as those words shot like poisoned darts down the phoneline. Disbelief? Shock? Fury? Maybe all three. I know she dropped the phone.

Mum got onto Kathryn, relating the strange phone call. I can picture her, trying not to panic, taking a few deep breaths, staying calm while she spoke to Sissy. Clyde would have fetched her dressing-gown by this stage, maybe got her a chair if she didn't have one already.

Sissy would've taken charge. 'Leave it with me, Mum. I'll find out what's going on.' She was always great like that, my big sister. Just the same as when we were kids; when the chips were down, she was there. It was Sissy who rang the hospital while Mum waited anxiously for clarification. Soon, panicked phone conversations were flying back and forth.

'We need to get down to Sydney as soon as possible. Donna's real bad, Mum. She may not live through the night.'

At dawn the next morning, Clyde drove my frantic mother the 70-odd kilometres from Laurieton to Killabakh, just outside Wingham. He stayed at Sissy's place to mind her two children, Jennifer and Patrick. John, Sissy's husband, was laid up in hospital with a broken leg.

Mum and Sissy headed south along the narrow, twisting Pacific Highway and onto the Newcastle freeway, joining the ant-like procession of vehicles zipping and dodging through the giant sandstone towards the city. Mum says they stopped only once, for sandwiches and fuel outside Newcastle, before Sissy plunged back into the traffic flow, heading straight for Westmead Hospital.

'Just hang on, Donna. Hang on until we get there,' Mum murmured, over and over.

※

The ICU was a hushed, surreal environment, the stuff of science-fiction movies. In my tiny room, medical staff glided back and forth, all in white, gowned and masked and capped, with only their eyes exposed. Without their protective layers of skin, burns patients are especially susceptible to infection. Anyone in their space must be made as germ-free as possible.

Nurses sat beside patients who lay like corpses, partially obscured by screens. There was a smell too, an airless mix of sharp chemicals and potent body fluids. My dad called it the smell of death.

'Your daughter's been very seriously injured,' the nurse explained behind her mask as she led Mum and Sissy, similarly scrubbed and shrouded, into my room. 'So be prepared.' This was the sum total of her counselling.

'How did it happen?' Sissy asked.

The nurse turned and raised her eyebrows. She tossed her head in the direction of a uniformed police officer, stuffed tightly into a hospital gown, posted like a statue outside one of the rooms. 'Her bloke's in there. Donna's just next door, in isolation.'

Sissy fainted as she entered my room. From the sight of me, or the smell, or perhaps a combination of both. She was given oxygen and escorted back to a chair. I'm not surprised she passed out.

I was encased in dressings, a bulbous monster. I couldn't have looked even remotely human, let alone like myself. There was a cradle frame over my body. I was surrounded by flashing machines and lay unreachable in a spaghettied network of plastic tubes and wires. I was unable to speak, unable to move. I could hear though, but no one knew. Disconnected noises swirled around me – nurses chatting, a telephone ringing, alarms, trolleys, doors opening and closing, footsteps around my bed. I was trapped, awake and terrified, in a dark, gauze coffin. This is what it's like to be buried alive, I thought. Just below the surface, with the sounds of the living only centimetres away.

Mum sat beside my bed and wept. She couldn't stop crying, or looking. She was searching for me, she says, underneath the layers of oozing gauze. She remembers seeing the tip of my burnt nose, and my hands – charred claws wound around splints and encased in plastic bags. One ear, still intact, protruded through the dressings.

'There's an ear. I can see she's still got her ear,' she told Sissy.

Later, one of the doctors came by and called Mum to one side. She has recounted the conversation many times since, with a proud sort of chuckle.

'You must prepare yourself for the worst. It's likely she won't survive,' the doctor told her gently. 'And it's perhaps more humane that way. Even if she were to live, her quality of life would be very bleak.'

Mum looked at him blankly, and he continued. 'You'll never take your daughter home.'

Mum drew herself up to her full height, and I imagine she tipped her chin forward in a small gesture of defiance. 'Well, one thing's obvious,' she said quietly. 'You don't know our Donna.'

On Sunday, Mum and Sissy drove to my house in Geurie, stopping first at Wellington Police Station. The constable couldn't give them many details about the incident at that early stage, but verified that somehow petrol was ignited and Coe had phoned the ambulance. Sissy asked if she could take some of my jewellery for safekeeping, and also whether Brian was entitled to any of the contents.

'I've already spoken to Brian. He isn't interested in taking anything apparently,' said the constable. 'It's probably a good idea you collect any valuables and keep them for your sister.'

As Mum and Sissy turned to leave, the constable cleared his throat. 'Oh, by the way, you might find the place a bit of a mess. We had to do a search.'

'What for?' Mum asked.

'Anonymous tip-off. A man phoned up and told us there were drugs on the premises.' He shrugged. 'Didn't find anything, but we had to ... you know ... go through cupboards and the like. Just so you know ...'

Inside the house, total devastation awaited them. Every room had been turned upside down. In the kitchen, the stove had been pulled apart, the cupboards flung open and their contents strewn across the floor, along with the washing. Yvonne Ford was standing down the hallway, a broom in one hand and a longneck in the other, trying to clean up.

'Coppers did it,' she said with disgust. 'Looking for drugs apparently. Had some sort of anonymous tip-off. They didn't find nothing, but look at this place! Bastards.'

'Yeah, the police warned us,' said Sissy, gazing at the mess. 'I didn't expect it to be this bad though.'

'Who would've rung up and said something like that?' Mum asked Yvonne.

Yvonne shrugged and took a swig of beer. 'This place is full of bloody troublemakers. People have already started helping themselves to stuff. Her collection of windchimes has gone. Outdoor furniture's been pinched.'

The petty pilfering was to get worse in the following weeks. At one stage my unregistered car was even jacked up, and the wheels taken. One of the locals needed four new tyres for his sister's vehicle, so he thought he'd help himself to mine, seeing as I wasn't using them. Later someone also saw fit to ram the garden hose under the back door, turn the outside tap on full bore and flood the house. Betrayal was everywhere.

John and Shirley Heller tried to rally the townsfolk in a gesture of support. John offered to donate a pig on a spit and help organise a fundraising night at the bowling club. Apparently, it was all too much trouble. Apathy, John told me later. Apathy, yes, but judgement too. I can hear them now:

'What can you expect, going out with a bloke half her age?'

'Just inviting trouble, that sort of behaviour.'

'Always blueing. We expected something like that to happen eventually. Stupid woman. Shoulda known better.'

John and Shirl eventually sold up and moved away. 'It was sickening, Donna. Made me think, if anything happened to me or Shirl, we'd be in for the same treatment.'

Back in my kitchen, Sissy was now wondering what else had gone. 'Donna's handbag and wallet? I suppose that's disappeared too,' she said. 'I know it wasn't taken to the hospital.'

Yvonne gave a scornful grunt. 'Brian took that, along with all the kids' belongings. Helped himself to some photographs beside Donna's bed as well. Packed the lot into Donna's car and took that too.'

'Bet he left the bills,' Mum muttered.

'Oh, by the way, Don had a video out. The people at the shop want it back. It's overdue.' Yvonne stepped over to the VCR and pressed the eject button. 'Here it is.' She slipped it back in the empty case lying on top of the television, where I'd left it on Thursday night.

'Is that all they're worried about?' Mum snatched the tape out of Yvonne's hand. 'Give me that. I'll return their tape all right.'

At the shop, Mum let them have it. 'My daughter, the girl you've known for years, lies dying in a hospital bed in Sydney and you're worried about your bloody video!' She slammed the tape down on the counter in front of the horrified customers. The owner stared at her, open-mouthed and blushing.

'Well, here's your rotten, stinking video! So sorry it's late!'

While Mum and Sissy gathered up my possessions, cleaned out the fridge, sorted through bills and tried as best they could to set things straight, Dad and his wife Bea were flying in from Indonesia. They'd been holidaying in Java with her family when they'd received a message from Bea's grandson, Albert, in Australia. Just as Mum and Sissy had found, the initial information was scant.

'Donna's been very badly injured. You need to get back to Sydney as soon as possible.' That was about it.

Frenetic preparations to leave the country followed. Relatives had garbled phone conversations with travel agencies while Dad and Bea shovelled their luggage together. With tickets for the next available flight to Sydney organised, they were bundled into a relative's decrepit four-wheel drive for the mad dash from the mountains down to Jakarta. The journey from Bogor to the airport normally took three hours, but they did it in just under two, reaching the boarding gate with only seconds to spare.

Dad has different recollections from Mum's about the first time he saw me in Westmead. He was there the day after her, and hadn't been given a single clue as to my injuries. I could have been stricken with pneumonia or a badly broken leg for all he knew. It was on the Sunday morning, and my face was unbandaged when he walked in. He described my head as being like a translucent white balloon, swollen and swirling with fluids. My face was one big blister, so puffed up that none of my features were visible. It was probably just as well because the end of my nose had been destroyed, I had slits for eyes, and my lips were gone, although there was a ventilator tube poking out from the vicinity of my mouth. For a while no one knew if I'd be blind because the swelling was so bad.

As Mum had found, it was hard to get anywhere near me because of the bank of blinking, flashing machines around my bed, and the pipes and wires sprouting from my body. Anything that needed to enter or exit my system was done so by clear plastic tubing, stitched carefully into my body where they could still find skin. I had a mainline sewn into my groin, a necessary but dangerous option because of the likelihood of infection.

These tubes hooked up to different bags, which hung around me like a bizarre supermarket display. One, filled with maroon lumps, looked like kangaroo meat and flowed down my feed tube, entering my body via the nasal passage. There were other concoctions too: glucose, morphine, blood. Some tubes expelled matter: I had a catheter for urine, and they would sometimes use a pipe to suction my lungs, dragging out mucus, soot and blood from my blackened insides.

Like my sister, Bea fainted when she saw me, and was carted off to the waiting room. Dad was also devastated.

'What happened?' he finally managed to ask the nurse.

'The bloke's in the next room,' she whispered.

Dad was overcome with a surge of fury. 'I'll kill the bastard, I'll kill the bastard,' he growled, over and over again. He stopped after a while, and probably stood gazing down at me for a second or two, before he began again, pacing and muttering. 'It's all my fault. I should've been there at Easter but I went away. Why did I go away? He wouldn't have done it if I was there.'

Don't blame yourself, Dad. I love you, Dad. Get me out of here, Dad. My brain was screaming but I lay silent as the dead, muzzled by the ballooning layers. Fix it, Dad. Make the pain go away, Dad.

The pain was indescribable. Despite being pumped with painkillers, I was in constant agony when I was awake. And I was boiling. I can't remember ever being so hot. My cooling system had been destroyed and I was smothered in bandages that oozed with body fluids: blood, sweat, pus. The tiny, windowless room had no fresh air. I felt like I was dying of thirst yet I wasn't allowed to drink.

Dad didn't stay long that day. I don't think he could take it.

My condition had been deemed 'unstable', and my blood pressure was plummeting. I was given Haemacel, for fluid resuscitation, with no significant effect, then dopamine, which made my heart rate soar, then more Haemacel. This was followed by increased oxygen via a ventilator and another round of suctioning. Later, the intensive-care nurse leaned over me. Her voice was soft but clear.

'Donna,' she said. 'I'm going to ask you a question. Nod your head if the answer is yes. Shake your head for no.'

She knows I'm awake, I thought. She's trying to get me to communicate. I concentrated as hard as I could through the haze of drugs and pain.

'Is your name Donna?'

Slowly and painfully, I forced my enormous head to bob up and down. Yes. I can hear you. And yes, that's my name.

'Do you understand what's happened to you?'

Again, I forced my head to nod. Yes, I know.

'Did Garry do this to you?'

I was exhausted now, but I had to do this. I had to respond. Slowly, painfully, I managed to tip my head up and down. Once. Twice. It was Garry, all right. Garry did it.

She paused for a few moments. I thought she'd gone, but after a while she asked me another question. A stupid question.

'Is your name John Smith?'

I knew this was a deliberate 'no' answer. I tried to shake my head, but it was impossible to twist my neck back and forth. Instead I lay still.

'You can't shake your head,' she murmured. 'But at least you can nod. It's a start.'

Although I was mute, two nights later I surprised the nurse on duty, posted like a ghost at my bedside. I'd been morphine-dreaming, chased through a dark labyrinth by an army of Garrys, with eyes like devils. Tattooed Nazis thundering closer and closer in big, black boots. I looked over my shoulder and saw that each had a lighter in their outstretched hands. Flick, flick. I was trying my hardest. My legs were pumping as fast as they could go, but I just couldn't get out of the tunnel.

Suddenly, I surfaced, and began to scream my lungs out. 'He did it! He did it! Garry did this to me! I tried to run but I couldn't! I rolled over and over! My son told me to roll, Mum, roll! Why does he hate me?'

The nurse tried to calm me, and then called other nurses to help her hold me down as I fought to climb out of the bed and escape Garry. They managed to restrain me, but I wouldn't stop screaming. 'Garry did this! He set me alight! He did it!'

Someone must have slipped a sedative into one of my lines. My records say '1 mg IV Haloperidol given with effect'.

Two days later, I once again screamed my message. 'Garry did this to me! He did this to me!'

At this stage the nursing staff informed the police. They were told that the officers on the case were already aware of the situation. The police investigation had quashed the suicide pact theory. Within the week, newspaper headlines stated unequivocally: 'COUPLE DID NOT PLAN SUICIDE PACT: POLICE.'

I was oblivious to the story of the double suicide pact tucked away in my files. It was a theory that had erupted in the wake of the assault, emerging from a tangle of facts and half-truths, as well as one or two calculated lies. Now, I think of it as a marathon game of Broken Telephone. You know the one, where kids sit in a circle and the first child whispers a message to the next, and so on. Round goes the message, becoming hopelessly distorted on its journey from one child to the next. The more distorted it ends up, the better – some kids deliberately whisper mistakes, others just muddle it by accident. But at the end of the game, everyone hears both the distorted version and the original, the truth.

I assumed my truth would be glaringly obvious at the end of the game, and so it was, to the police at least. But for a variety of reasons, creating and then maintaining the suicide pact distortion suited a number of people who assumed I was as good as dead anyway.

I ruined the game though; I decided to live.

On the Friday night, in the wake of the assault, a forensic team had combed my house and property. The yard was lit up like Christmas. They noted several items in their report, including a melted four-litre plastic fuel container, a partly burnt, red disposable cigarette lighter, a bedspread and a white doona, a length of garden hose, pieces of black crocheted top and fragments of burnt human skin.

Coe and Bodean had been taken over to the Fords' place across the road. There were many people there that night, according to Coe. He said it was like a big meeting. There would've been my old friend Yvonne and her husband Colin, their daughter Sue and her husband Adrian, who was, of course, a close friend of Garry's. Garry's pirate brother Mark would have been there with Yvonne's other daughter, Sandra. Brian was also present, anxious, along with everyone else, to discuss the fate of his drinking buddy and ex-wife. His brother Danny had dropped him off, only hanging around long enough to reef Bodean out of Yvonne's arms.

'Donna told me to hang on to the kids until her mother arrived,' Yvonne cried, as Bodean kicked and screamed in terror. 'He doesn't know you!'

Danny refused to hand him back. 'I'm his uncle and he's coming to Parkes with me. Brian'll bring Coe tomorrow.'

I will never know exactly what was said that night, apart from what Coe told me many months later. Coe said the adults 'ranted and raved' at him for hours. Coe, the only witness. Tired and stressed out beyond belief, worried about the statement he had to give to the police the very next day.

He said he remembers lying on a mattress in their big, dark lounge room in the hours before dawn. He could hear the adults in the next room still debating, throwing in ideas, different scenarios. The door was almost shut but, as he lay under a blanket on the floor, he could see a thin yellow line of light around the doorframe.

He said they talked on and on, around and around and around. He managed to recall a few phrases, although who said what will always remain a mystery.

'We've got to save Garry's arse.'

'He's not a real bad bloke. He doesn't deserve this.'

'He's family.'

'We've got to live in this town.'

'She's as good as dead.'

Coe didn't believe this last bit, which was just as well. He thought I'd be out of hospital in a week or two. He couldn't sleep, although by this stage it would have been close to daylight.

More than a year later, when he made a second statement, Coe told the police, 'I loved him.'

'Can you tell me why you wished to change some details of your statement?' the detective asked.

'Yeah, cause, um, before, I was trying to protect Garry because I thought he might get into more trouble.'

'Can you tell me what you meant by that?'

'Yeah, like, I love him, he was like a dad.'

Early the next morning, the day after the assault, my friend John Heller arrived at the Fords' place. Brian and Coe were out the front of the old weatherboard, getting ready to drive to Wellington Police Station. John told Mum and Sissy that, as he approached, he overheard Brian talking to Coe beside the car.

'Remember, that's your story and you stick to it,' Brian said. 'Don't say nothing about Garry. He's in enough trouble as it is.'

John cleared his throat. 'I heard the news. Thought I could drive you down to Westmead. You know, be closer to Don. I'd be happy to pay for petrol, accommodation. The lot.'

Left: The pre-school years – aged two and a half.

Below: Sissy and me – in matching South Sydney Swimming Club costume – in the backyard at Redfern.

Top: The gang of kids from Redfern, about to hop in the Valiant for a birthday picnic on the South Coast. I'm in my beloved Souths football jumper, at the front.

Bottom: Friends then, friends now: Deb and I on campus at Mitchell College in Bathurst, in 1975.

Left: The old me, in 1991.

Below: Bodean and Coe in our front yard in Geurie in 1993.

Top: My kindergarten class of 1994, nine days before the assault.
Bottom: Garry Clynes.

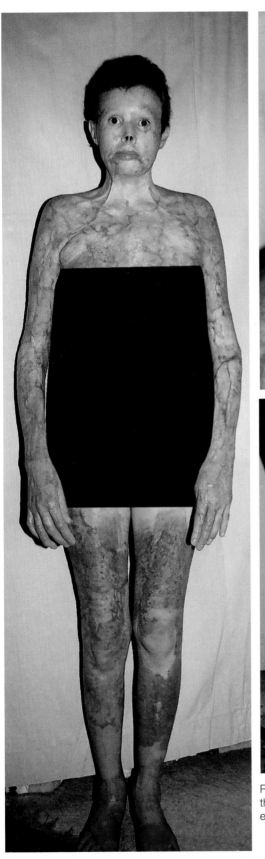
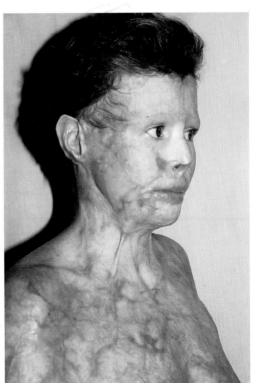
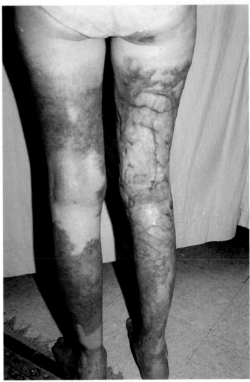

Ray Paterson, a nurse at Wingham Hospital, took these photos in February 1995 to document the extent of my injuries.

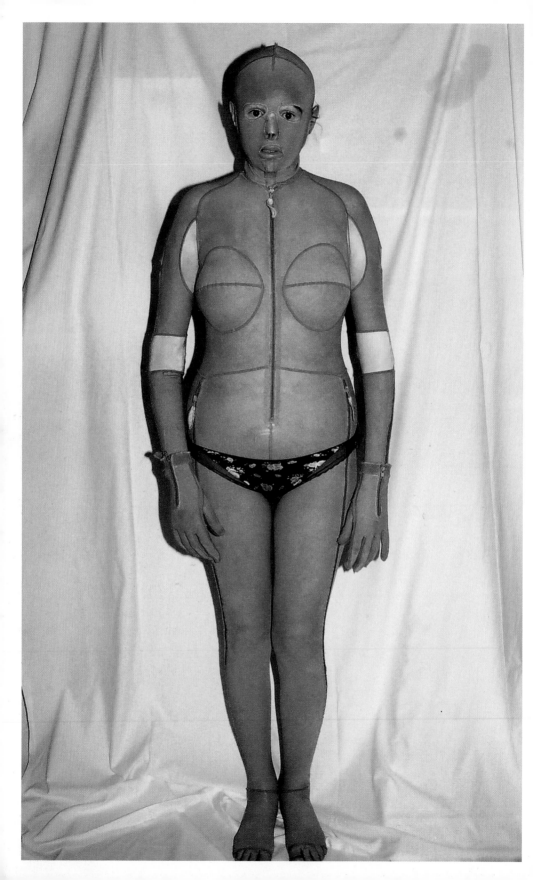

Left: My new and improved burns suit.

Below: Westmead Hospital, 1996: the 'big and thick' skin graft needed to release tightness in my neck. Dad had to sit down after taking this photo.

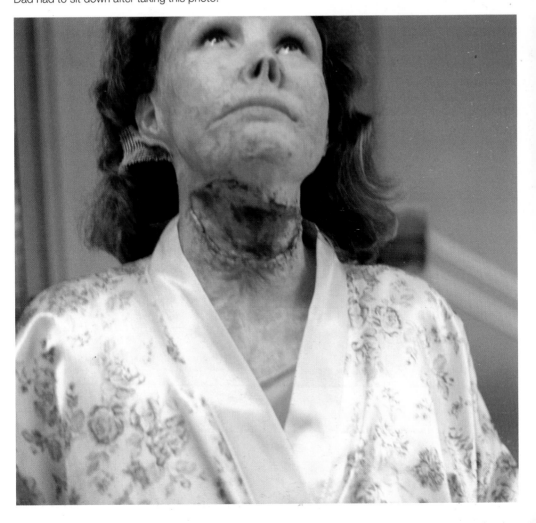

My wish list: With Coe at Thredbo in 1996 (right), and with Bodean at Uluru in 1998 (above).

Back with my boys in 1998.

Top: Inside the Women and Children's Safety Room at Taree Courthouse.

(Courtesy Bob Weeks and *Coast Living*)

Right: At a domestic violence protest in Taree, in 2000.

Top: The New South Wales finalists for Australian of the Year, at Government House in Sydney in 2003 (L to R): me; Steve Waugh, Australian of the Year; Thomas Keneally, Senior Australian of the Year; Sarah Dunbar, Young Australian of the Year; Jeff Gambin, Metropolitan Local Hero.

Bottom: Accepting Australian of the Year, Local Hero in 2004.

Hitting the pavement: I was selected as an Olympic Torch Bearer for the Athens Olympics in the Sydney relay in 2004. VOCAL were kind enough to buy the torch for me to keep. (Courtesy Newspix)

Top: With two amazing Aussies at Government House in Canberra in 2007: Steve Waugh and Dr Fiona Wood, Australians of the Year 2004 and 2005, respectively.

Bottom left: Bodean with footballer and burns survivor Jason McCartney at Camp Phoenix in 2005.

Bottom right: With CEO and founder of KIDS Foundation, Susie O'Neill, at Camp Phoenix in 2002.

Camp Phoenix 2006: With Alison Hirth and Georgette (top), the baby she was told she couldn't have after suffering extensive burns; with Sophie Delezio (bottom), who suffered burns to almost 85 per cent of her body when she was just two years old.

Above: With John Lewis and Lizzy Graham, who both survived a shed fire. They're now engaged to be married.

Left: Still friends: Gabby Mazzali and I in 2002. (Courtesy Peter Carrette)

Top: With Mum at Camp Phoenix in 2004.

Bottom: Three generations and a crop of sunflowers: Coe and Zane, aged one, and me and Bodean outside our home in Wingham in January 2007.

Brian thought for a moment. 'Nah, mate. Thanks all the same, but I got a party on tonight in Parkes. Twenty-first birthday. Free grog and all that. Sort of promised I'd be there.' He would've been puffing on a cigarette while he spoke, or stamping one out, or lighting one. 'Nothing we can do anyway, mate.' There'd be a shrug then, a shake of the head, an averting of eyes.

Outside the police station, Brian had one more thing to say. He switched off the ignition and turned to face his son. Coe remembers it clearly.

'By the way, son, do you know your mother was carrying on with Garry for years? The bitch. While we were married. That's why I started drinking. That's why I left. That's why you lost your father. It was your mother's fault.'

Coe, bewildered, exhausted and now fizzing with anger towards his mother, followed his dad into the police station.

I have the statement that Coe made, but I almost can't bear to look at it, even now, years later. He talks about arguing and petrol being spilled, but mainly by me. He talks about pushing and pulling, but again, mainly by me. The focus is off Garry and on me.

Coe then states that I asked for a lighter. I didn't even have a lighter – I didn't smoke, the house was all electric, the wood heater out of commission. On the rare occasion I needed a flame I used to ask Garry, or Brian before that. Coe said he refused to get a lighter and that Garry took one from his pocket instead, but he didn't see him use it.

'I knew Garry did this to you, but I didn't tell because no one asked. I failed you. I betrayed you, Mum,' he said later.

'No, darling. You were only twelve. You didn't betray me. The adults around you did that.'

The police questioned two other witnesses, both closely connected to the offender and both on the scene soon after the incident. Their statements include the following:

I looked around and I could see both Donna and Garry huddled together, lying on the grass ... Garry got up and started to walk around. He then said, 'Where's Donna, is she all right? What happened?'

In fact, I had run from Garry and was many metres away from him when I fell to the ground. We were not 'huddled together' in some bizarre death embrace at all.

The police were used to dealing with this sort of thing though, or so they told me later. In their search for the truth they often had to sift through rumours and lies and bits of fact that had been bent out of shape. They knew beyond all doubt that I was the victim of a violent assault.

The Department of Community Services (DOCS) were not so sure. On 2 April they received a notification from the Dubbo Mental Health Team stating that Garry and I had doused ourselves in fuel and lit ourselves deliberately in front of Coe and Bodean. DOCS clung to this story tenaciously. As I lay in hospital on life support, their investigation was hurtling forward like a runaway truck, aided by a few individuals with their own agendas. In exactly one month's time I would be branded a long-term alcoholic and a violent and emotionally abusive parent.

Six

'We can smell you, Donna. You know what that means.' Nurse Iain was standing beside me in his mask, gown, gloves and cap. 'You're going off. Your chest graft has to come down. It has to come down now.'

I blinked at him through a silicon mask, worn constantly to flatten scar tissue on my newly reconstructed face. Despite the heat, I began to shake. Tears welled up. I couldn't take much more of this, I knew I couldn't. But I had to get better, for my boys.

With their images in mind, I had survived the first few weeks, amazing the medical staff. I was, for the moment, out of ICU and back across the corridor in the Burns Unit. I had a tendency to seesaw back and forth between the two, depending on how close I was to death. The room I was in now was not much bigger than a cupboard, but it was right next to the nurses' station, where the staff could watch me and do the sniff test as they walked past. They were always sniffing, like mice looking for cheese. If there was a bad stink emanating from my bed, it inevitably meant that my latest skin graft hadn't taken, and needed to be stripped down and cleaned. Today it was my entire chest and midriff area – a big one.

I couldn't answer, but Iain chatted away as he unravelled the outer dressings, dumping them in a large bin beside him. He worked rapidly and was soon down to the final layer, a thick pad glued to my chest area, encrusted with blood and ooze. A horrendous odour rolled up from my body, the stink of rotting meat.

'James,' called Iain through his mask. 'Can someone find James? I need another pair of hands here.' He went on to explain that James was a junior nurse on a temporary visit, getting some experience in the Burns Unit.

Experience? I'll be an experience all right.

James came in. My eyes were working now and I could see he was tall and slim, and appeared very young. Even though he was shrouded in sterilised hospital garb, I noticed he had fair hair and skin, a peaches-and-cream complexion.

Iain introduced us. 'Donna, James. James, Donna.'

James blushed. I nodded. Pleased to meet you.

'Right. Let's get this over with. You know the drill, Donna. You know it's going to hurt. James is going to hold your feet down while I pull this final bandage off. I'll do it on the count of three.'

Red-faced, James stepped carefully around my lines and positioned himself at the foot of my bed. He grasped my feet nervously, steeling himself. I closed my eyes, feeling woozy with fear and drugs.

Iain began the count. 'One, two –' He didn't get any further. With an almighty sweep, he ripped the final dressing off my chest one number early, leaving a vast expanse of congealed blood and minced flesh. It's grisly, but it always reminded me of pizza topping.

The sight and smell of my chest was too much for James. He took one look and hit the deck, crashing onto the floor and banging his head on the leg of my bed. Iain steadied my shaking, screaming body with one gloved hand, and held the slab of stinking bandage high in the air with the other.

'Cathy! Isabella! Somebody get in here now! I've got another casualty.' He turned to me and raised his eyebrows in mock disgust. 'Christ, it's hard to get good help around here.'

When I'd first seen my chest, before this latest failed operation, I'd thought they had me in a corset. I could have sworn I was wearing a black, chest-hugging piece of lingerie. Like Madonna, I'd thought. But it wasn't underwear at all. It was charcoaled skin, black after the initial bleaching.

Burnt flesh does not grow back. It becomes poisonous, polluting the body with toxins, and has to be debrided, or cut off, in the first few weeks. This happens in a series of operations. The surgeons then staple thin sheets of fresh skin over the debrided area. In 1994, before the advent of artificial skin, they got the good skin from unburnt parts of your body, which in my case was a challenge. My left leg had been partially shielded by my right as I'd curled up into the foetal position, so this, as well as my buttocks and back, was a favourite area to harvest skin.

They used something a little like a motorised cheese slicer to take thin films of skin during the operation. This skin was run through another machine that cut fine holes across it, so it would stretch like crepe paper, making what little skin I had go further. The surgeons were so pressed for time that as soon as the donor site healed a little, they'd have to skin it again, carving it like a leg of lamb. The donor sites hurt more than the grafted areas.

I was operated on many times in the first month or so. Initially, the nursing staff would need to take me right down. 'Taking me down' meant removing all my dressings. It involved firstly unwinding the outer bandages as I lay shivering on the bed. Then they'd disconnect me from my bags and machines and, with a nurse at each corner of my bedsheet, they'd hoist me onto a shower-bed, roll me from side to side to remove the sheet, and wheel me into a large, tiled bathroom to scour away the final layer of dressings.

Water sprayed from a hand-held nozzle like dozens of tiny ice picks while six nurses tugged at the gluey dressings stuck to my new skin. They used sponge pads and some sort of foamy antiseptic to clean the good grafts, the ones that were taking well. (New grafts would be sealed in plastic, kept dry for seven days to take.) The pads didn't feel like sponge. It felt more like I was being scrubbed with wire brushes and turpentine to get rid of the yellow ooze, dried blood and remnants of dressing. The nurses would stop at times to dig out staples.

There was a limit to how much morphine I was allowed. The nurses were usually able to give me one 'top-up' during this process, which would provide a little extra pain relief, but only for a short period of time. I was allowed to choose whether it was administered when I was first wheeled into the shower, or later on. There was no getting around it though. The whole procedure was hell, from start to finish, and happened daily.

For many years after, tiled bathrooms terrified me.

I couldn't see the nurses' faces because of the masks, but I came to recognise some of them in other ways. Cathy had Michelin Man around her neck, a tiny gold figure made of rings, which dangled from under her uniform and bobbed about as she bent and scrubbed.

Isabella had soothing words: 'All the negatives are being washed away. Just imagine them flowing out of your body, floating away ...'

Iain had dark eyes and an even darker humour: 'Is it bad enough yet? Do you want your hit yet?'

I would have laughed if I could.

Rebecca had a stiff British accent and a matronly manner that bordered on brutal: 'Do as you're told, Donna. If you're not going to cooperate, we may as well just pack you off home in a taxi.'

She would have been great on the battlefields at Gallipoli; she was just about old enough to have been there. 'So you've lost an arm? You've got another!'

Normally, after being stripped and cleaned, I would have expensive cream and fresh dressings applied, but on operating days I'd be returned to my room like a skinned rabbit, waiting under a sterilised sheet to be loaded onto a trolley and wheeled up to theatre.

Everything about hospital was a ritual, and the trip to the operating theatre was no exception. I'd be feeling hazy as they trundled me along the corridors towards the lift. I would pass a sequence of framed prints, which I came to know by heart. The last one was a butterfly poster, a burst of blurred colour in the hospital corridors.

As we moved closer to our destination, the air would become colder. I imagined myself in a fridge, blue with ice. By the time we reached the waiting room, I'd be twitching under my sheet.

'Would you like a blanket?' the nurse would always ask.

In the beginning I couldn't speak, but she'd give me one anyway. She'd remove it from the warmer carefully and place it over me, crisp white and warm as toast. This was the best of the worst. It was like crawling into bed on a freezing night, those first moments as your icy toes press into the hot electric blanket.

The nurse would have already checked for dentures, as well as jewellery. A little later the anaesthetist appeared. He would croon to me like a hypnotist, telling me I was getting sleepy, asking me to count backwards from ten. He would slip the drug into my mainline or insert a new needle. I don't remember exactly. I'd black out and wake up in recovery much later, another operation completed.

There was an exception to this, a single occasion when I lay inert but fully conscious on the operating table as voices discussed my alarming loss of blood, and the likelihood that one ear may need to be removed. Generally though, I awoke in recovery, with the same nurse by my side. She would murmur a prayer as my eyelids fluttered. I had begun to pray often as had those around me, asking God for things on my behalf, like courage, strength, fortitude. 'Fundamental fortitude', as old Jackie Bartholemew used to say. Did I have enough of it? Could I keep doing this? I had to. My boys needed me.

As I lay in hospital, I was inundated with support from friends and acquaintances in the outside world. My small space soon looked like a cross between a florist and a kindergarten classroom as flowers, letters and cards, as well as art and craft from students at Orana Heights, came streaming in with the daily mail. Bronwyn, the Burns Manager, grumbled about falling macaroni, glitter and coloured paper on the floor, but I lived for those daily deliveries. The outpouring of grief from my workplace was so great that the school had to appoint one of the assistant principals, Di Hannigan, as the coordinator for enquiries and support from staff, parents and children.

As rumours of a double suicide pact spun throughout the district, my workplace publicly declared their support in a school newsletter. One of my colleagues, Robyn Denkel, put her disbelief in writing:

We were all shocked by the events that took place. Rumours ran rampant. Rumours of suicide and the like. I was with Donna the evening before the accident. We were both at Dubbo Base Hospital … She was definitely not suicidal. Her main concern whilst having her stitches out was for her children, who were waiting for her to take them home.

In early May, soon after another one of my organs had packed it in, Sissy sent out a letter to everyone, acknowledging their kindness.

> Dear Friends,
>
> I would like to thank you for your kind regards, prayers and best wishes for Donna's speedy recovery.
>
> As you might not realise, Donna is back in Intensive Care being assisted by the ventilator for breathing, but still fighting. She drifts in and out of consciousness but at times knows we are talking to her. She responds by either blinking or nodding her head.
>
> All cards and letters are read to Donna both by the staff and by one of the family when we visit her. The cards or letters are then taped onto her window where we hope that she might be able to see them.
>
> If you would like to continue writing to Donna, I am sure that she would greatly appreciate your kind thoughts and best wishes, and we will continue to read all letters to her several times.
>
> I will keep you informed of Donna's progress as time goes along.
>
> Once again, we would like to thank you, and I am sure Donna would also, for your kind thoughts for her speedy recovery.
>
> Yours sincerely,
> Kathryn Daly, Donna's sister

Although I was unable to receive general visitors, family members kept a vigil by my bedside, both in ICU and back in the burns ward. Sissy was often there, and Mum and Aunty Dassie would make daily visits, while Dad and Bea took the night shift.

Sometimes the medical staff tried to temper the dreadful reality for my family.

'We have a surprise for you,' a nurse said as Mum and Aunty Dassie entered the ward one day. 'Your girl's looking good. We've prettied her up for you.'

They walked in to find the usual gauze-bound mummy, but this time I was wearing a pretty pink bow on top of my head. Dark humour for dark days.

Aunty Dassie would rub my toes and talk softly to me. 'Everything's going to be all right, love. You're doing great. We love you.'

Mum would fix the flowers, changing the vase water and arranging the blooms beside my bed. I couldn't speak, but my eyes followed them around the room.

Uncle Ronnie always made their lunches.

'What you got on your sandwiches today, Dass?' Mum would ask.

'Corned beef and pickles today. And this one's cheese and tomato. What about yours?'

I listened to them and closed my eyes, imagining I was with the two sisters, sharing a picnic in the park on a sunny day.

Mum found me some thick wooden pencils. On my stronger days, I was able to grasp one between my clawed fingers and manoeuvre it drunkenly across a notepad, or make scrawled progress notes on my wall calendar:

Watched TV.
Sat in chair.
Holding pen better.

I often used writing to communicate my frustration.

I'm so sick of being here. Can't talk, always in pain, can't move. It's driving me mad. I'm running out of inner strength.

Then there were instructions to the casual staff, unfamiliar with my treatment:

> Could you put my left axilla splint on, please? I have to wear the
> left more to stretch it.

On 24 May, I wrote in Mum's birthday card.

> To Mum
> I love you.
> Love Donna XXX

There were plenty of tears after that one.

Mum was my protector in hospital. One day, at the end of April, she and Kathryn arrived at the ICU. Here, close to death, patients were only allowed one visitor at a time.

'I'm sorry,' the nurse said, 'she already has someone with her. You'll have to wait.'

Mum wanted to know who my visitor was. It was Brian. Mum looked at Kathryn, and marched into my room to discover Brian crouched over me, holding a pen between my bandaged fingers, trying to force me to sign something.

'Just put a cross on it,' he urged.

Mum swept over and snatched the pen away. 'What the bloody hell are you doing? Get out!'

The paper he'd been waving in front of me was a cheque for $45,000 that, prior to the assault, I'd arranged to borrow from the Teachers Credit Union to pay Brian out for his half of the house. I probably would have been entitled to a lot more than 50 per cent of the family home, but I'd just wanted to get him off my back, split things down the middle and be done with it. Of course, I now had no way of repaying the loan, but that didn't seem to worry Brian.

Sissy contacted my solicitor, Ann Kinghan, who assured her that even if I'd managed to sign the cheque, it would have been invalid under the circumstances.

At this time Mum also became suspicious that enquiries had been made about my superannuation – Coe made a passing comment a couple of weeks after Brian had visited that I'd be worth a lot of money if I died.

'Where did you hear that sort of talk?' Mum asked him.

Coe looked down at his shoes and remained silent.

'Your mother isn't going to die, darling,' she said firmly.

But Coe was certainly being lured by the dollar. Many months later I read some unnerving entries in his school diary dated late April and early May.

Yesterday dad got his $45 000 cheque, but the problem is Mum needs to sign it ...

Me and dad have been looking in the paper for land. We have found these two: 4,800 acres of mountain and grass fields. The other one is 30 acres and woodland, 2 dams and a small creek. Both propertys are $25,000 and Between Bunderburge and Marybrough in Queensland.

I was looking in the paper for property when I found this real good bargain ...

Even Mrs Blakemore had her bit to say when she came to see me.

'It's a dreadful thing you've done, Donna. Leaving Brian with all those bills. You'll have to set it right. You'll have to tell your sister she'll need to look after Grace Bros and HFC.'

Mum wasn't there when Mrs Blakemore came in, but she found out about it later. 'What did that old witch want?'

The bills Mrs Blakemore referred to were from a credit card in Brian's name, and another in our joint names, with Brian the main borrower. Brian should have been the last person to accuse me of leaving him with bills, considering all those years I'd spent as the sole provider. These accounts were minuscule compared to the money I'd put into that marriage. His family could deal with them.

Mum also used to help with my facial exercises, following the instruction sheets carefully as I tried to entice my muscles to work, forcing my face to grimace, smile and frown.

Donna Knapp, my round-faced and sweetly determined occupational therapist, or OT, was more brutal than Mum. 'Your mouth's open, Donna. Close your mouth, remember?' she'd say as she strode into my room. 'Raise your brow. Come on. One more time. You don't want a deadpan face for the rest of your life, do you?'

Physio begins almost immediately with burns patients. They need to get your joints moving before you seize up completely. Almost from the start, Amanda Hughes, my physiotherapist, was bending things that felt like they should never be bent.

'This is for your own good,' she'd insist, working away at my clenched fingers or manipulating knees or toes or elbows and shoulders as I writhed under her grasp.

She was even at it when I was on the operating table, and oblivious to her twisting and pulling.

'You did well,' she'd say afterwards. 'We got your arms to 90 degrees yesterday!'

The OT and the physio joined forces and organised a neck collar and splints. They were blue plastic, like chunks of pipe cut in half and moulded to fit my arms, legs, feet and fingers. During the day they would sit tucked away in a candy-striped calico bag that hung innocently on the wall in front of me, under the clock. But at night I would be splinted up and staked out on my bed in a cross formation to prevent my muscles from contracting and distorting even more.

Oh Jesus, I know how it feels to be crucified.

New modes of what appeared to be custom-designed torture were constantly invented for me, including a mechanism that hooked to either side of my mouth at night, stretching the corners of my new lips. Another contraption fitted around my wrists and onto each finger in a series of elastic bands, designed to bend my unbendable digits. The candy-striped bag started to bulge.

For five and a half months, Dad did the night shift with me. He'd work all day, installing fire sprinklers in city office blocks, then drive through peak-hour traffic to Westmead. He caught a few hours' sleep back in Redfern before heading off to work again early the next morning.

He regularly brought in five-kilo bags of lollies to replenish the staff jar on my behalf. For me, he brought stories: tales about work, about my childhood, about his growing up. He was my entertainer. He'd bring me orchids from his garden too, and report how many snails he'd found over the weekend. He'd talk about what was happening out there, in the world beyond my tiny room. Nelson Mandela had been elected president in South Africa. There had been a massacre in Rwanda. O.J. Simpson was under arrest following the murder of his wife and her friend. There was talk of the latest Disney animation, *The Lion King*, which would eventually be released in Australia. Bodean would like that one, he reckoned. Maybe he could take the boys to see it when he saw them, he said.

And when will that be? I wondered. When will you see them?

Sometimes, when the long, monotonous nights got to him, he'd sneak a wheelchair from around the corner and ride up and down the corridor, whizzing past my room with a mischievous grin and a wave, until one of the nurses stopped him.

'Traffic warden got me,' he'd whisper, sitting back down beside my bed.

Dad was also the one who held the mirror up to my face.

Apparently people had been talking about it for a while, the nursing staff and my family. They all knew it had to be done, but no one quite knew how to tell me. Mum simply refused. Dad stepped in.

'Give me the mirror. I'll bloody well do it,' he said one evening when his visit coincided with Mum's and Sissy's.

It's hard to describe what you feel when you realise you have lost your original face forever. When you see that the familiar, comfortable features you lived with every day of your life no longer exist, but have been replaced with a hideous, grinning skull straight out of a horror movie.

My forehead and the bridge of my nose jutted out over the rest of my face. Most of my nose was gone. Instead I had two large black holes. One had a feed tube poked into it.

I couldn't close my mouth. All my teeth were exposed, like a braying donkey. My new lips were thin, lopsided rolls of flesh – tiny, crooked-rimmed sausages. My skin was an angry mix of purples, pinks and maroons, a violent patchwork of scarred tissue, a legacy of the many grafts. A few strands of brittle brown hair sprouted from my skull. My eyes, deeply embedded, were the only familiar things left.

I can't do this, can't do this anymore, looking like a freak. My thoughts spiralled into a deep, dark pit as fresh tears fell. I now saw what my visitors saw. And I understood that initial flash of shock, the struggle to hide it, and the secret they had all been keeping from me. I was severely distressed, not only by my appearance, but also by the grief it had caused others.

I remember Bea was there as I stared at my reflection. 'Don't cry, don't cry,' she said. 'No good. Face go red.' She frowned and shook her head.

What face? I wanted to scream.

'It'll be okay, love,' Dad said, pulling the mirror away. 'We can get you a wig. We can fix your nose. The things they can do nowadays – they do it in America. Unbelievable what they can do, it can all be changed. We can get you a whole new face in the US.'

It was a fairytale, but I was good at believing them. They're what got me here in the first place.

As my parents, my aunty and my sister spent countless hours beside my bed, I was aware of the two members of my family that I hadn't seen. Mother's Day came and went without so much as a phone call. My imagination was in overdrive. Had Garry come back to get them? Had they been burnt too? Were they dead?

I missed Coe and Bodean dreadfully. Their photos were pinned to a noticeboard near my bed and, when my parents visited, my eyes would travel up to their sweet faces, then back down to Mum or Dad sitting beside me. I asked about them all the time.

My boys? How are my babies?

'The kids are fine, love. Don't you worry about them. They're being looked after. You just get better. That's your job.'

I couldn't help but worry though. Call it mother's intuition. I knew something wasn't right.

Seven

I'm propped up in bed, gazing at a small television screen. There's a tape in the VCR and the nurse has just pressed play.

'So kind of the Blakemores to send this, Donna. They know how much you're missing your children. This'll cheer you up. Just buzz if you need me,' she said as she slipped out the door.

The screen is still black, but now I can hear the rusty squeak of a swing.

I recognise Brian's drone. ' Whoa! Careful, look out! Not too high. Easy.'

A picture flickers in front of me. Even though it's rolling a bit at first, I recognise its my blond baby, sitting on one of those long swings with a seat up either end. He's laughing as the swing seesaws back and forth, higher and higher.

'Slow down, leadfoot.' It's Brian again.

My stomach lurches as I watch Bodean, only two years old, soaring up and plunging down, laughing wildly. Hold on, darling! Hold on.

Now it's Mrs Blakemore's turn. I hear her Irish lilt in a soft aside to Brian, which I'm sure I'm not meant to hear. 'He's too high, Brian.'

'He's right. He can handle it. He holds on, Mum.'

For a moment the screen goes black, and then Bodean flashes on again, this time sitting non-plussed in the centre of a trampoline, his finger in his mouth. His eyes look at me, navy blue, like mine.

It's Denise's backyard. There's a rotary clothesline and a few towels and pieces of clothing are flapping about in the wind. Their shadows dance darkly on the bare earth. There are a few dogs: a big St Bernard, a scruffy little mongrel and maybe one other, a cattle dog perhaps. A galah sits in the bare branches of a stunted tree and there's an old caravan up the back, near the high metal fence. This would be Brian's home.

Other things are scattered about in the dirt: a red bucket, an empty beer keg, a rusty rocking toy, a toddler's pink trike, a hose, a wheel off a bike and a cricket bat. A heap of junk has been piled up at the mouth of a tin shed.

Brian is filming and calling out to Bodean, who stares blankly at the camera, still sucking his fingers. 'What's the matter with you? Go on! Bounce on the trampoline. Show your mum how you can bounce. Go on. Get up and bounce. Bounce. Come on!'

So Bodean stands up and begins to teeter around on the springy surface. He sways dangerously close to the hard metal edge.

'Nice and easy,' murmurs Mrs Blakemore as Bodean tips drunkenly about.

I'm edgy, knotted with panic. Why doesn't someone sit on it with him, hold his hands and help him jump?

'Watch it!' calls Brian. 'Oh, there he goes. Oh, he's over.'

I'm sobbing now, squeezing my eyes shut so I don't have to watch anymore. I open them and buzz for a nurse, catching a flash of Bodean slipping down between the trampoline pad and the springs attached to the metal frame.

'Turn it off,' I mouth. 'I can't bear it.'

※

I had been in hospital almost two months, sealed off from the outside environment like a lizard in a jar. I was confined to the climate-controlled, antiseptic wards and corridors of hospital-land. How I longed to see the sky, feel sunshine on my face, run my fingers over tree trunks and grass, breathe in fresh air, rain, earth.

My voice had come back, a raspy whisper.

I would tug weakly at my mother's sleeve. 'Get me out of here, Mum.'

'Where, love? Where could I take you?'

'Take me home.'

On 21 May, I had my first visit from Coe. Brian brought him in. Coe said, months later, that he'd wanted to visit earlier but no one would bring him. Finally, after endless requests, Brian had agreed, although I believe Denise was not happy.

A while before his visit, Coe had spoken to Sissy on the phone. 'How's Mum? Aunty Denise says she's critical and could go at any minute.'

Sissy tried to reassure him. 'She's being well looked after, Coe. The nurses are changing her dressings and putting special cream on her. She's hooked up to a lot of machines, but she's going to be all right.'

'How long will she be in hospital?'

'About six to eight months,' Sissy replied.

'That long!'

'Yes, maybe, but then again she could get better quicker so maybe only three or four months. When will you and your dad be coming down?'

'In a couple of weeks. He has to arrange transport first.'

As Brian and Coe entered the Burns Unit, Coe asked about my appearance. 'What does Mum look like, Dad?'

There were some particularly gruesome pictures of burns patients on the wall in the foyer, and they stopped to have a look.

'Can't really describe it, son, but she's bad all right. Maybe like this. Or this.' Brian pointed to one or two of the more mutilated faces. 'It's not pretty, anyway.'

Coe says that I wasn't as bad as the photos, but I looked pretty shocking all the same.

'It's difficult to describe,' he said, many years later. 'You were in bed, all bandaged up except for your face. The first thing I noticed was that your nose was gone. Then I saw your teeth. Your hair was thin and crinkly.'

'Did I say anything?'

'You couldn't talk much. You just cried. You couldn't stop crying, you were so excited about seeing me.'

It's true. I remember being overcome with emotion. I had missed both my boys so badly and worried about them so much. Now at least Coe was here.

He and Brian were gowned up, of course, but I could see Coe was grubby. His hair needed a wash and a brush and his fingernails were dirty. He had never looked unkempt like this before.

'Brian, I'm worried about the boys,' I said.

'Look Donna, they're okay. They're fine. But as soon as you're well again, the kids are going back to you. That's a promise.'

'Are you sure?'

'Absolutely. They're your kids.'

To give Brian his due, I did find out later that he was at least partly sincere in what he'd said. Although he didn't say anything in support of me, DOCS records state that he wouldn't hear a word against me either, and he felt that the children belonged with me.

Coe sat and talked while I hung on his every word. This day must have been one of the hardest for my brave 12-year-old, realising his mother was not going to get better in a few days or weeks, or even months, and having to carry on a mostly one-sided conversation with a seriously ill parent who could do nothing but weep. He did his best though. He told me he'd started playing footy and he didn't mind his new school. He talked about his teacher, Mrs Kenyon, and also some of the friends he'd made. And Bodean was okay, he said.

Slowly, I felt reassured. It seemed everyone was right – they were okay with the Blakemores. And when I was well enough, I could resume parenting.

Coe didn't mention that his old school had forwarded some photos of me, and that when Bodean saw my face he began pointing and crying, 'Mummy! Mummy!' He didn't tell me that Denise shut my photo away in a drawer or that she refused to show Bodean again. He also didn't tell me about the 'smacking stick' – I found out about that months later when Bodean saw me take a wooden spoon out of the drawer to stir a casserole and began to shriek, 'No, no, no! I'll be good!'

Coe didn't tell me that, in early April, his uncle Danny took him by the scruff of the neck and pushed his face into a newspaper headline: 'COUPLE IN SUICIDE PACT'.

'See that?' he said. 'You've got it wrong. She did it to herself. We told you your mother was mental.'

In the beginning Coe refused to believe what his aunt and uncle were saying, but as the months went by he began to doubt his memory. He had nightmares and felt anxious and scared, not only about me, but also about his and Bodean's uncertain future. He was discouraged from talking about me or asking about my progress and he hadn't been taken to counselling, despite the Department's continued strong recommendation for psychological intervention. But he didn't mention any of this during his visit.

He also didn't tell me that his cousin sneered at him – 'At least I belong here. I'm not bludging like some people.' – or that Coe got less and his cousins got more: the squashy child's seat in the rear of the car while they got the front, hand-me-down clothes while his cousins' were brand new. The Blakemores had been given finances through DOCS to assist with Coe's and Bodean's needs. Had my boys seen any of it?

At one stage, when Brian left my hospital room to get coffee, Coe leaned forward, his grubby face lit up with excitement.

'I got something for you, Mum,' he whispered. He dug around under the gown searching in the pockets of his jeans. 'I went back and got it the day after the fire. Here.' He held out a hand towards me.

In his outstretched palm lay the gold filigree heart he'd given me for my birthday, almost two months before. It was no longer attached to my silver chain. Instead it hung by a piece of white ribbon.

'Don't cry, Mum,' he whispered. 'I love you.'

'I love you too,' I mouthed.

'Here, Mum, I'll put the heart on your table here, where you can see it.'

One of the nurses slipped in soon after, to check vitals and increase my morphine.

'I'll be out of it in a minute, but keep talking to me, darling. Keep talking …' My eyes rolled back into my head as I slipped into morphine dreams. 'Off with the fairies', Mum called it. If only! Off with the rats, lawnmower blades, monsters and flames.

'I hated it when they switched the morphine on,' Coe said years later. 'I'd never get a chance to say goodbye.'

At the end of May, soon after this visit from Brian and Coe, DOCS officer, Maria Williams, phoned my father and then my mother. This was hidden from me; my family just kept repeating the same suspicious script: 'Nothing's wrong, Donna. The kids are fine. You just get better.'

Apparently Denise had complained to the Department that my parents were hassling her with phone calls, agitating to have the two boys in the holidays, to be closer to their mum. It was something that the Blakemores seemed determined to block.

'The children need to stay where they are at present,' Ms Williams told my father over the phone. 'Please stop harassing the Blakemores about holiday access.'

Dad quickly became irate. 'I don't know who you are or what you're on about, but the Blakemores have done nothing for those kids. We're family! We've got a right to have the kids, and Donna has a right to see them!'

'The children would benefit from your continuing to visit, but they're settled where they are and managing well. They shouldn't spend time away from home at the moment,' she insisted. 'The children's wellbeing has been the concern of the Department since the fire. As for Donna, it's the Department's view that incinerating yourself in front of your children is a horrendous act of abuse and of course we need to ensure ...'

Dad told me much later that he saw red at her accusation and began shouting over the top of her. 'My daughter didn't bloody well do this to herself. You better get your damned facts straight before you go around shooting your mouth off!'

'Your daughter incinerated herself! She's an abusive mother and, as far as the Department's concerned, she may never get her children back!'

At this point Dad lost it – eloquently. 'If you're not going to listen, fuck off!' He slammed the receiver down. Seconds later, when the phone rang again and he heard the DOCS officer's voice, he slammed the phone down a second time.

Ms Williams then rang Mum.

Poor Mum wasn't used to dealing with departmental types. Ms Williams identified herself and then told her that she, Dad and Kathryn were to stop annoying the Blakemores with requests to have the children for the holidays. Mum was floored. She burst into tears.

'I just want to help my daughter get well,' she said. 'Seeing the children and knowing that they're with our family will help her get well.'

Ms Williams had her answer ready. 'Of course we understand you want to see your daughter get well. However the Department's foremost concern is the stability and emotional welfare of the children, rather than their mother. It's not appropriate for them to visit you when they're already settled with the Blakemores.'

'But they're not close to the kids. We're their family. And as for Brian, he's never looked after them,' cried Mum. 'Donna's always had that responsibility, and she worked because he could never hold down a job with his drinking.'

'Nevertheless,' Ms Williams said, 'Donna set herself alight in front of the children, and this is clearly extreme emotional abuse. Obviously she was unfit to be a parent, even though you say she worked and provided in a financial way.'

The fact that Ms Williams saw fit to inform my parents that I was an abusive mother was not recorded in the Department's running notes on these telephone conversations. I was to find out eventually, when I finally obtained my file, that this part had been conveniently left out.

So alarmed were my parents by these calls from the Department that they decided to seek legal advice regarding access to their grandchildren, as well as the Department's misinformation over the assault. The solicitor quickly backtracked once he knew that Children's Services were involved. He told my parents they had no rights. It would have been plain to him anyway that my parents had little money to pay for expensive legal intervention. It seemed my parents were powerless against the Department.

Kathryn took matters into her own hands and phoned Ms Williams to tell her that I had explained the facts to my parents. I hadn't set myself alight. Garry had done this to me. But DOCS rolled on regardless.

Ms Williams might have been vocal about my 'self-incineration', but she didn't tell my family about certain allegations that had been made against me, the character assassinations happening behind my back, the biased nonsense that DOCS had collected from interviewees who either didn't know me or had a personal axe to grind. Later, much later, I would find out just who was delivering these Judas kisses as I lay in the hospital bed.

On the afternoon of Friday, 24 June, Vera Reiner, a social worker at Westmead, received a message that a DOCS officer was coming to see me on the following Monday. Peter Whincop, my usual social worker, was not in. Vera didn't know me, but she was curious – this was Children's Services. Whatever it was, it had to be important. She found the name of my solicitor, Ann Kinghan, in my files, and decided to ring and tell her about the message.

Concerned and confused, Ann immediately phoned the Department's Parkes office and a care application for Coe and Bodean was served to her over the phone. It was supported by a statement of alleged brief facts, the main one being that I had deliberately incinerated myself in front of my children. Ann could not respond on my behalf, however, unless I gave her instructions. At about 3 pm, she phoned me at Westmead.

A nurse stood at the end of my bed, frowning above her mask. 'Donna, your solicitor's on the phone. She needs to speak to you now. It's about the kids. It's very important.'

Oh God, what's happened? My mind was in overdrive as the nurse called for assistance to heave me off the mattress. It took me at least ten minutes to get to the phone at the nurses' station – half dragged, half carried by the two staff. My legs were throbbing with pain by the time I reached the phone, as the blood rushed through my veins and into my feet. I could barely remain upright. Everywhere the nurses touched was agony.

I've got to do this. God help me do this.

With a nurse either side to prop me up, I tried to concentrate while the receiver was held to my ear. I couldn't hear properly at first, apart from the words 'court' and 'your children'. The word 'DOCS' was not mentioned, or if it was, I didn't notice. I had no idea what was going on, but I knew it involved my kids and it was something serious.

'Do whatever you have to do,' I gasped, 'but don't let anyone take my children.'

'Where can they live while you're in hospital?'

'My sister's,' I managed to say.

I had spoken. Now my solicitor could act.

A DOCS representative had been scheduled to come on Monday, after court at Forbes, to tell me my children had been taken into care. It was only by chance that I was able to intervene: a social worker's gut feeling that she needed to make a phone call. As it was, Ann had to scurry around on Friday afternoon, confirming Sissy would take the children and organising representation for me on Monday. Her information from the Department, which they faxed to her office, was scant, and left her no time to investigate before Monday's hearing.

On Monday, 27 June, the Children's Court at Forbes made orders adjourning proceedings until 10 August. Although Ann was ill-prepared to counteract the Department's ambush, she had at least bought some time with this adjournment. Meanwhile, the court declared the children wards of the state and placed them in the temporary care of Denise Blakemore.

I was unaware of the results of the court hearing and knew nothing about Denise being pronounced the official carer of my children. But I realised something wasn't right because my solicitor had become involved.

With so many assurances that the boys were fine, I'd accepted the fact that they were with the Blakemores for the moment. My solicitor's phone call had changed all that, prompting me to nominate Sissy as their carer. The Department had forced my hand. I had no idea, though, that I'd been accused of igniting myself, and that I'd been labelled an abusive mother. I had no idea just how serious things had become.

Towards the end of June, as I lay oblivious to the Department's actions, Denise brought Bodean for a visit. Brian had come to the hospital with him soon after Coe's visit, but I have to say I don't remember. On the day Bodean and Denise came in, Mum was there and her grandson recognised her straightaway.

'Nanna, Nanna.' He held out his arms.

'Come here, love,' crooned Mum. Denise deposited him on Mum's lap and he began to play with the gold chain around her neck.

Naturally, he did not recognise me. He probably couldn't even figure out that I was human, let alone his mother. But it was so good to see my baby. I began to cry and, once I started, I couldn't stop.

I was shocked at the way Bodean looked. A thick river of snot dribbled from his nose, and his head lolled to one side. Mum said he felt feverish. His hands were filthy and his clothes were encrusted with food and dirt. His trackpants were way too small for him, and cut into his chubby little legs. His shrunken top rode up above his waist leaving his soft, white midriff exposed. His feet were crammed into tiny pink sneakers, clearly second-hand.

'Show Nanna your new shoes,' Denise instructed, smiling over at him.

Bodean, on cue, stuck one little leg up in the air and pointed proudly at his filthy shoe. Mum pursed her lips, saying nothing.

'Denise, I don't understand about the children,' I whispered. 'I don't know why my sister can't have them now, until I'm well.'

Denise pushed her blond hair back from her face and gave me a small, patronising smile. 'They need to be with their father, Donna. The kids are fine.'

Tears were still streaming down my face. 'I want to see my boys, but I don't want Brian here again.'

A long time later I found out that Denise reported back to the DOCS worker on her visit, like some sort of Departmental spy. I found details of her phone call to them embedded in my DOCS file.

Denise said that Donna knew nothing about the care application. She said it was obvious that the family law court action had not come from her.

There were also comments about my emotional state.

> Denise was shocked at how poor Donna was emotionally. She said that she was not capable of saying more than four or five words together, and was crying all the time. Denise described her as 'an emotional and mental wreck'.

Under the circumstances, I think anyone would have been an emotional wreck, especially if they'd had to endure what happened next. At the end of the brief visit, Denise took Bodean back from Mum and stood at the foot of my bed looking down at me, encased in tubigrip and oozing bandages. Bodean was clinging to her like a koala, his little head of curls leaning into her chest. He looked up at her then and said something that shook me to the core.

'Mummy,' he said. The word boomed and bounced about the tiny room, over and over in a loop. *Mummy. Mummy. Mummy.* He called her Mummy. She turned away from him, looked me hard in the face and smiled.

Eight

The wall calendar told me it was July. Someone had turned another page over, and a whole new sheet of numbered squares sat waiting to be crossed off. The calendar was an important measure – in hospital, time was slippery. Encased in bandages and sprouting plastic tubes tethered to an array of machines, there was no clear demarcation between one day and the next. The hours rolled into one another, a continuous ribbon of fluorescent lights, jangling trolleys, pain and hallucinations.

Through the fog, I thought about Bodean's visit, his pasty face, his runny nose and lolling head, his clothes too tight, his sturdy little boy's feet squeezed into lolly-pink girl's shoes. How he'd called Denise Mummy.

On 7 July it was noted in my medical files that Coe and Brian came to see me again. I remember very little about that visit, only a vague awareness of their presence and the usual fear that, like before, Brian would try to force me to sign something I shouldn't. I know he repeated his assurances about Coe and Bodean. 'The kids are fine. When you're out of here, the kids'll be going back to you.'

Soothing words aside, I knew things just weren't adding up. If the kids were fine, why had my solicitor called me? Something had to be wrong. Still, without any information to the contrary, I clung to the idea that, in the end, logic would prevail. It had to. It was the thought of having my children back that was keeping me alive.

I didn't know it, but DOCS were in the process of interviewing Sissy and John, asking them to prepare documents such as character references, and plans and photographs of their house – each room, the adjoining gardens and land. This was supposed to be a placement option, a procedure that should have been carried out before any court action, but my children had been legally handed over to Denise. It wasn't until many months later that I realised DOCS must have already been in damage control.

After the shock of my solicitor's phone call, I was descending into a depression. I was sure the nurses hated me and were trying to kill me. So I stopped drawing attention to myself in any way. I didn't buzz for help; I didn't make requests or complaints; I didn't ask questions. I tried hard to be invisible. But, in my condition, I couldn't avoid medical attention for long.

I dreaded any of the staff coming into my room, whether they were bullying or benevolent. Were they going to roll me over, triggering a new level of pain, or would they be unclogging a blocked feed tube? Would they have to force another into the hole where my nose had been, pushing it down my throat as I tried to swallow the pipe between vomits? Or would they be changing the dressings, the most torturous daily ritual of all, taking up to six hours to complete? Four capped and gowned nurses tugging at bandages, scrubbing at the rotten flesh, digging out staples, creaming and re-bandaging. Faceless medical staff, jostling for space, tripping over my tubes, having to halt proceedings to reinsert catheters and drips.

I was having other problems too. It was around this time I picked up an eye infection, which placed my sight at risk. Breathing, always difficult, was becoming more laboured. My severely burnt windpipe was a mass of mucus and scorched tissue, which had to be pumped out of my lungs. Coughing was vital, but so hard to do. My throat felt like it was on fire, yet I was forbidden a drink, because the flap that normally stopped food and drink going into my lungs had gone on strike. Dad would sometimes carefully rub ice around the edge of my newly made lips, but I was desperate for water.

'Now, I'm going to clean your teeth to make you feel better, Donna, but you must promise not to swallow the water when you rinse. You must spit it out,' Nurse Isabella warned in her soothing voice.

In July too, the nightmares returned. I dreamed of being trapped and trying to run away, of being chased, caught and bashed up, or shredded to pieces by a lawnmower. The hospital sounds, the buzzers and bells, the rattle of the staff lolly jar, the cries of other patients, even the click of a biro, all seeped in and became part of whatever story was unravelling in my subconscious.

With my declining state, the nursing staff decided something needed to be done. They had a quiet word with my mother, explaining that my progress had slowed and I was fretting badly for my children. I was sinking. Could she think of something to say to me that would bolster my will to live?

Unfortunately, they neglected to explain the sort of things she might mention to get me to rally. They forgot to say that I needed hope, encouragement, a light at the end of the tunnel. I suppose they assumed she understood. As in my younger years though, despite loving me dearly, Mum wasn't one for pussyfooting around with too much sentiment.

I had my eyes closed behind a silicon mask when I felt Mum's breath on my ear. Her voice was an urgent whisper. 'You have to get well. You've got to get better. You have to get up out of that bed because they're taking the children.'

Even in my fragile state, I was well aware, from my years growing up in Redfern, just who 'they' were. Welfare – the infamous, many-tentacled government department that struck fear into the heart of any parent – now known as the Department of Community Services.

As a child, I'd visited the Jenolan Caves, where we stood in one of those luminous caverns while they turned the lights out. I remember it was so dark I couldn't see my hand in front of my face. I was terrified to move in case I stepped off the edge. There was nothing to hang on to – no handles, nothing. In hospital, it was like being back there, but up until now there had been a faint light far in the distance. My kids. As those words were spoken to me, the light was extinguished. My nightmare had been confirmed. My children had been taken from me, and my spirit finally doused.

A few days later, on 16 July, Nurse Iain had a gut feeling about me and decided to make a routine check. I was very quiet – too quiet. I'd stopped breathing.

'Don't do this, Donna! Not on my shift!'

Other staff came running. 'Breathe, Donna! Breathe!'

I remember those words, muffled and distant, as though I were lying underwater with someone screaming from the surface. They began to work on me as I was wheeled across the corridor into ICU. For three days I lingered, critical but stable.

Although I was meant to be out of it, certain things pricked my consciousness. I had a mouthful of tubes right down my throat. They were tied in position but the tape was so tight it had ripped into the flesh at the back of my neck. This was eventually discovered by a nurse doing my daily dressings.

'What's this here? Hasn't anybody noticed this is too tight? It's caused a wound in the back of her neck!' Then to me she murmured, 'Dear, dear, that must have been painful.'

Unable to move, or even open my eyes, I thanked her mentally. Little did I know, wounds like this left unattended were more than just painful. For burns patients they were often fatal.

On 19 July, still in ICU, my condition worsened and I was given an emergency tracheotomy. They cut my throat, pulled open my windpipe and inserted a fat, hollow tube in my neck; a hideous, gurgling contraption, oozing yellow phlegm, through which I would need to learn how to breathe, cough and speak.

As I regained a little movement and opened my eyes, I became aware of a nurse sitting beside me. In ICU there's always a nurse with you, usually eating sandwiches or writing notes. I beckoned for my pencil and paper. I grasped the pencil in my bandaged fingers and managed to scrawl him a very brief message:

Please help me die.

Nine

It was clear, from the look of surprise and disappointment on the nurse's face, that if I were going to do away with myself, it would have to be without anyone's help. I felt deeply ashamed for trying to involve a stranger, but I was determined to end my life. I was sick of moving one step forward only to be dragged back again and again. Let's make it a bit harder, a bit harder. Let's take her children away now. Oh, that's not enough. Let's give her a trachy to learn to speak through. Let's make it permanent.

The one thing that had kept me going was the thought of my children. I had to get well for them. Now, apparently, someone had decided they didn't need me and I didn't deserve them. I presumed they would stay with their father, Denise and Danny, and they would all live happily ever after without me, thanks to the Department of Community Services. So what was the point in living?

I became preoccupied with finding ways to kill myself. How did people usually do it? I wondered. There was carbon monoxide poisoning, but I needed a car and a hose for that. There was gas, but that required an oven. There was drowning, but that needed water. There was wrist-slashing, but I had no knife. Even if I had a car or an oven or a swimming pool or a knife, I couldn't move. I couldn't roll, I couldn't sit up, I couldn't even bend my fingers. Could I hold my breath? Would that work?

Perhaps, if I had an accomplice, they could put a pillow over my face and smother me. But no, I had the trachy to foil that one. Maybe if they put the pillow over my trachy that would do the trick. Or not even a pillow, but just a finger ...

All this time in hospital, nothing had been funny. Along with my face, my hair, my skin and muscle, voice, kids, career and life as I knew it, I had also lost my sense of humour. Now, at the most unexpected time, through all those layers of despair and depression, my humour came bubbling up. Death by breath holding? Right! A finger over my trachy? Who was I kidding? These images were the most amusing things that had jumped into my head for months. And all the while my heart monitor continued to skip along. With a heart as big as Phar Lap's, it seemed, and no way of killing myself, the situation had an appealing irony to it.

Right, I thought, seeing that even killing myself is going to be a bloody struggle, let's make a little deal, old heart. As long as you keep going, so will I.

It was then that I decided that whatever it took, I would learn to walk, talk, eat, breathe by myself and be a mother to my boys again. Because, damn it, I *was* their mother, and a good one too!

'We'll see. We'll see who can't do this and can't do that,' I murmured to myself, intubated and isolated in ICU. We'll see.

My environment may not have changed much, but one thing was different. My attitude had shifted. It wouldn't be a smooth trip, but I'd been in training all my life, and I knew at that moment that I would make it. It looked like my mother's whispered message about DOCS taking the children was going to save me after all, though it had nearly killed me first.

Meanwhile, the Department was hastily putting things in place that should have been done as part of normal procedure long before their care application for Coe and Bodean went to court. They had obviously not expected a last-minute intervention by my solicitor, resulting in a six-week interim care order rather than their planned 12-month care order. It had not been the done deal that the Department or the Blakemores were expecting.

My own family knew now that my emotional stability and my ability to be a parent was under question because of some left-field story that I had willingly doused and ignited myself in front of Coe and Bodean. I was still unaware of this, and just assumed my children were being put into care because I was too ill to look after them.

On 24 July 1994, Sissy and John and their two kids, Jennifer and Patrick, were asked by the Department to travel to Lake Canobolas in Orange, where they would meet with Coe and Bodean. Then they would take them to McDonald's. The idea was that the boys would be observed by a psychologist as they interacted with their aunt and uncle, as well as their two cousins.

Sissy, much later, said it felt like a set-up. Why, she wondered, did they have to travel to a place so far away from their home near Wingham, a place that was unfamiliar to any of them. Why not Dubbo, or even Parkes? Why not Sissy and John's place at Killabakh, where both the boys had been before?

DOCS officer Maria Williams, psychologist Janet Webster and temporary carer and aunt Denise Blakemore huddled together behind a tree and watched while Coe and Bodean chatted and played happily with my sister, brother-in-law, niece and nephew.

'It looked totally weird,' Sissy said later. 'They were like three conspirators in cahoots. They were peering over one another behind this tree trunk, staring across at us. God knows what the kids thought of it all.'

Sissy was puzzled about other things too. Janet Webster was meant to be an independent observer. Why was Maria Williams there and, more importantly, why was Denise with them? Why didn't the psychologist just sit at the picnic table as an acquaintance and do her observing, rather than prowling around like a spy?

Despite the weirdness of the situation, everything went smoothly, and Sissy and John were observed as being 'responsive and understanding' towards Coe and Bodean. However, Janet Webster would end up supporting the Department's decision to place the boys in the care of Danny and Denise. She was concerned that Denise allowed Bodean to call her Mummy rather than Aunty but she would ultimately state to the Department that both Coe and Bodean were better off in Parkes, where they could have close contact with their father. Brian had in fact left the Parkes area and was living in Sydney, but someone forgot to mention that.

Janet Webster had not been told that I was a victim of crime, but was led to believe I was an abusive parent. I'm sure she was also unaware of the fact that my own family had had far closer ties with Bodean and, more particularly, Coe, prior to the assault. Danny and Denise had played minor roles in their lives. Janet Webster was making decisions based on dangerously incorrect information.

Sissy and John had assured the Department that they would support Coe and Bodean in a variety of ways. They were happy for Brian to visit his sons, as long as he wasn't drinking. They would encourage Coe's love of sport, take Bodean to playgroup, seek counselling for the boys as necessary, and provide a comfortable living environment for them and also me, their mother, once I was out of hospital. This would be an ideal situation to maintain the strong bonds between my sons and me.

Maintain bonds? Not if the Department could help it.

DOCS decided to hold a family conference at Westmead, ostensibly to discuss different placements for the children. Like the observation of Sissy and John the previous day, this was something that should have been done well before any court involvement, even according to the Department's own procedure.

The conference took place in a large room filled with a jumble of chairs and cupboards. Bronwyn, the Burns Manager, neat and efficient in her navy blue suit, wheeled me in on my giant waterchair. It was a cross between a wheelchair and an enormous recliner rocker with padded cushions and a big steel bar on the back for pushing. Various bags of fluid were hooked onto the side of my chair. More hung off my dolly trolley, a contraption that looked a bit like a mobile coat rack.

Despite my shift in attitude, I was physically weak and far from well. I had not yet learned to speak effectively through my trachy so, before the conference, I had scrawled my one wish on a piece of paper for Bronwyn to read out at the meeting. This was that my boys should go to members of my family to be cared for until I was well enough to do so myself.

I was the last to enter the room. There seemed to be lots of people, all seated in a big ring. Bronwyn pushed my chair in to join the circle and she took a seat on my left. Sissy and John and Mum sat in front of me, a little to the left. Further around sat the Blakemores: Denise, Danny, Brian and Mrs Blakemore. Maria Williams, the DOCS officer, sat between the two family groups. I noticed two figures sitting in a corner of the room, right up the back away from everyone else. One was Richard Gray, the DOCS manager from Parkes, and the other my solicitor, Ann Kinghan, who was allowed to observe but not participate.

This was the first time Maria Williams had seen me. She looked at the notes in front of her and cleared her throat. 'We should get underway now that everyone is here. Of course, we've met today to discuss placement options for Coe and Bodean Blakemore. Would anybody like to offer a comment?'

Bronwyn, the Burns Manager, took the opportunity to speak. After introducing herself to the group, she explained I was unable to talk and that she would be my voice. 'Donna has only one wish that she would like people to know about. I have it here on this paper.' She held my scribbled message up briefly. 'That one wish is that her children are to be cared for by members of her own family until she is able to do so herself.'

'What about the father? He has a right!' shouted Danny, leaning forward.

'Brian's never been there for the kids,' said Mum. For a moment her eyes locked with Danny's.

'He's the father,' said Mrs Blakemore, pointing at Mum. 'It's only right they should be with him.' She hunched her back and began to wring her hands.

'Yeah, I'm their father,' Brian echoed.

Now it was Sissy's turn. She sat up straight and squared her shoulders. 'Yes, we know that,' she said, 'but what have you ever done for the boys? Donna's always been the major carer and provider –'

At this stage, all hell broke loose, as though a starter pistol had been fired. Maria Williams sat back, unable to control the melee.

Bronwyn, ever professional, was trying, once again, to speak on my behalf. 'As Donna is the mother, I think it's important that we understand her wish –'

But Danny wouldn't let Bronwyn finish. 'Brian's the father. He needs them. It's his right!'

'We didn't say he doesn't have a right,' Sissy said. 'If the children came to live with us we wouldn't mind if –'

'The kids are fine where they are,' Denise butted in. 'They're okay. I don't mind looking after them.'

'Yes, but we're the only family they've ever known,' Mum pointed out.

'What about me? I'm their father!'

'Yeah, he's the father!'

'Brian needs the children!'

As the shouting continued, and as my family retreated into appalled silence, I was becoming more and more distressed, gagging, crying, struggling for breath. I tugged at Bronwyn's sleeve. Do something, make them stop. Make them listen. Make them shut up.

I felt like I did all those years ago when I first came to Geurie. I was becoming invisible, smaller and smaller until I turned into a tiny white dot, drowned by the combined forces of Brian and his relatives.

No one seemed to be making any attempt to run the meeting. With a disgusted glance around the circle, Bronwyn finally stood up and shouted over the free-for-all. 'Listen to me everyone! This is over right now. My patient is my priority and if you haven't noticed, her breathing has become very laboured!'

As she spoke, an uneasy lull was cast over the room. The Blakemores stared at me in hostile silence. Mum was holding back tears, and my sister was white with shock. John, taciturn as usual, tugged at his neatly cropped ginger beard, hanging his head and staring at the floor.

Bronwyn came around and seized the back of my chair as I sat fighting for breath. 'This meeting's over as far as I'm concerned,' she repeated, wheeling me out the door.

Back in the Burns Unit, as Bronwyn settled me into my room, my family gathered outside in a state of disbelief. Ann Kinghan was also there. Mum said she looked shell-shocked.

'That meeting was a complete whitewash,' she told my family. 'They're just going through the motions. The fate of those children had obviously been decided long before today.'

An hour or so later, as I lay recovering in my room, Brian poked his head around the corner. Once again, I began to cry. What was he doing here? He shuffled closer to the bed in his sterilised hospital gown and pulled up a chair. His eyes, pink and watery above the mask, slid past my face in a kind of restless embarrassment. 'Just take it easy, Donna. Everything's gonna be all right.'

'No, it's not,' I mouthed, gasping for air through the pipe in my throat. 'Why are you doing this to me?'

'Look, it's happened, and we just have to make the best of it. Forget all that stuff that was said.' He waved one hand in the air dismissively. 'When you get out of here, we'll all go back home to Geurie. I'll put some ramps around the house for your wheelchair. You'll have your kids. I can help look after you. We can forget about what's happened, go on as before.'

I looked at him and blinked back more tears. He was making himself sound so generous, so full of forgiveness, that I suddenly felt beholden to him. He was offering a way out. A great tide of relief swept over me. At least this was a possibility for the future. It was *something*. I would have my children and a home. If it meant putting up with Brian, I'd done that before. I could do it again. A bizarre vision of me pushing the lawnmower in my wheelchair flashed through my mind. I smiled. It was ludicrous.

Brian mistook my smile for joy. 'See,' he said. 'Everything's gonna be okay.'

His generous offer was never mentioned to me again, although apparently he did a fair amount of boasting around Dubbo and Geurie about how he was going to look after his poor, repentant wife, build ramps and rails, take her for outings in her wheelchair, care for the children and reinvent himself as the self-sacrificing family man.

On 10 August, a further hearing took place at Parkes. I knew the matter of who would care for my children was going back to court, and I knew things weren't going well, but it was still a shock when Mum and Dad came to see me the following day.

'We lost the kids, Don,' said Dad, squeezing my gnarled hand. 'There's nothing we can do.'

A care order had gone through, placing both Coe and Bodean in the custody of Denise Blakemore for the next 12 months. Denise had been encouraged to give an 'undertaking' to facilitate my access to the boys. Access to my family – my hands, eyes and ears – was not included in this undertaking. It was me and only me. How was I expected to organise access in my state? Begging Denise seemed the only way. She was the conduit to my boys.

After court, Mum and Sissy had taken up the offer of a cup of tea back at Danny and Denise's place, following William Burke's advice. Organised by Ann Kinghan, he had been my legal representative in court on the day the care order was passed.

'Keep the lines of communication open,' he'd said to them. 'The children's contact with you and Donna will be largely at their discretion.'

Coe had greeted everyone at the front door. 'Who won the battle?'

'We won the war!' Danny told him.

William Burke had been refused access to my DOCS file, and was only given ten minutes to read the affidavits of Maria Williams and psychologist Janet Webster. He was not allowed to submit any character references on my behalf. Like Ann, he had done his best in the face of DOCS's railroading, but the might of this government department was apparently impossible to overcome.

Many weeks later my sister showed me William Burke's report following the court decision:

In summary, it seemed to me a waste of time and effort in Court to initially stumble and then find oneself hitting a D.O.C.S. brick wall, which would have remained regardless of preparation UNLESS the fundamental D.O.C.S. belief of self-incineration damaging the children emotionally could have been shattered by contrary evidence. Donna's references were objected to and hence could not be tendered.

... If Donna was truly assaulted by petrol and flame by Garry, then the injustice done will seem minor to the injustice now being done by D.O.C.S. assumptions and its 'brick wall' determination to preclude maternal extended family access ... On hearsay, D.O.C.S. has effectively condemned Donna.

At this stage, however, my family were too scared to disclose to me details of the Department's accusations. They had nearly lost me back in July with Mum's whispered message of DOCS's intervention and they were afraid that too much more bad news would kill me. Even in my befuddled state though, I knew they were hiding something. I'd lost my children, but there was something else. What were they keeping from me?

'Our hands are tied, love,' was all Mum would tell me. 'It's up to you now. You have to get better. You have to get yourself out of here and fight for those kids.'

Ten

Although my determination to escape was slowly growing, thoughts of suicide were never too far away, lurking in the shadows. Days filled with optimism and tenacity collided with days of abject misery and defeat. I knew I needed help, and Chris Basten, my hospital psychologist, was one of the professionals I requested to see.

Chris was meant to be imbuing me with the strength to move forward. He'd been helpful in the past but, today, he just wasn't doing it for me.

'I know you can get through this,' he said. 'You have so much to live for.'

I glared at him. He looked like he'd just stepped out of a *Vogue* magazine: golden hair, even tan, immaculate suit, polished shoes and Italian leather briefcase.

'You just don't get it, do you? They've taken my children. I've been hanging on, for my boys' sake, only to be told, "Don't bother, we're taking them." I've lost everything.'

'I know how you feel, but you mustn't think like that.' He glanced at his watch. 'I want you to visualise you're out of here. Visualise walking along a beach, or sitting in the middle of a rainforest.'

'Don't tell me what I should be thinking,' I whispered, tears rolling down my face. 'It's okay for you. At five o'clock you'll get to leave this place, jump in your sports car and drive home to your beautiful wife and your 2.5 kids and your perfect home. When you're sitting around the dinner table tonight surrounded by your family – your life – you visualise me here. You visualise that!'

I apologised for my outburst a little later and, to give Chris his due, he did go home and think about me. He told me that he couldn't eat his dinner that night and had trouble sleeping, at least for a night or two. There was another thing that puzzled him, he said – how did I know he drove a sports car?

The psychologist wasn't the only person who pushed my buttons. A fellow burns patient had been flown up from Tasmania some weeks after my arrival in Westmead. They said he was almost as bad as me. When I found out he was being discharged, I was devastated.

'It's not right,' I sobbed hoarsely to Iain as he pushed me towards the bathroom in my wheelchair. 'That guy was here after me, now he's going and I'm still here. When can *I* go home?'

'You're not ready to be discharged.' Iain steered the wheelchair into the shower and took out his scissors. I could tell he was tired and cross.

'I want to go home!'

'Come on, Donna, I need to cut these bandages off. Stop complaining and help me by sitting up.'

I shook my head and hunched over in my chair, taking a gulp of air through my trachy. 'I'm not complaining. I just don't understand.'

Iain's voice was tight. 'It's just the way it is. You'll get out when we know you're ready.' He leaned forward with the scissors.

'No!' I whispered, with as much venom as I could muster.

He tossed the scissors onto my lap. 'Here, then. You have a go. Cut yourself out. I'm going for morning tea.' He knew full well that I couldn't even hold the scissors let alone make the blades open and shut.

Iain did come back. Eventually. 'Oh,' he said, with feigned surprise. 'Are you still here?'

Iain was bossy at the best of times, sometimes downright harsh, but I believed he had my best interests at heart. Soon he was making me shuffle along on foot rather than use the wheelchair.

'Come on. You've got to walk if you want to get to the toilet.' He waited while I lifted my legs out of bed, an agonising manoeuvre as blood poured into my feet. Then he'd brace his toes against mine and take hold of my hands, tugging slightly while I tried to push myself up. 'That's it. You can do it.'

I had such a weak bladder from the catheter that sometimes I didn't make it to the toilet in time. 'Don't worry about it, Donna,' Iain would say breezily. 'This is nothing compared to some of the stuff we have to clean up. At least you're on your feet.'

My young physio, Amanda, would also take me for walks in my frame; I'd edge along the corridor and into the lift on my way to and from the physiotherapy room. Because my bandages left so many gaps, most embarrassingly around my bottom, Amanda had to tie a second gown around my neck to mask various sections of bare flesh.

'Come on, Caped Crusader,' she'd say as I tottered along like a geriatric mummy.

It was only a matter of time, though, before Amanda decided my strange costume just wouldn't do.

'We have to get you looking *normal*,' she declared, as though I *wanted* to lumber around the hospital masquerading as some weird superhero. 'You need proper clothes, and shoes too.'

This proved to be a lot more difficult than it sounded. Trying to get regular daywear to fit over the top of all my bandages and tubigrip was fraught with problems. I couldn't twist my limbs to get things on and off, and the heat was excruciating anyway without extra layers being added. Finally one nurse came up with the idea of making an entire outfit out of tubigrip. It was already almost impossible to bend; with a boob-tube dress over bandaged arms, legs and torso, I'd have so many layers on I'd never be able to move. The thought of this, together with my stylish new size-15 joggers fitted for swollen feet, was just too much to bear. I'd be a cross between the abominable snowman and Krusty the Clown, clomping around the corridors of Westmead. Was this what they meant by 'normal'?

※

People continued to put energy into finding ways I could occupy myself. Some weeks after my admission to Westmead, the staff had found out I liked to draw, and Mum and Dad were asked to buy some crayons and art paper. Unfortunately, I couldn't grasp the crayons and was in no state to produce works of art.

What about listening to music? After all, it could be therapeutic as well as entertaining. Off went Mum and Dad to find the necessary equipment but I couldn't work the cassette player. Couldn't put the tape in, couldn't turn it on or switch it off.

Reading then – brilliant idea! But hang on, I couldn't hold the book. No problem; the occupational therapist unearthed a bookstand. With the book in place, things looked promising. Until a nurse walked in to check my progress an hour or so later.

'Oh dear. Still on the same page. Perhaps a magazine would be easier to manage.'

Away went the book. Out came *New Idea*. The subscription had been a present from a colleague of mine, Christine.

One hour later …

'She's a slow reader. Been on that page for a while.'

Two hours later …

'Hmm. Still reading that tampon ad.'

Five hours later …

'Fallen asleep on the tampon ad! Must have had enough reading for one day. We'll just pop it away now.'

Once it became obvious I couldn't turn the page, my occupational therapist decided I needed a stick with a rubber tip. This would solve all my problems: I could simply hold the stick in my mouth and use it to turn the page. But what would I do with the stick between turning pages? Would I drop it on the bed? I could, but then I wouldn't be able to get it back into my mouth. Would I keep it in my mouth for the day then, like a dog guarding its favourite bone?

By this stage, with no way to distract myself, I was slowly going crazy. I had a constant monologue playing in my head; I couldn't shut it up. I worried about the children, about my ability to care for them. I worried about my family and the toll my own dramas were taking on them – I knew my mother had lost more than ten kilos. I worried about my house back in Geurie, about finances, about Garry coming to finish me off. The negative thoughts churned around and around without respite. No sooner had I got rid of one concern, than another would wriggle its way in. It was hard not to spiral back down into depression.

To break the cycle of pessimism, I decided to make a wish list in my head, a series of promises that I would keep to myself when I got out of this place. It would help me focus on the future in a positive way.

Some time before, Bodean had come in clutching a sad bunch of artificial sunflowers. I had them pinned to my noticeboard but they were the ugliest plastic flowers I'd ever seen. I vowed that when I got out I would plant sunflower seeds with Bodean and show him how magnificent the real flowers were.

My next promise to myself was not to put life on hold anymore. For a long time before the assault I'd been talking about taking some long-service leave and travelling to the Red Centre with my boys. I'd never done anything about it though. When I got out of hospital, I'd take Coe and Bodean to see Uluru. In the future, whenever they saw that big red rock they'd think, 'Mum took us to see that.'

This made me think of other places I wanted to show them. I began to plan a bank of memories for my boys: we would eat snow together, I decided, and we'd explore Victoria. We'd visit the Gold Coast theme parks, travel to Tasmania, to the Great Barrier Reef. We'd research the history of each destination as part of our adventures. Once I got out of here, I would not put these things off any longer.

Of course, the most important item on my wish list was simply to get better. Without this, nothing else could happen. There would be no Coe and Bodean in my life. There would be no travelling, no sunflowers, no life worth living.

Coaxing myself along the road to recovery, I began to make a mental note of 'firsts'. Actions that seemed minor to most people became major achievements to me. Being able to travel around the hospital in my wheelchair with Mum or Dad driving was probably the most significant step, and one that led to many other firsts.

Like everything else, my wheelchair travels soon became a ritual, a daily routine with Mum and part of my nightly amusement with Dad. They were always a welcome escape from the confines of my room, and a diversion for both my visitors and me. When Mum arrived each morning, the first thing she'd do was hunt for a wheelchair.

With the help of nursing staff, I'd be loaded into my chariot and disconnected from various bags. Some would go with me, attached to the side of the wheelchair. The nurse would tell Mum how long I had before I would need to be reconnected. We felt like gleeful prison escapees as we took off down the corridor towards the lifts.

We would explore different areas of the hospital: the dentistry section, or the foyer with its chemist, florist and gift shop. We'd study the large model of the hospital in the entranceway, planning where to go and what to see. We soon came to know by heart what was on each floor as we wound our way around the labyrinth of antiseptic corridors and dove-grey wards. Mum was a terrible driver, banging into the lino kickboards or swiping walls and architraves as she steered the wheelchair around corners, through doorways, into or out of lifts.

'I'll never get off me L plates,' she'd say, tugging crossly at the chair as we made our way around the giant hospital complex.

But it wasn't long before I grew weary of being limited to the stale confines of the hospital interior. Escaping from my tiny room was wonderful, but it just wasn't enough.

'Take me outside, Mum,' I pleaded one day when she and Sissy came to visit. 'Please, I just want to get out of here.'

Sissy and Mum held a whispered conversation at the foot of my bed, and then Sissy disappeared, heading in the direction of the nurses' station. In a few minutes she was back with one of the medical staff. I had to keep out of the wind. I had to stay away from the sun. I couldn't get too hot. I mustn't become too cold. But yes, I could go outside.

In preparation for my first trip beyond the four walls of the hospital, I was wrapped in several layers of white sheets and blankets. My face, too, needed to be almost entirely covered, with just a narrow slit in the sheeting for my eyes.

Sissy and Mum took me down in the lift, through the foyer and out the main entrance. I scrunched my eyes against the dazzling light as we followed a path just outside of the building, bordered by a low brick wall with gardens beyond. Soon we had found a sheltered area under a tree to park the wheelchair. Mum and Sissy perched next to me on the wall while I took in my surroundings.

For months I had endured acute sensory deprivation. My senses of smell, of taste, touch, sight and hearing had all been starved. Now, finally outside, I was overwhelmed. I squinted about as Mum gently eased the sheets away from my hooded face. The sun was blinding, the blanket over my lap a radiant white. The air smelled so different, fresh and cool on my raw skin. I wanted to bathe in it, to drink it into my dried-up body. I gazed up at the brilliant blue sky and the leafy canopy above me.

'Mum, have the trees always been that green?'

'Mmm,' she murmured. I could barely hear her reply. I wondered if she'd heard.

I took another mouthful of real air through the pipe in my neck. 'Mum?' I gasped. 'Have the trees always been that green?'

'Mmm, mm,' she repeated softly. She was doing her best not to cry.

'I never cried in front of her,' she'd tell people later. 'I saved that for when I was by myself.'

Mum was proud of her stoicism, and often appeared hard-hearted when really she was just trying to hold herself together. I remember one day, about the same time as my first trip outside, I begged her to come down to physio before she left for the afternoon.

'Come on, Mum. Please, I want to show you something.'

'Takes a long time to get back to Dassie's. Can't miss the train you know,' she grumbled.

Just the day before I had finally mastered walking down two steps in the physio room, a vast hall filled with mats, ramps and various other pieces of equipment. Navigating a couple of steps didn't sound like much, but it was a major triumph for me to complete the series of complex movements.

'Look, Mum! Look at me!' I whispered as I shuffled to the end of the ramp then lifted and lowered one foot after the other.

Once at the bottom of the steps, I glanced over at Mum and grinned.

'She's working really hard,' Amanda said. She knew it had taken months to conquer those two steps.

Mum, however, did not seem so impressed. 'Yes, well, is that it? I've got a train to catch, you know.'

Mum managed to cry later, when she was relating the story to friends and family. But right then and there, it seemed that my latest feat hadn't moved her at all.

※

Towards the end of my daily wheelchair jaunt, Mum and I would end up in the canteen. The ladies there soon came to know us.

'How's our girl today?' they'd call out from behind the counter.

'Oh, not too bad. Getting there,' Mum would answer, parking me at a table and moving towards the food display.

'The usual?'

Mum, Aunty Dassie or Sissy would have coffee and something to eat, huddled over their food like battle-weary soldiers. I'd have a cup of tea.

At first, Mum fed me the tea with a spoon, like soup. Nurse Iain caught her one day.

'That's not good for your daughter, you know. If you keep doing things for her, she'll never learn.'

'We tried a straw, but she hasn't the breath to suck the tea up,' said Mum. 'She can't manage by herself.'

'She's never going to manage like that. If you think it's hard here, wait until rehab – it's like boot camp.'

From then on, Mum held the cup up and I bent over to take a sip. In a few weeks, I graduated to lifting the cup myself, with Mum's hand underneath to steady it.

'Let me have a go,' I whispered one morning. We'll see. We'll see who can't do this and can't do that.

'Okay, love. I'll put your sugar in first.' She picked a sachet from the cup in the centre of the table.

'No. Give me the sugar.' I held out a shaky hand. 'I'll do it.'

Mum placed the sachet in my gloved palm. After several attempts and intense concentration, I managed to pick it up between my new, grafted fingers. With my other hand I tugged at the tiny packet, trying to rip the paper. Mum and Aunty Dassie looked on in silence.

Suddenly, with one last tug, I ripped the packet in half and sugar sprayed out over the table. I smiled at Mum and Aunty Dassie.

'She did it!' said Dassie, clapping her hands together. 'You did it, Don!'

Mum pursed her lips, gave a few rapid blinks and said nothing.

Awkwardly, I shook the remainder of the sugar into my teacup and, after a few attempts, managed to pick up a teaspoon and stir.

'Don't touch it,' I said, as Mum leaned over to help me get the cup to my mouth.

I wrapped my hands around the teacup, hunched over the table and lifted the drink all the way to my mouth. I wore quite a bit of it down my front, but I didn't care. This was the day I had, for the first time since the assault, managed to tear a sachet of sugar open, tip it in my tea, stir it, lift the cup to my mouth and drink. All by myself.

Eating was another thing altogether. I had been on bag food for so long, I was out of the habit of eating. The feed tube felt like a garden hose: threaded through my nose and down my throat, it made me gag constantly. With a stomach full of protein mix, a raw throat and a diminished sense of taste, eating was the last thing I felt like doing.

The nursing staff became obsessed with getting me to eat. They brought in a series of protein shakes every morning – ghastly concoctions flavoured with imitation strawberry or chocolate – and tried to coax me to swallow. They brought sandwiches and ice-cream, fruit drinks and jelly, and then came back half an hour later to inspect what I'd eaten. They wrote down everything: one nibble of sandwich, a spoonful of ice-cream.

Sometimes I'd manage to con my visitors into eating for me. Dad would always polish off my dessert at least, looking innocent when the nurse came back in.

'Very good today, Donna! A whole dish of ice-cream. Well done!'

The nurses soon co-opted my family into tempting me. Mum and Aunty Dassie would arrive with punnets of strawberries and containers full of Uncle Ronnie's rice custard. Dad would bring soft-centred chocolates and offer me pieces of his toasted sandwich down in the canteen. I remained recalcitrant.

'Donna, you can't live on bag food for the rest of your life,' Isabella told me one day. 'You have to start eating.'

'Take the feed tube out and I might get my appetite back,' I whispered. 'I'm too full with that stuff being pumped into me day and night. I'm full up to here,' I said, pointing to my chin. 'And the tube makes me sick. How can I eat? If you take the tube out, I promise I'll eat.'

Isabella was having none of that. 'We can't remove it, Donna. You have to show us you're going to eat before the feed tube goes. You have to try harder. I know food tastes of nothing right now, but I promise you, you'll get your sense of taste back, and you will enjoy food again.'

Isabella had another talk to Dad. 'What does she really enjoy eating?'

'She always liked a Chinese meal,' he said. 'With a beer.'

'Why not bring in some Chinese takeaway and a beer then?'

'A beer?' Dad asked, astounded. 'Into the hospital?'

'After what she's been through, a beer isn't going to kill her,' said Isabella.

The following Sunday, Dad smuggled in a prawn omelette, a bottle of beer and a bottle of lemonade. It was a hot day. We sat in the sheltered courtyard and Dad cut my meal up. I managed to get a few pieces of omelette up to my mouth with a fork, dropping three-quarters of it over my hospital gown. Dad leaned down to open the lemonade and the beer bottle sitting on the ground beside his chair. Soon he was mixing drinks in a couple of glasses borrowed from the canteen.

'What you got there, Dad?' I asked, trying to peer over the edge of the table.

He gave me one of his best smiles. 'What do you usually have with a Chinese feed?'

'Not beer?' I asked, as he passed me the cup. 'The nurses'll have your guts for garters.'

'Nurses *told* me to do it! Anyway, it's a shandy, so only half as bad. Cheers,' he said, holding his glass up. 'Here's to continued health and happiness.'

I rolled my eyes. 'If you say so.'

I had three sips and for the first time in months I became euphoric, overcome by a burst of light-headed optimism. The beer was ice-cold. The sky was spread high above us, a bright, cloudless blue. I had fresh air in my lungs and sunshine all around. Life was suddenly better than it had been in a long, long time.

As my health began to improve, I was allowed more visitors. Most were welcome, although some I could have done without.

Soon after the care order had gone through, all the Blakemores, apart from Brian, who was living in Sydney, travelled down to see me on an all-expenses-paid trip to the city.

I could hear them long before they found me, clattering along the corridor searching for my room. They streamed in en masse, without gowns, without scrubbing up, ignoring the strict protocol. The Burns Unit was not like the broken bones ward or the plastics department. You couldn't just come traipsing in, running along the corridor, calling out, poking your head into each room as you passed.

'Found her,' called Denise, coming through the doorway with Bodean clamped to her hip. I noticed that, like before, his clothes were grubby and far too tight. His curls had been cut off, leaving a harsh crew cut. Danny mooched in beside his wife and hung around at the base of the bed.

Coe came in next. I was horrified at how he looked: his hair was long and untidy, and he wore shorts and a ragged shirt. The sleeves had been ripped out and the material frayed around both armholes. A seam gaped open from his armpit to his waist. He looked like a street urchin. Even in his old weekend play-clothes, he had never looked unkempt like this.

Denise's two kids, Steven and Jason, were spick and span. Their neatly cut hair had just been combed. They were dressed in fresh, collared shirts, new shorts and clean lace-up shoes.

I was mortified. I'd been boasting to the staff about my two beautiful boys, and now here they were, resembling unwanted state wards. Denise gave me a smug look. Her two boys hadn't seen me in hospital before and were obviously fascinated.

'Wow! Look at her!' exclaimed Steven, creeping towards my bed. 'Look at her face!'

'That's pretty bad, all right!' Jason said, elbowing his way in front of Steven.

I began to cry, and Coe, with red cheeks and downcast eyes, edged forward to stand awkwardly beside me.

'Hi Mum,' he mumbled. I think he was embarrassed by the whole situation, not the least at his cousins' reactions.

Fortunately, Mum walked in with Sissy. Both were gowned up.

'You can't all be in here, with no gowns or nothing,' Mum told them. 'She can't have too many people at once. It's too much.'

Danny scowled at her. 'Fine, I'll wait downstairs. Come on, Steven, Jason. We'll have a look around the shops.'

'From now on, I think it'd be better for Donna if she just had her two boys visit,' Sissy said to Denise. 'If we're here, we'll take the boys while they visit with her, and you can come back and get them after an hour or two.'

My family grew vigilant in heading the Blakemores off at the pass, so I could enjoy some quality time with my sons. During their visits, my family would either perch Bodean on my lap as I travelled around in the wheelchair or they'd get him to help push me along, while Coe walked beside me, holding my hand.

'Here, Bodean, help push Mummy,' Sissy would say, or, 'Come and sit on Mummy's lap, Bodean.'

Bodean was happy to hang on to the chair, or to sit on my lap, but as for calling me Mummy, he would have none of that.

One day, as I was being wheeled through the foyer with Mum, Sissy and the two boys, we stopped to look in the florist. By the door, above the buckets of daffodils and roses and multi-coloured dahlias, floated a bright bunch of helium balloons. Bodean began to squirm on my lap, pointing and shouting at a big car-shaped balloon.

'Car! Car! Look, car!'

I stared at him in surprise as a sudden memory from before the assault flashed into my head. Every second Thursday, on payday, I'd take the boys into Orana Mall after work to do the grocery shopping. As a special treat, Coe would get two dollars to buy a matchbox car from the bargain shop, and Bodean would get a helium balloon.

I'd tie the balloon to the shopping trolley, and Bodean would tug at the string, pulling it down and letting it go. Pulling it down, letting it go. At home, I'd fasten a ball of wool to the end of the ribbon so he could continue his game. As the week passed, the balloon would slowly descend to the floor. Bodean loved this game. One of the last balloons I'd bought him, the day before the assault, was a red and silver racing car, identical to the one floating in the doorway of the florist's.

'Car, car! Look!'

'Come on, darling. Not today,' said Mum, pushing the chair past the display. 'Nanna's broke.'

'Stop,' I said, gesturing stiffly. 'That car balloon – I'm buying it.'

Mum looked at the price. 'What? For twelve dollars?'

'I don't care. I'm buying it.'

Mum tut-tutted as she tied the balloon to the side of my chair. Bodean laughed, wrapping his tiny fingers around the ribbon and tugging at it. Pulling it down, letting it go.

'Do you remember?' I asked Coe.

'Yeah, I remember. Thursday night shopping.' He smiled at the memory. 'I wish we were back there. I wish things were like before.'

'I'm getting there, Coe. I promise, I'll be out of here soon.'

He gave me a small smile but looked unconvinced.

Mum parked the chair under our favourite tree, and she and Sissy sat on the garden wall with Coe. After a while, Sissy glanced at her watch. 'It's nearly time to meet Denise and Danny in the foyer. We'd better be making our way back.'

'Mum, can I take the balloon off the chair and hold it?' Coe asked.

'Sure, go ahead. Just don't let it go.'

'I'll tie it round my wrist,' he said, undoing the ribbon. 'Just to make sure. Can you help me, Aunty Sissy?'

Sissy fastened the ribbon carefully on his arm, and he began to wave it back and forth as he walked, tipping his head up to watch it slip around in the air above our heads.

'Look, Bodean! Look at the car. Brmm, brmm, it's a flying car,' he laughed, tugging it about and making more motorcar noises as Bodean clapped and squealed.

I gazed at my two boys. For a moment it was like we were back in Orana Mall, with a trolley full of food, a matchbox toy and a balloon, heading home to Geurie. Then Danny rounded the corner.

'Ooh, look at the little baby, playing with the balloon,' he said, his voice heavy with sarcasm. 'Now, isn't that cute?'

Instantly, the light was extinguished from Coe's face. His smile was replaced with a sour, squeezed look, and his lip curled as he scrambled to undo the string from his wrist.

'I was just holding it for Bodean,' he muttered. 'Here, Bodean, take it.' And with that, he shoved the balloon towards his startled brother.

Fortunately, I had other visitors who made my time in hospital more bearable. The school community had continued to support me, and a week never passed without bundles of letters, photographs, cards and posters arriving. Chris Gorton, a fellow teacher, had even organised a video from the school, with children and staff wishing me well and sending the latest news. Helen and Julie Brown from Orana Heights School travelled down to be with me, and my friends Fran and Sue even brought a selection of costumes they'd designed and sewn for the school musical. I'd begun sketching ideas for backdrops and costumes just before the assault.

'Now you're not there, everyone's starting to realise how much you did.' Fran grinned, holding up a pair of gold and purple harem pants and a spangly pillbox hat. 'What do you think of our handiwork?'

'I'll give you ten out of ten for effort,' I said.

I loved seeing my workmates, but there was sadness in their visits. I would never be well enough to go back to teaching. I'd worked hard and enjoyed it so much but those days were gone. I knew I could never return.

I was also embarrassed. I was a victim of domestic violence and felt ashamed, as though some nasty little secret had now been laid bare before the entire school community. In the years that followed, I would experience this shame over and over, first in my own mind, and then in the minds of others. I know now that victims of domestic violence often feel this way. Much of society reacts, perhaps unconsciously, in an unfortunate pattern: be attacked by a stranger and the community is outraged; be attacked by someone you know and it's viewed differently. Somehow, the responsibility shifts and it becomes your fault.

In my last couple of months at Westmead, I had a visit from Deb. She had been in contact with Dad and would ring the night staff to ask about me and pass on her love. She sent an enormous bouquet of flowers very early on, and then a series of cards. Dad let her know she could come and see me in August.

Deb was so upset after the visit that she went out the very next day and bought a diary to write in, her usual solution to any problem. 'I have a lot of half-empty diaries,' she told me once. 'I've devoted a whole shelf to them in my study.'

Much later, she showed me what she wrote:

When I came into Donna's room, I looked at her a long time. I guess I had it in my head that I must look her straight in the eye and show her I could take it. A tear, and then more tears, slid down her cheeks.

'Don't look at me.' Her voice was a whisper, breathless.

I couldn't find Donna in the face. It was skinned, translucent and very, very tight and small. The sides of her nose were burnt away. There was just a little of it left, and some orange baby hair growing back. No eyelashes or eyebrows, a swollen mouth and stiff, partly bandaged hands. I held a hand.

As I sat there, I kept expecting her to turn back into the normal, funny, bubbly Donna I'd always known. Now, as I write this, I can't believe Donna isn't Donna anymore.

In the hospital bed, her arm moved slowly, like an old person's, as she pointed to a bulletin board. There was a photo of her a few months before she was burnt. In it she's sitting on the front steps of her mother's house with the family. I got up for a closer look.

When I looked back at her, I could see her shadow somewhere in the burnt face. I could see the old Donna. And later I picked up her drawl through the whisper. Just now and then. She's still in there somewhere, I thought.

Apart from my family, my most frequent visitor was Pat, the Westmead Hospital chaplain. She was a small, grey-haired woman. Under her gown she wore sensible blouses and pleated skirts, flat brown shoes and thick stockings. A gold cross was pinned to her lapel.

Pat was an enormously comforting presence: kind, gentle and reassuring. She was the one member of staff who never asked anything of me. Sometimes, when the daily dressing change or physio session had left me even more ragged than usual, I'd mouth to Pat, 'Not today,' and she'd slip away down the corridor. But most times she was welcome. She sat at my bedside and held my hand, waiting for me to speak if I chose. She did not come to preach religion. She was there, willing to travel with me wherever I chose to go.

As I got to know her better, I began to tell her the story of my life: my upbringing in Redfern, my marriage, life in Geurie, teaching, motherhood, but most of all the deep love I felt for my boys and the devastation I felt at losing them.

I also talked to her about Garry, the man I had adored and trusted. I told her what I could tell no one else: that his betrayal was every bit as painful as the physical trauma of burns survival. I hated Garry for what he'd done, yet grieved for the Garry I'd loved.

Pat listened to me without judgement. This was a gift.

'You've come so far, Donna. The Lord's with you,' she'd tell me. 'Would you like me to say a prayer?'

I'd nod. Usually I was crying. I'd close my eyes and listen to Pat's simple message: 'Every day I need you, Lord, but this day specially. I need some extra strength to face whatever is to be.'

Sometimes she'd leave a poem or prayer for me. 'Throw it out if it doesn't help, Donna. Don't feel you have to keep it.'

But it inevitably helped. Throughout childhood I'd had a hefty dose of religious training – Sunday school, church, Girls' Brigade – but as an adult I hadn't thought much about God. I believed, but my faith wasn't strong. In hospital, however, I clung to the notion of God's presence. Even without Pat by my side, my thoughts were often occupied by little prayers. I'd pray before my dressings were changed, before I was wheeled down to the operating theatre, before physio. I'd pray for strength, endurance and optimism, both for fellow patients and for me. I'd pray to get well enough to leave the hospital and get my children back. For me, prayer became a balm, a soothing mantra to get me through one hellish moment after another.

In September, a new visitor came to see me. It was Bruce Levet, a barrister from Sydney, who had come to discuss what further action I could take in the continuing saga of getting my children into my family's care. Ann Kinghan, my Dubbo solicitor, had contacted his chambers on my behalf after the care order had gone through.

Bruce walked in, dressed casually in trousers and an open-necked shirt. His manner, however, was all business. He didn't appear fazed by my appearance as he pulled up a chair beside my bed and took a yellow legal pad from his briefcase.

He launched into a lot of technical jargon at first, concerning recommendations by Burke and Burke, following the court order in August. I had no idea what he was rattling on about. Eventually he began to speak more plainly.

'The Department is under the impression you did this to yourself,' he said, gesturing in the general direction of my mutilated body. 'They're calling you an unfit mother.'

Strangely, it wasn't the first part that stuck in my head. Did this to myself? Everybody knew that was nonsense: the hospital staff, the police, my family, an entire school community. That 'mistake' could be sorted out easily, I thought. It was the unfit mother accusation that immediately set my imagination in overdrive. I knew they didn't mean 'unfit' as in 'ill'. That's not what the term 'unfit mother' meant. They must have some sort of dirt on me, I thought frantically, but what?

Anything that I had done wrong in 37 years began to spin through my head. Was it the affair with Garry? Was it the abortion? Was it the fact that I'd left Coe to babysit Bodean on the day of the fire? What the hell could it be?

'You need to get out of hospital as soon as possible,' Bruce continued. 'By Christmas time we want you up and driving a car. You need to be cooking meals, dressing yourself, shopping, walking normally.' He counted each instruction off on his fingers.

I stared at him in disbelief. What planet was this guy from? I couldn't even bend my arm to wipe my own arse. I couldn't brush my hair or walk more than a few steps without a break. My voice didn't rise above a whisper. And as for a car – what car? Bruce's instructions were tantamount to saying I had to have a million dollars in the bank by Christmas.

'Do you understand?' he asked. 'The longer these people have your children, the more settled they'll become, and the less likely it is that you'll get them back. Ever.'

Call it divine intervention, or just strength of will, but things progressed quickly following his visit. My breathing began to improve and my trachy was removed. I knew I could do it. They told me I had a hole in my neck but it was better than a tube sticking out of my throat.

On 17 September 1994, almost six months after the assault, Bronwyn told me I'd be moving to the Plastics Ward. Plastics was largely concerned with reconstructive surgery, which didn't really apply to me at that time, but I needed to be put somewhere and it seemed like the best place.

I was worried about leaving the Burns Unit. Sure, it had been hell, but it was a familiar hell. I knew the drill. I knew the various tortures and the different personalities of the staff – when to lie low, when to make conversation. A whole new ward would have its own peculiarities to get used to.

'Plastics will be so much better, Donna,' Bronwyn said. 'You can take all your things with you: your photos and cards and such. And you won't be regimented like in here. It's much more casual and relaxed. You'll still have your own room with a window and an ensuite. You'll be able to shower at your leisure. Your morphine will be reduced. You'll be on tablets instead, so the nausea will ease. Your feed tube will be taken out. And best of all, it's one step closer to going home.'

Despite my initial fears, Bronwyn was right. Compared to the rigid, savage world of the Burns Ward, Plastics was like relaxing in a five-star hotel. I had been there for three days when one of the medical staff came in with a pen and clipboard.

'You'd better start making travel arrangements,' she said, standing at the end of my bed and flicking over papers.

I looked at her, startled. 'What do you mean?'

'You're being discharged from Westmead, Donna. You're going home.'

Resurrection

Eleven

After all those weeks of asking when I could go home, it was finally happening. 'Home' would not be Geurie though. I would be going to stay with Sissy and John at Killabakh, a tiny community on the New South Wales mid-north coast. Before being discharged into Sissy's care, however, I needed to spend a short time at Manning Base Hospital in nearby Taree.

Iain's warnings that rehab was like boot camp were still ringing in my ears as Sissy, Mum and I made our way out of Sydney and headed north along the Newcastle freeway. I lay on the back seat in silence for most of the trip, worrying about the new hospital environment. I was heavily sedated and bandaged, but the long car trip was still agony, every bump jolting my fragile new suit of skin.

I needn't have worried about Manning Base Hospital. Like the Plastics Ward at Westmead, it was a relaxed environment where I was left to fill in much of my day as I pleased. Dad had suggested planning simple activities to avoid time dragging. It was good advice, and I followed it religiously.

Once I'd showered and had my dressings changed for the day, I tackled a crossword puzzle before stopping for morning tea. Then I read for a while or watched television. After shuffling back and forth to the toilet, it would be time to write letters.

By this stage I was sending a steady stream of communication to my boys: scrawled messages of love, news of my progress, questions about their lives, and simple drawings to amuse Bodean.

I also wrote to the Department of Community Services on two occasions, directing my communications to Richard Gray, manager of the Parkes cluster. I had decided to play DOCS at their own game – my first letter was to say that Denise had had Coe rebaptised in a Catholic church without consulting me. Why was this allowed to happen when he'd already been baptised years before in the Anglican church in Geurie? I received no reply. My second letter objected to the fact that Bodean was calling Denise Mummy. Once again there was no reply.

After letter writing it was time for lunch and then bed rest. The hospital was situated on a hill and my room was high up and sunny, with a magnificent view of the mountains from the window next to my bed. I soon took to lying upside down on my mattress to vary the view from my window.

'It's okay,' I'd reassure the nursing staff when they gave me odd looks and asked if I was all right. 'Things look different depending on which end of the bed I lay my head. I'm just entertaining myself.'

My sleeping arrangements weren't the only thing the nurses doubted. They hadn't experienced a patient in my condition before and much of my ongoing treatment was new ground for them. In here, I was now the expert.

'Does that wound look okay to you or do you think the doctor should look at it?'

'Am I scrubbing you too hard or do I need to be firmer?'

'Is this enough cream or should I apply more?'

My physio was not so trusting of my opinions. On my arrival at Manning Base, he had measured me up for two burns suits: skin-coloured pressure garments, each comprising a long-sleeved top, long pants and a full face mask made out of tough, elasticised material designed to flatten scarring over time. I would need to wear one of these suits under my normal clothing for two years.

The physio demonstrated little experience at measuring people up for pressure garments, and when the finished items arrived there were several problems. The breast area sat in two hollow bumps over the bottom of my rib cage, but the top itself was too short, and clung above my waist like an unflattering crop top. The crotch of the trousers dangled down towards my knees like a pair of ill-fitting pantyhose. The top's sleeves were way too tight, ripping my delicate new skin whenever I tried to squeeze my arms down the narrow channels. The material cut into the crooks of my elbows, armpits and the backs of my knees whenever I tried to bend. My skin was being destroyed, leaving raw, gaping slashes around my joints. Every day the physio changed the garments, trying to squeeze my arms and legs into places way too narrow.

'Stop! You're hurting!' I'd cry. 'Can't you see it doesn't fit properly?'

'Don't be ridiculous. This is your pressure suit, and you've got to wear it,' he'd say, struggling to do the zip up my back.

'It's too small,' I'd insist.

'It's been measured up. They're meant to be tight. That's how they're designed.'

After a week at Manning Base, it was decided that I could be discharged into my sister's care if I attended daily rehab at Wingham Memorial Hospital, overseen by Dr McClean and Nurse Heather Russell. Perhaps I would find a physio who would listen.

But it was not to be. My new physio was just as pig-headed as the previous one and insisted I stop complaining and wear my suit. His solution was to put more padding over the wounded areas, causing more bulk, more friction and fresh wounds when the pads were removed, together with strips of bleeding skin.

One afternoon, returning to Sissy's place after another painful day of rehab, I decided I'd had enough. I took to both my burns suits with the kitchen scissors, slicing the entire armpit section out of each pressure garment.

My physio was furious. 'You can't go and do that!' He stared at the gaping holes in my suit. 'These garments cost a lot of money!'

'Well, I did do it,' I said calmly. 'I told you about the wounds. I told you they were getting worse. You wouldn't do anything so I fixed the problem myself.'

'You've made a complete mess of them. They were perfectly good suits.'

'If you like the damned things so much, you wear them.'

'Listen, you've been told time and time again – if you don't wear your garments, your scarring will be raised. Don't say you weren't warned.'

'I'll wear the bloody things if they fit! Please. Find someone who can measure me properly.'

And so the hospital arranged for me to meet with Ms Walsh, a representative from a company involved in the manufacture of specialist support garments from the German Jobst range. As luck would have it, she was going to be passing through Taree on her way to a conference in Tamworth.

'Let *her* have a go at measuring you up,' the physio said.

When Ms Walsh arrived a few days later, I showed her my ill-fitting suit – which I had refused to wear again – and the various wounds I had sustained from it.

'Good God!' she exclaimed, staring wide-eyed at the suit. 'No wonder you can't lower your arms. You can have gussets put in at all those joint areas, you know – soft material that won't cause any damage to your skin.'

I blinked back tears. 'Thank God someone's listening to me.'

She turned the suit over. 'Where are the zippers on this thing?'

'There's just one. Down the back of the top.'

'But there should be zips down either side of your arms, and also down each leg. That way you don't have to tug your limbs through the material.'

'You mean I just lay the sleeves out flat and then zip them up around my arms?'

'Exactly. No pushing, no shoving. The design of this suit is abysmal.' She shook her head. 'It should be in one piece too, so it doesn't cut you in half, and it needs feet. Let's get you measured up properly.'

Within a few days, I had two brand new Jobst pressure suits, complete with gussets and zips in all the right places. They were a perfect fit.

〰

I was settling into life at Sissy and John's place. I had been visually starved for so long that their 25-acre property was paradise. Sissy made me up a bed in the sunroom, a cosy nook with windows looking out onto a wooden pergola draped with wisteria, the blooms hanging in fat purple bunches. On still days, with the windows open, I could hear the drone of bees gathering nectar. On the lawn, orange and grapefruit trees sagged with golden fruit, beds of lavender scented the air and, further on, cows wandered through paddocks with grass up to their flanks. In the distance sat three mountains, Coxcombe, Killabakh and Goonook, which alternated between a rich, earthy green, a deep plum and a dark grey, and were either shrouded in mist or sharply silhouetted against the sky.

In the early weeks at Killabakh, I spent a lot of time in bed, weary from my day at rehab. After another painful physio session at the hospital, I'd be delivered to Nurse Ray Paterson, a bear of a man with a wiry ginger ponytail, a red, woolly beard and a beatific smile. He reminded me of a Viking, even in his pale blue nurse's uniform.

After taking down my dressings, Ray would lift me into a warm bath, perching on the side to bathe my wounds, and then he'd pat me dry, check my injuries, apply cream and reapply bandages. It was Ray who took graphic photos of my scarring when the investigating officer finally requested them the following February.

By the time I came home, I was totally drained and needed to lie down. My niece Jennifer would tiptoe in and sit on the edge of my bed to talk.

'What can we do this afternoon, Aunty Donna?'

She was a typical 15-year-old girl; I knew what she wanted. 'How about we go through one of my bags of clothes?'

Sissy and Mum had rescued some of my possessions from the house in Geurie, including several tonnes of clothing, which had been packed away in garbage bags that were now stacked in the shed.

At my prompting, Jennifer would grin, jump up and disappear out the back. 'This one, Aunty Donna?' she'd ask, dragging her chosen bag into my room.

'Any one you like,' I'd say. 'There are plenty to choose from.'

She'd tip the jumbled contents out on the floor and I'd spend the next hour watching her pull out jeans, jumpers, tank tops, blouses, dresses and skirts, tugging things on and off, skipping back and forth to the mirror in her room to assess the fit and style of each item.

'This is so cool, Aunty Donna,' she'd say, whirling around in front of me in a lacy black cocktail dress or a sleeveless top and denim skirt. 'What do you think? Can I borrow this sometime?'

I'd smile at her from my bed. 'You can have it, darling. Looks much better on you than me.'

When would I ever wear a strappy evening dress? I thought. As for skirts and tank tops, I could barely tolerate Mum's baggy clothes on my skin; my old clothes would be impossible.

As Jennifer pulled each piece of clothing on and off, I was reminded of my days out west: a part of my life that seemed, in some respects, just a heartbeat away. Each dress, each pair of narrow, high-heeled shoes, each skirt and blouse, caused a rush of memories painful to recall.

I'd bought the black evening dress for my 30th birthday, which I'd celebrated with the Geurie community into the early hours of the morning. The next year I'd worn it to a fancy-dress do at the local hall, with a pointy black hat and black cloak. I'd done Brian up as Count Dracula, gelling his hair back and adding a widow's peak, sideburns and a pair of fangs.

Jennifer unearthed my swimming costume, worn only once the previous summer, on a holiday at Mum and Clyde's place with the kids. With the costume, Jennifer found a pair of purple denim overalls and a pink tank top. I had a photo somewhere of me in this outfit, standing on a pier with Bodean and Coe on a sunny day in January. It was one of the last pictures I had taken before everything changed.

※

In the beginning I couldn't help with anything around the house, but by amusing Jennifer, and sometimes Patrick, I felt I was lending a hand. My physio said that I should engage in at least 25 minutes of exercise a day, following my sessions at the hospital. He suggested going for regular walks around the property. I tried to explain to him that the farm was on a hill – fine for walking one way but, with my breathing problems, a struggle back up the slope to the house. He dismissed this concern, so I found other outlets.

I started with making my bed each morning: a time-consuming and tiring exercise. Sometimes Jennifer came to help with the tucking in as I couldn't even manage to lift the mattress a centimetre. Without her assistance I would make my way around the bed, poking the edges of the sheets under the mattress with one crooked finger.

We'll see who can't do this and can't do that. We'll see.

I wasn't able to try washing up because of my gloves, but I would put the dishes away once the kids had dried them, taking one thing at a time from the bench and walking across the kitchen to the correct drawer or cupboard.

'Let the kids do it,' Sissy would say. 'It's taking you so long, walking backwards and forwards all the time.'

Bruce Levet's voice rang in my ear: 'By Christmas time we want you up and driving a car. You need to be cooking meals, dressing yourself, shopping, walking normally ...'

'It's good for me. I'm walking and doing something useful. Soon I'll be able to take two cups or two plates at once.'

Whenever my determination wavered, I thought about my children. 'The longer these people have your children,' Bruce had said, 'the more settled they'll become and the less likely it is that you'll get them back. Ever.' I needed to get better. I just had to. I continued to push myself, designing my own practical physiotherapy program, paving the way to looking after my boys and myself, and becoming a fully functioning adult once again. Soon I was managing other tasks: setting the table; putting the cereal and spreads away after breakfast; wiping up the dishes; making cups of tea; doing the laundry; hanging out the washing.

We'll see who can't do this and can't do that! We'll see.

These simple tasks took me ages. Hanging out a load of washing could while away most of the afternoon. Even squeezing a peg or opening a carton of milk took a lot of effort, and things like using a knife to cut or peel vegetables and meat were just too difficult at this stage.

Sometimes I would go shopping in Wingham or Taree with Sissy after she'd picked me up from rehab. I wasn't much help but I could push the trolley if it wasn't too full, and take groceries from the shelves as long as they weren't too high.

I always preferred shopping in Wingham as nearly everyone in the town was aware of my presence. They'd either heard about me through the hospital grapevine or at the neighbourhood centre where Sissy worked. They knew Sissy and John were looking after me, and that I'd been involved in some sort of terrible accident. The various shop assistants and local professionals greeted me with warmth and sympathy.

Still, whether I was in Wingham or Taree, dressed in my burns suit with Mum's clothes on top, I looked and felt a freak, stooped over like a little bird-lady trying to ignore the stares of passers-by. For a long time, I simply didn't look at people. If I looked, they were looking. I just focused on where we needed to go and shuffled after Sissy, my eyes on the pavement at my feet. I was meant to be wearing my facemask too, but I refused to put it on in public. The stares would have tripled in number.

Mum and Clyde often came to visit, especially on weekends when Jennifer and Patrick were home from school. Saturday night was film night, a family ritual. Sissy would slip the tape in the machine before turning the lights out and drawing the curtains, like we were at the cinema.

'Everyone got their bag of chips? Everyone right for cordial?' John would ask. I never lasted to the end of the movie; I'd be fast asleep inside half an hour.

One weekend, Mum brought her own video and was obviously excited about sharing it. 'I hired this especially for you, Don,' she said, producing the video from a plastic bag. 'Been wanting to show it to you for ages.'

'Oh yeah? What's it called?'

'*Man without a Face*!' she replied triumphantly, brandishing it in the air.

Sissy was horrified. 'God, Mum! Why would we want to see that?'

'It's about a schoolteacher who has half his face burnt off in a car accident. The locals think he's a child molester and they run him out of town. I thought Don would enjoy it,' Mum said huffily. 'Her being a schoolteacher and everything.'

'And her face too,' Patrick added. 'It's pretty much gone.'

Sissy gave her son a hard stare.

'Patrick!' Jennifer clapped a hand over her mouth.

'What?' he asked, looking indignant.

'How about you collect the dishes and take them to the sink, son,' said Clyde, standing up. 'I'll help you.'

I held out a hand. 'Come on, Mum. Give us a look.'

Taking the video from her, I was amused to see Mel Gibson posing on the back cover, sporting a half-melted face, but still managing to look quite rugged.

'Looks like a good show, Mum. Let's see how Mel handles it.'

While dealing with the reality of my alien body and new face – or lack of one – I still managed to find small joys. Two days before my discharge from Manning Base Hospital, my boys came to stay for a week with Sissy and John on an applied access visit.

Both Bruce Levet and Ann Kinghan had advised me to push for as much contact as possible, not only by ringing and writing to the boys but also by requesting that they be allowed to visit. When I applied, I reminded DOCS that Denise had promised, in court, to facilitate access for bonding purposes.

Sissy had helped me write the request to DOCS while I was still in Westmead, but they remained ominously silent. Once I'd been discharged from Westmead, I rang DOCS's Parkes office, clutching the receiver as I waited for someone to answer. I had rehearsed my speech over and over. It was a simple enough request, but still I was riddled with fear. Don't stuff up, I told myself. Whatever you do, don't stuff up. Be calm. Be polite. Don't cry!

Finally someone picked up. I regurgitated my story, adding an assurance that I'd be happy for DOCS to send an officer out at any time to check that the boys were being cared for properly.

'My family have nothing to hide. I'm still in hospital, but I'll be able to see Coe and Bodean every day when my sister brings them in to visit.'

'That all seems fair and reasonable,' said the officer. 'We'll see what we can do.'

After this positive response, I was elated. At last the boys were going to have some extended time with my family and me. There was one last thing to do before I lost my nerve. I rang Denise.

'How are the boys?' I asked.

'Oh, they're fine,' she replied. 'Bodean's asleep at the moment. Coe's in town with Steven and Jason. They like to ride their bikes after school now that the days are longer.'

'Just give them both my love and tell them I'm doing fine,' I said, trying not to think about Coe zipping around the streets of Parkes.

'Yeah, okay then. I'll tell them you phoned.'

Her dismissive tone gave me more motivation to get to the point. 'By the way, seeing the school holidays are coming up, I've applied for an access visit. The boys will be able to stay with Sissy and John.' I kept my voice cool.

Denise snapped out of casual mode. 'No! That's not right. You can't do that! We've made other plans.'

'The Department thinks it's reasonable, Denise. Like the court said, it's important for Coe and Bodean to see me for bonding purposes, and this way they can visit me every day.'

So there!

Denise brought Coe and Bodean to Manning Base Hospital on Sunday, 25 September at 4.40 pm and then rang Sissy to let her know they'd arrived. I was discharged from hospital on the following Tuesday; the thought of having my kids under the same roof for the rest of the week filled me with a dizzying combination of extreme happiness and emotional fragility.

The week flew past and when I wasn't being tortured in daily rehab, I spent as much time with my boys as possible. Bodean still refused to call me Mummy; he was oddly remote and difficult to engage in simple conversation. He was also given to uncharacteristic outbursts of wild behaviour. He would snatch and grab food during the evening meal, and quickly took to smashing various household items as soon as he could get himself around a corner and out of sight. He threw tantrums at the slightest provocation. I was so preoccupied with having my baby back that I tried not to focus on this behaviour, explaining it away with excuses – it was just his age, or a temporary reaction to strange surroundings and comparatively unfamiliar carers.

Coe was also different: quiet and sullen. Apart from occasional glimpses of the boy I remembered, my happy, outgoing and considerate son seemed to have disappeared, leaving a brooding stranger in his place. The only real enthusiasm he showed was when he talked about his high school plans for the following year. Denise and Danny had talked about sending him to boarding school with his cousin Steven, which would be, according to Coe, 'like a giant camp away from home'. To counteract this, I launched my own big sell of Wingham High. We took a walk around the school, and Jennifer talked enthusiastically about her agricultural course, the friendly kids, great teachers, top facilities and sound academic record.

'But I won't know anyone,' Coe said. 'Maybe I'll start at school with Steven, just for the first term, and then come here later in the year.'

'Well, darling, the thing is, if you go away and come back, you'll be the new boy. If you start in first term along with everyone else, you'll all be in the same boat.'

'S'pose so.'

He was keen on sport, so I pushed this aspect. 'You can do whatever sport you want.'

'What? Even football?'

'Sure, why not?' I said, feigning enthusiasm for a sport I dreaded him playing. 'There's football, soccer, squash, basketball. There's all sorts of things to choose from in town.'

He conceded, grudgingly, that this was something positive, but refused to discuss it further. Whenever I brought up the subject of his relocating to Wingham, he'd snap.

'Just get off my back, will ya! I don't want to talk about it.'

It was soon obvious to me that I wasn't the only one to bear the brunt of Coe's moods. He seemed irritated by Bodean too, and would often wind him up to frustration level by making games too hard, deliberately holding things out of reach, taunting and teasing him. This cruelty towards Bodean was totally unlike Coe. He had always been caring of his little brother. As with Bodean's unsavoury behaviour, I simply didn't focus on these worrying aspects. I would be forced to confront the emotional damage of my kids later, but for now, it seemed best to ignore it.

On Saturday, 1 October, the day before the boys were due to be returned to Denise's care, Brian rang, wanting to speak to Coe. It was a little after seven in the morning, and Sissy answered the phone, telling Brian that Coe or I would ring him back when we were awake.

Within 15 minutes he had phoned again, obviously agitated.

'Listen, I'm coming over now,' he told Sissy. 'I'll have a cup of tea with Donna and see my kids.'

'It's 7.30 in the morning. They're still asleep, Brian.'

'Bullshit! Anyway, they're my kids. I've got a right to see them.'

At this stage, Sissy hung up and came to my room. She poked her head around the curtain that sealed my area off from the rest of the house. She was still in her nightie. 'Don, you better get up. Brian's performing.' She explained the phone calls. 'God knows how you put up with him for so long.'

'I'll give him a call.' I struggled to get myself out of bed in my elasticised suit and arm splints. 'I can't even spend a week with my kids without someone from that bloody family interfering.'

Sissy helped me into my dressing-gown. 'Take it easy, Donna. Don't let him get to you.'

'He should probably be allowed to come and see the kids. Do you mind if he visits, Sissy?'

She put her hands on her hips and frowned at me, and I was struck by just how much she looked like Mum, with her dark, wiry hair and full lips pressed into a straight, emotionless line. 'As long as he behaves himself.'

John was hovering nearby, already in his work clothes, his unkempt hair sticking out at odd angles. 'I was going to do some work down in the paddock after breakfast, but I'll hang around the house today. I'll have a word to him when he arrives. We need to set some ground rules.'

Sissy and John went into the kitchen to make tea while I rang Brian and requested he come out at nine o'clock to see the boys. He seemed to have calmed down.

John met Brian at the gate and had a brief chat, telling him that his earlier rudeness was unacceptable. I stood at the door as he shambled up the path behind John, in a grubby shirt, shorts and thongs. Determined to be civil, I asked him in for a cup of tea.

Coe was ecstatic about seeing his father, jumping around him like an excited pup, his face wreathed in smiles. It was the happiest I'd seen him all week. He idolised his dad with a fervour I found hard to understand, considering all the times Brian had let him down with broken promise after broken promise. Following the popular advice of the day, I had resisted pointing out the truth about Brian to Coe, and assumed that one day Coe would see his father for the person he was, rather than as an elusive hero figure.

Bodean was less interested in his father, but hung on the outskirts of the conversation as Brian and I sat talking at the dining room table.

'I'd like to take the kids for a drive, Don. I haven't seen them in a while. I been in Sydney.' He took a sip of his tea and looked at me warily. His eyes, a washed-out blue, were shadowy and bloodshot. His hair was going grey and lay flat on his head, with a fringe that had been hacked short in a jagged line. He turned to Coe. 'What do you reckon, son?'

'That'd be cool, Dad! We can go to the park and have a game of footy,' said Coe, jumping from one foot to the other.

Brian ruffled his hair. 'Okay, okay. Calm down. Your mum has to say it's okay.'

I thought for a moment as the pair of them looked at me.

'Well, Mum? Can I go?'

'Yeah, how about it, Don? Just for a little while. I miss 'em.'

'I know what that's like, not seeing your kids. I guess there's no problem.'

'Maybe I could get them fish and chips in town and we could go to the park, like Coe suggested.'

I was trying hard to be reasonable. 'They'd enjoy that. Be a bit of a treat for them. But you'll have to bring them home straight afterwards.' I gave him a hard look.

'No problem. I'll have them back here by one o'clock.' He scratched his bristly chin and glanced around the room. 'Don't suppose you lot smoke. I'm dying for a fag.'

I sent Coe off to have a shower and Brian and I sat on the porch while he had another cup of tea and found a smoke from his car.

'So what have you been up to lately?' I asked. 'You said you've been in Sydney. Coe mentioned you'd been away for quite a while.'

'Yeah, I picked up a bit of work in the city, and I had to get out of Parkes. HFC and Grace Bros are after me, and me solicitor's screaming for money, thanks to the divorce proceedings.' He shook his head and took a long draw on his cigarette.

I refused to bite.

'By the way, Brian, next time you ring here, make sure it's at a reasonable hour. Seven o'clock is way too early.'

He shrugged. 'I don't have a watch. Can't afford things like that. How would I know what time it was?'

'You seemed to be able to get here at nine o'clock when you were asked.'

'You've always got an answer, haven't you?' He drained the last of his tea and put the mug down at his feet.

'Just remember not to be so demanding in future. I've never had a problem with you seeing the boys and neither has my family, so next time, instead of waking everyone up and inviting yourself out here, try using some manners instead, and wait to be asked. This week is meant to be my time with Coe and Bodean.'

'What about me? I haven't seen them much either.'

I glared at him. 'You can see them anytime. I can't. Besides, I've got a letter from Denise that clearly states that the children will be with me until Sunday, 2 October. The week is up tomorrow.'

Brian held up his hand. 'Okay, okay. Get off your high horse. I'm just taking them for a drive and lunch. Calm down.'

As it turned out, Brian had no intention of bringing the boys back that day. At 11.20 am he rang to tell us not to expect the boys back at 1 pm, and if we tried to get them he'd call the police. I begged him to return them.

'You promised,' I sobbed. 'You said you were only taking them for lunch. Please, Brian, don't do this to me. Please bring them back. My dad's coming all the way from Sydney tomorrow to see them.'

Brian's voice was gruff. 'I phoned Danny. He told me I had to keep them. He said you had no right and your time with the kids was up.'

By this stage I was beside myself. I could barely speak. 'You promised, Brian. Please!'

'They're staying with me.' He hung up.

I replaced the receiver and wiped my eyes. 'Bastard! Bastard, bastard, bastard!'

'What's happened?' asked Sissy, coming into the room.

John was behind her. 'Who was that?'

'Brian's refusing to bring the kids back.' I filled in the details as Sissy and John stared at me. 'I'm ringing Danny, seeing as he's so bloody free with his advice about where my children should be.' I knew Denise and Danny's number off by heart and punched it in. Danny picked up on the second ring. I wasted no time in getting to the point.

'It's Donna, Danny. Brian's just phoned me. What's going on?'

'If this is about Brian taking the kids, the arrangement was for Brian to pick them up on Saturday. Your week is up.'

'That's not what Denise's letter said. Sunday was the pick-up day. Sunday to Sunday. A week.'

'That's not a week. That's eight days. Saturday is collection day.

'That's not true! Let me talk to Denise.'

'She's in transit.'

Once more I burst into tears. I pushed the receiver at Sissy and buried my face in my hands.

Sissy snatched the phone. 'This is Kathryn Daly speaking. What's all this nonsense with Brian and the kids?' She sounded crisp, businesslike. As she spoke, she beckoned for me to listen to what Danny was saying. I pressed my head close to hers, so my ear was near the receiver. Even though I was crying, I doubt that Danny could hear me over his own ranting.

'... a right to see his kids. And while we're talking about the kids, apparently the care order is being contested. That your doing?'

'Donna's contesting the court's decision. The whole thing's ridiculous – this stuff about suicide and igniting herself. She was the victim of a crime!'

'Not according to the Department. Tell her from me that she doesn't have a chance. A whole lot of dirt's gonna come out and she'll lose everything. Tell her DOCS is getting a QC.'

'She's their mother and they need her,' said Sissy, her hand shaking as she held the phone between us.

'This whole court shit can be avoided, you know. We'll give her back her kids when I've seen her at least half a dozen times to check she's good enough. When I think she's ready, she'll get the kids back.'

Sissy had started crying. She held the mouthpiece away from us and whispered to John, 'I can't handle much more of this.'

'Just listen. Don't say anything,' he mouthed back.

Danny was frenzied by this stage. 'Donna's only causing more trouble for herself with another court case! I'll decide when to give the kids back!'

Finally, unable to get a word in, Sissy hung up. It wasn't even lunchtime yet and my final weekend with the boys was in tatters.

We phoned the police, but apparently they could do nothing. John, Sissy and I decided the day's events should be documented, including Danny's abusive phone call, and that we should ring DOCS's 24-hour hotline to report what had happened. After jotting down detailed notes, Sissy rang the number and spoke to Lorraine Prentice. Ms Prentice promised to record the incidents and send a copy to the Parkes office. Much later, when I finally obtained my DOCS file, there was no record of our complaint.

On Sunday morning Brian phoned again. Once more, Sissy answered. She got straight to the point. 'Where are the boys, Brian?'

'Put Donna on, will ya. I'm not speaking to you.'

Sissy handed me the phone. I was immediately on the attack. 'You've gone too far, Brian. I want my children back.'

Just like his brother, Brian began to yell and I was forced to hold the receiver away from my ear. Both Sissy and I could hear him loud and clear.

'I'm not happy about the boys staying with that bitch of a sister of yours!' he shouted.

'That's where I'm living, Brian, so if you don't like my sister, that's too bad. You don't have to be here, so what's the problem?'

'She'd be badmouthing me in front of my kids. I know what your family's like.'

'Actually, Brian, my family is extremely controlled when it comes to you. There's no badmouthing going on from this end. Now, what about my boys?'

'Denise is up from Parkes. She's bringing them out to your place mid-morning,' he said sulkily.

Sure enough, an hour later, Denise arrived with Coe by her side and Bodean clinging to her like a koala.

'Hi Mum,' Coe said, giving me a hesitant smile.

'Hi darling. Take Bodean from Aunty Denise, will you, and get him something to eat, and yourself too, if you like. Put the kettle on while you're at it. Would you like a cuppa, Denise?' How painful it was, having to be nice to this woman.

Sissy went to make tea and I sat at the big table with Denise opposite me, her arms folded in front of her.

'Brian was wondering when you were going to sell the house in Geurie, Donna. You'll be getting half each, won't you. It'd be a help for you to get a place of your own, maybe.'

I know who it would help, I thought, deliberately sidestepping the question. 'I think I'll be here for a while yet. By the way, what were Brian and Danny up to, taking the kids like that?'

She leaned forward and blinked at me from under a curtain of blonde hair. 'Brian was totally out of line, Donna. I'm real sorry about the mix-up. I told him he shouldn't have done it.'

I wasn't in the mood for her innocent routine. 'Time with my kids is precious, Denise, and I don't appreciate being robbed of it.'

'Well, you'll have them back soon anyway,' she said, leaning back and crossing her arms again. 'They're your kids, Donna. I never wanted to keep them. I'm just looking after them until you're okay.'

How many times had I heard that? 'My family should have had care of the children, Denise. It was completely unfair of the Department, denying them access and getting me to grovel just for a visit. Apparently they think I'm an unfit mother.'

'I wouldn't know anything about that,' she muttered. 'I didn't want your kids in the first place. I'm on your side.'

'If that was the case, why didn't you just say that my family could look after them?'

She ignored the question, but I could see her cheeks were reddening. 'It's all in the past anyway.' She waved one hand casually in the air, like wiping the slate clean. 'I know you've got a barrister now, but there's no need to go to court to contest the care order. When I go back to Parkes, I'll see DOCS and tell them how much better you are and how you should have your kids back. You'll have them by Christmas. Like I said, there's no need to go to court. We don't want any dirty washing aired in public.'

I glared at her. 'What do you mean, "dirty washing"? Danny said something similar. I don't know about you, but my family hasn't got any dirty washing.'

She shrugged her shoulders and fiddled with a strand of her hair, breaking eye contact. 'Oh, you know. Just private family stuff.'

I was puzzled. Why were she and Danny warning me off court? And what was this business about dirty washing? Was she referring to some mysterious past indiscretion that had labelled me unfit to be a mother?

And why was Denise suddenly so helpful? It was straight out of left field. I began to get the feeling that she was hiding something. Had she been an innocent relative who'd offered to care for my boys because I couldn't, or had she played a more sinister role in the Department's interference? I wondered if I would ever find out.

Denise changed the subject and once again made enquiries about when I'd be selling the Geurie house. 'You and Brian are just going to do a fifty-fifty split, aren't you?'

'Is this really any of your business?' I asked. 'That house was financed almost entirely from my wage and plenty of my own blood, sweat and tears. He's lucky to be getting half. My solicitor's already advised me he's not entitled to that much, but I've decided to be generous. I'll organise the sale when I'm ready to talk to Brian about it and, after yesterday's little performance, that doesn't look like it'll be anytime soon.'

'I don't blame you for being mad at him.' Denise smiled apologetically and stood up. 'I'd better be going, but how about the kids stay today? Brian can come out later this afternoon to get Coe, and Bodean can stay on for a couple of days. I could get him Tuesday, before I head back to Parkes. I'm visiting with Mum and Dad for a few days at Mount George. It's funny how our families have all ended up in the same area.'

'Yes,' I said. 'Hilarious.'

As Sissy and I walked her to the gate, Denise turned towards me. 'Think about what I said, won't you?'

I frowned. 'What do you mean?'

'Think about not going ahead with the court case. When I get back to Parkes I'll send someone out from the Department to assess you. I'll sort it out. I can see you're getting better. You'll have your kids back soon, I'm sure.'

'Should we be talking about this?' interrupted Sissy. 'Isn't it something that needs to be left to the Department?'

'Donna's the one who keeps saying she wants her children returned. I thought she'd be pleased to hear what I'm going to do.'

'I'll be happy to speak to any DOCS worker who comes out, Denise,' I told her as she opened her car door. Maybe, finally, DOCS was going to see reason. But Denise's sudden backtracking seemed odd to me. What was going on?

Twelve

More pieces of the DOCS puzzle fell into place in October, when I received a letter from my Dubbo solicitor, Ann Kinghan. She had sent me the affidavit by DOCS officer Maria Williams which had been used in the Department's care order application, along with the psychologist's report from Janet Webster, who, back in August, had hidden behind a tree in a park making notes on my kids. Ann requested that I read over both documents and comment as necessary.

I sat on the edge of my bed in the warm spring sunshine and unfolded the affidavit and the report. The more I read, the more I became paralysed by a strange, icy shock. My gut began to twist and once again I found myself struggling for breath. I was horrified by the pages in front of me.

'Oh my God, oh my God. How could they say this?' I flicked back through the papers. 'What a bunch of lies!' For a moment I sat, stunned and silent, before hurling the bundle of documents down in front of me. I tugged at my pressure mask, pulled it off and tossed it on top of the papers. Then I burst into tears.

'What's the matter?' asked Sissy, appearing in the doorway. It was becoming an all too common question.

'Take a look for yourself.' I nodded towards the heap of papers at my feet.

Sissy picked up the affidavit and the report, sat down beside me on the bed and began to read. As she digested the contents, I could feel my distress seeping away, quickly replaced by cold anger.

'I'm going to deal with these liars if it takes every last ounce of strength I've got,' I said. 'If they think they can steal my children and blame me for it, they're in for one hell of a shock.' I struggled to my feet. 'I'm getting a pen and paper and I'm going right through this bullshit and exposing it for what it is. Ann's going to be very interested in what I've got to say.'

Later, as Sissy and I sat at the big table going through the documents, I said, 'You were in court. You must have known what they were saying about me. Why didn't someone tell me?'

'I was shocked at the accusations, and I knew you'd have to deal with them sooner or later. We wanted you out of hospital first.' She wiped a tear away. 'You were just so down and, when you started to progress, we didn't want to hit you with another shock. It was bad enough having to tell you we'd lost the kids without going into details.'

'Great, now my own family's lying to me.' I couldn't look at her.

'It wasn't like that and you know it. Anyway, Bruce Levet warned you that the Department thought you'd done it to yourself.'

'That's a nice way of putting it, though, don't you think? "Did it to myself." I mean, look how they've phrased it in the affidavit here.' I reached for the pile of papers. 'It says I doused myself in petrol. It says I participated in some sort of suicide pact in front of my children, deliberately inflicting emotional abuse on my two boys.'

Sissy nodded and said nothing.

'So this isn't just some little mistake that the Department has made, some small slip-up about the assault.'

'I did my best, Donna, I really did. They wouldn't listen.'

I shook my head. 'I find this all incredible. How could they stuff up like that? And what about all this other crap? It's character assassination on the hearsay of a handful of people.'

'Let's go through it properly then. Pass me the notepaper. You comment and I'll jot down what you say.'

And so this is how Sissy and I spent the rest of the afternoon and a good part of the evening. I was worn-out from rehab, but somehow that didn't matter. I was so mad my fury had transcended everyday weariness.

The following day, Sissy typed up my response for the solicitor:

Witness: Constable Adderley

Allegation: 'Donna and Garry were drinking most of the day.'

Response: Untrue. Garry had certainly been drinking quickly. Yes, I was at the club. I'd had a few drinks. It was my birthday. Bar staff would be able to verify the quantity of alcohol I had consumed.

Allegation: 'Donna and Brian were always drunk and fighting.'

Response: Brian was the one with the drinking problem, not me. On a couple of occasions I'd needed to phone the constable late at night because of Brian's drunken behaviour and violence towards me. One of these times he came to the house to assist me. I had been home looking after the kids. I was in my pyjamas and sober.

Allegation: 'Coe did most of the caring for Bodean. Neither parent would be capable of caring for the kids.'

Response: I had always been the main carer for my two boys. Coe sometimes babysat for a small amount of money. He was definitely not Bodean's carer though. While Coe and I were at school, Bodean was minded by a registered day-care mother.

Witness: Denise Blakemore (sister-in-law)

Allegation: 'He (Brian) has always been a very heavy drinker. Since the fire incident he has managed to stop drinking and is trying to think of the future.'

Response: Brian is a long-term alcoholic. It would be highly unlikely that he has suddenly cured his drinking problem.

Allegation: 'Up until Coe was five, he spent most of his time with Brian's parents.'

Response: Coe was looked after during the week by his paternal grandparents because I worked. I was having so many financial problems with Brian drinking and largely unemployed that I was forced to save money by removing Coe from day care. Brian's alcoholism prevented him from caring for Coe himself.

Allegation: 'He (Bodean) is very pale, but he's a good size.'

Response: Bodean was born fair-skinned and has always been so.

Both he and Coe have a paediatrician and a GP and both of these professionals can vouch for the fact that I made medical appointments whenever either of my boys had a health issue. Bodean and Coe were in good health before they moved to Parkes.

Allegation: 'He (Bodean) doesn't talk much.'

Response: He was talking when he was in my care and in the care of his day-care mother. Did anyone think he might be traumatised?

Allegation: 'He's very demanding and not in any sort of routine at all.'

Response: Bodean was in a very structured routine while in my care. With a working mother, he had to be. He was also in a routine when with his day-care mother.

Allegation: 'I have shown him photos of his mum repeatedly, but he shows no recognition of her. It worries me that he has not fretted for her at all.'

Response: According to Coe, the school sent a framed photo of me to the boys, and Bodean had pointed to my face persistently, calling, 'Mummy! Mummy! Mummy!' Denise finally put the photograph away in a drawer.

Witness: Ann Blakemore (mother-in-law)

Allegation: 'We looked after Coe most of the time. The little fellow preferred to be at our place.'

Response: The grandparents looked after Coe while I was at work. At his grandparents' house he was often spoilt with chocolates and lollies. He was totally indulged.

Witness: Janet Webster (psychologist)

Allegation: 'Coe told me that he can talk to his father when things are troubling him, that they are good friends. He described his father as friendly and generous. He also stated that if he does anything wrong his father only lectures him whereas, according to Coe, his mother used to hit him a lot.'

Response: All parental responsibilities were left up to me. This included administering discipline. When either of my boys did the wrong thing I would speak to them at an age-appropriate level and

very occasionally use one or two smacks as a last resort. This does
not constitute child abuse!

It was clear. The DOCS 'investigation' had been flawed, supported by a
hotchpotch of biased opinions and transparent lies. There were so many
individuals who could have vouched for my character and parenting
skills. Yet the Department spoke only to a handful of people who either
had a skewed view of me, like Constable Adderley, or a vested interest in
tarnishing my name. DOCS, too, had their own agenda. They needed me
to be labelled an abusive parent because it went with their suicide
conclusion. It was a perfect fit.

It seemed that the Blakemores had desperately wanted care of my
children. If I had died, my boys would probably have been entitled to a
sizeable superannuation payout, which Danny had tried to verify,
according to Coe. There was also the house in Geurie – all of it, if I died.
Could money have been the motive for their attempt to keep my
children? The sickening possibility was slowly dawning. Was this a
paternal family conspiracy? A conspiracy that had gone pear-shaped
when I'd decided to live?

Soon after replying to Ann's letter, I had a visit from Bruce. He
congratulated me on my progress. He toured the house and grounds,
discussed at length the viability of having my boys stay with me there, and
unleashed a lot of confusing legal babble. I do remember him saying one
thing: 'It's going to be very difficult to change the status quo and get your
children back. Very difficult indeed. You are taking on a powerful
government department. They have unlimited resources. You are just one
woman, in fragile health, with limited funds. I don't doubt your
innocence, or their negligence. I have to say, though, our chances are not
good.'

That was definitely plain enough to understand. In the face of such
negativity, I only had one thought.

We'll see who can't do this and can't do that. We'll see!

Thirteen

I am back in Redfern, in the lounge room that looks out onto a dull 1960s streetscape. I am sitting on Garry's knee. He gazes into my eyes, and I stare back into his soft blue irises. There's a mist around us and music plays. It's orchestra music and it swells about the room like the crescendo to a love scene in a Hollywood movie.

Now Garry is stroking my arm. His fingers are gentle. He's smiling. I continue to return his gaze. Then his eyes grow darker, steely. I'm reminded of storm clouds hanging low, about to break. Suddenly his eyes flash red and the music changes. AC/DC's 'Thunderstruck' belts through the room and the windows rattle with the force of screaming guitars.

A few seconds into the song and Garry leans down and bites hard into the soft, pink flesh of my forearm. Blood spurts out in a scarlet jet. I am screaming my lungs out but no one hears. A woman clutching a straw shopping bag walks past the window, but she takes no notice of the racket. For a moment I think it's my mum, a younger version.

'Mum! Mum!' I cry, but the woman walks on, out of sight.

I look down at my arm and it's a mass of veins and mangled flesh. Garry is still going, gnawing up my arm towards my neck and face. I try to wriggle free, but his arms pin me to his lap. I struggle, flailing about as his gnashing teeth reach my face. Not my face!

As he bites into my mouth I wake from the dream. I'm safe, sitting upright in bed, eyes wide under my pressure mask, heart pumping, breath choppy.

The nightmares continued nearly every night, along with a stream of unanswered questions about the man I'd once loved and trusted. Did he think about me? Did he care? Was he sorry? Or was he going to come and finish me off? Creep through the dead of night with a lighter and petrol container. Bones and all, this time.

As the heat of summer hung over Killabakh, my anxieties increased. I knew why. It was time for me to front up to Taree police station to give my statement: my version of events on the afternoon of Friday, 1 April 1994. I'd never been inside a police station before. I didn't know what was expected of me and was terrified of saying or doing the wrong thing.

I padded through the labyrinth of corridors behind Sissy and Detective Sergeant Frank Kuiters, past offices and waiting areas, uniformed officers and a smelly old bloke cursing in a holding cell. My body was quivering. If my new skin were able to sweat, I would've been bathed in perspiration. Instead I was hermetically sealed in my stifling burns suit. It was 13 December 1994.

The interview room was sparse, similar to those on TV crime shows. I don't remember a window. There was a table and some chairs, a monitoring screen suspended in one corner and a video camera set up on a tripod. A police officer began fiddling with the camera as I took a seat. Sissy sat beside me; Frank sat opposite. He was square of build, clean-shaven with cropped, dark, wiry hair. He was gruff, self-assured.

I had spoken to him a few times on the phone, but this was the first time we'd met face to face. Despite his confidence, I could see he was shaken at the sight of me. He averted his eyes and began shuffling a pile of papers while the camera was set up.

The interview was very formal, and the formality made me even more nervous. Frank started off with things like, 'Do you agree there is only one door into the interview room?' and 'Do you agree that I told you that my questions and your answers would be recorded electronically both on video and on audio cassette tape?'

'Yes. Yes. Yes.'

I had not rehearsed what I was going to say. I'd just turned up with the knowledge I had in my head. After I'd given my name and age, details about where I was living, Frank asked me about my injuries.

'You've got facial injuries?'

'Yes.'

'Can you just tell me – without showing me – where the rest of the injuries are?'

'All down the front of me – my face, my shoulders, my legs, my arms, my hands, around my ribcage.' I forced my hands to remain on my lap.

'Abdomen?'

'Yes, my legs, tops of feet. A lot of skin grafts were taken from my back because it wasn't burnt.'

'Right. So it's ...'

'It's all down the front.'

'It's all down the front,' he repeated in his deep voice.

'Yes.'

'There's basically no burning on your – on your back.'

'Sixty-five per cent of my body was burnt.'

'Yes. But it's all restricted to the front area.'

Frank moved on to the lead-up to the assault, or 'incident'. We established that Garry and I had gone to the club, where, according to Frank, 'an excessive amount of liquor had been consumed'. He asked me how much I'd drunk; I told him about four drinks. I told him I always slowed down; I never tried to keep up with Garry.

'Could you, in your own words, tell me what happened when you returned from the bowling club?'

I told him I parked the car and took the keys. I didn't tell him about Garry's shaking and pushing, his ranting and raving as I drove. *Bitch, ya bloody old slag! I know you're fucking someone, ya bloody ugly slut!* I told Frank I checked the children and did some washing and put the tea on. I told him I was talking to Coe and Bodean. I forgot to mention the bit about Garry throwing Bodean on the bed. *Keep ya fucking kid away from me.* And the bit about Garry thumping and kicking the outdoor furniture. I told him that I put the laundry hose out though, and crept around to see what Garry was up to.

It was then my voice began to give out.

'Right,' said Frank. 'Well, just take a break for a minute. Your voice has changed.'

'Mmm.'

'You've got some ...'

'The ...' I couldn't get the words out. Out of the corner of my eye, I could see my sister watching me. She touched me on the shoulder. This compounded my anxiety; I couldn't have a coughing fit, not now.

'... bronchial tract burns, haven't you?'

'Yes, my throat was burnt,' I managed to say.

'Right. Are you having any trouble speaking for long periods?'

'Yes.'

'Right. Any time that you have any trouble, just take a break, take ...'

'Mmm hmm.'

'We're not in a hurry. Is that drink there all right or ...'

'That's all right, yes.'

After a while, Frank asked what Garry was doing when I came out with the washing machine hose. I explained that Garry was siphoning petrol from my good car into the unregistered Corolla. I was so nervous that I didn't mention Garry swearing at me. I was aware that in an effort to answer the question clearly and simply, my version was bleaching all the nastiness and accelerating violence out of those final moments.

'Can you remember any conversation that was had between you and Garry at that stage?' Frank asked.

'I asked him what he was doing and he said he was taking the Corolla. I objected to that because he'd been drinking and also the car was in my name, unregistered.'

Ho hum. I'd made it sound so civilised. *You can't tell me what to do, slut! I'll do what I fucking well like!* Garry's words bounced around inside my head, but I couldn't repeat them. If I said what he'd said, I'd be swearing – swearing into a tape recorder, with a camera pointed straight at me and a detective watching, listening, firing questions.

It's okay, I assured myself. They'll know what happened; they would have spoken to all sorts of people. Trevor Dunn, for a start, who was first on the scene and would have heard how Garry was going berserk. Dave

Hayward, who'd heard Garry going off at me the week before. The Fords – they knew what Garry was like, what he was capable of. And Coe. Even though the police had forbidden me to speak about the fire to my son, and I had kept my word, I knew he would have told the police what Garry had done. No need for me to rake over every single gory detail. I mean, it was obvious who was guilty, wasn't it?

I was making assumptions about the police investigation – foolish assumptions. I know that now.

Frank asked me about the petrol container. 'What sort of a tin was it, do you remember?'

I tried to imagine those minutes before the explosion, but my head didn't want to go there. 'I think I remember it being an old – like an old paint tin,' I said at last. As it happened, I had remembered incorrectly. It had been a plastic petrol container, the same one I'd bought years before. I don't know why I made the mistake. Perhaps I was thrown by Frank's use of the word 'tin'. Perhaps it was because the opening, just centimetres from my face, seemed so round and large, like an open tin. I didn't understand it then, but little inaccuracies like this, spoken innocently, could cause no end of trouble. Frank glanced at the papers in front of him. He would come back to it soon enough.

We talked more about time of day and quantity of petrol; I wasn't too sure of the latter, not knowing how many trips Garry had made back and forth, from car to car.

Frank asked what happened after I'd said no to Garry taking the car.

'Well, he started to – we started to – both of us started to argue over it. He said, "No, I'm taking it," and I said, "No, you're not." Back and forth like that.' *Bloody fucking bitch! I'll show you! Say fucking no to me, will ya, cunt!*

Frank nodded. 'Yeah.'

'I went to grab the tin, take the tin away from him. He was pulling back at the tin when some just splashed over our hands.' I failed to tell Frank that 'pulling' included grabbing and shoving, and ripping my clothing away in handfuls. I just gave the bare facts, no decoration. Wasn't that what I was meant to do? Just answer the questions as plainly and simply as I could?

I assumed Frank would have known how terrified I was back then, about the voice screaming in my head as I clung to the container, trying to stay upright. *If he gets you on the ground you're a goner. You've had it. He'll kill you.* Frank hadn't asked me what I was I thinking or feeling, so I didn't elaborate. Instead I swallowed, blinked and shuffled a little on the hard seat. I didn't want to be here, didn't want to think about it anymore.

'Right. And when you say "our hands", you're still talking about your hands and Garry's hands?'

'My hands. Well, I assumed it went on his hands because it went on mine.'

'Right.'

I went on to explain I was being pushed back to the rear of the house and that there was 'a bit of a struggle' and after that 'he seemed to have thrown petrol over me'. I told him about my eyes stinging, about how I had to rub them, and about hearing the click of a lighter and opening my eyes.

He asked me if I smoked; I thought it was a strange question. I said no. He asked if Garry smoked. I said that he did.

I told him I saw the lighter in Garry's hand and I ran. I told him I turned to look behind me and saw I was on fire. I told him about Coe yelling, 'Roll, Mum, roll!' I put my head down then, and bit my lip. I felt my chest heave and I pressed my eyes shut. I could hear the tape machine whirring softly. Finally Frank spoke.

'Are – are you right? Do you want a break? All right. I'll just suspend the interview.'

It took me a minute to pull myself together, to push away the picture of Coe standing by the back door hollering into the dusk. I tried to think of other things, like Dad skylarking in the wheelchair at the hospital, or Bodean tugging at a car balloon. A line of prayer from hospital drifted into my head: '... hold onto my trembling hand and be with me today.' Somehow, it helped.

'I'm okay now,' I said at last.

'You're quite ready to go on?'

I nodded and he asked what happened then. I told him about rolling over the long grass and being hosed. I said I remembered people tugging at my fingers.

Frank's next question caught me unawares. 'Do you recall any conversation between yourself and Coe about going inside and getting matches?'

I stared at him. 'No, I don't.'

'Do you recall anyone else asking Coe to go inside and get matches?'

'No, I don't.'

'Is it possible that you actually had hold of the tin of petrol yourself?'

'No.' I explained I had both hands rubbing my eyes.

'Right. Getting back to the tin, you've said to me it was a – a paint tin.'

'I think it was a paint tin.' Once more I tried to dredge up the image of the container, but fear and desperation were scrambling my memory.

'Right, so when we're talking about a paint tin, we're talking about a pot which is about that high?' Frank held one hand a little above the surface of the table.

'I think it might have been a four-litre one. I think … I …'

Frank frowned. Had I said the wrong thing? 'A four-litre. You know what a four-litre …'

'Yes.'

'… paint can is. All right.'

I gulped. 'I think it was one of those.'

'And …'

'I didn't really take much notice of it.'

'Yeah.'

I could see Frank wasn't convinced. 'But I think that was what it was.'

'Okay. Do you recall if it had a metal …'

'No, I couldn't,' I interrupted.

'… handle?' Frank finished.

I shook my head. 'I couldn't recall. I don't know whether it had it or not.' Why was he so fixated on the tin? I wondered.

Frank asked me more questions about the struggle. Were we on the ground? Were we standing? Did I break free? Or did he break free from me? And again, how much alcohol had we consumed? I told him Garry was drunk and I was moderately affected. I pointed out for the second time that I had been celebrating my birthday, but I also had family responsibilities.

'I knew I still had the children to look after, you see, and had to bath and feed and do the washing, like I said.' Did Frank understand I wasn't an irresponsible drunk? Did he believe me? I stared at my lap, my fingers neatly gloved, resting on my thighs. I was aware the interview was not going well. I'd made Garry's violent behaviour sound merely thoughtless, part of a lovers' low-key tiff. Then there was the questioning over the alcohol, the fuss about the paint tin. Did he think I was lying?

I jerked my head up. 'Another thing, you said about matches – mention of matches,' I blurted out. 'I don't have matches in the house.'

Frank looked startled. 'All right. You don't have any gas appliances?'

'No. All electric.'

'All electric. Okay.' Frank seemed satisfied about that at least. Soon he was back onto the struggle. He wanted to know if Garry had threatened me.

I frowned, as much as my skin would allow. 'That he was going to go and take the car whether I liked it or not.' Maybe that's what he meant.

'Right. But was there any talk or threat by him as to your personal safety? For example, did he say to you, "I'm going to belt you. I'm going to kill you," or, "If you don't leave me alone, I'll drive over the top of you," or something like that?'

I remember at this point in the interview being not only nervous, but also suddenly confused. Why on earth would Frank suggest Garry was going to run me over? I now know exactly what Frank was doing. To the best of his ability, and without 'leading the witness', he was trying to extract more information from me, to encourage me to reveal the unsanitised, horrible, violent truth of that afternoon. He wanted me to lay bare Garry's intent. He was on my side, after all. Being inexperienced, I just didn't get it.

'No, I don't think ...'

'Was there any threat like that?' Frank persisted.

'I can't recall anything like that.'

He then asked if I'd threatened Garry.

'I just didn't want him to take the car because he'd hurt himself or someone else,' I said, starting to tear up.

Frank asked if there had been any other violent incidents. Ashamed, I admitted that there had been. I mentioned bruises and the time I'd hurt my eye when he'd pushed me and I fell against the stove. He asked if I'd reported the incident, and I had to say no. Would he now conclude I was lying?

I told him about the jealousy, the possessiveness, and tried to explain the rising danger towards the end of our relationship, but it sounded like a lame attempt to bolster my position. 'If I was late coming home from work, he wanted to know where I was,' I said, unable to articulate the depth of his rage. *You're a fucking slut. You bitches are all the same. I know what you get up to behind my back.*

More sanitising.

He asked again if Garry had made any verbal threat to kill me or if I felt the situation was planned. Had there been an argument prior to the taking of the petrol? My fuddled brain replied no. No argument, I thought, only his tirade. Later I realised I should have explained Garry's seething temper, which was obvious at the club hours before. But surely others would tell Frank. Others would fill in the gaps.

The interview had not gone well, in part due to inexperience and nerves. But this wasn't the only evidence, I told myself. This was the New South Wales Police Department after all, dealing with a crime against society. Dealing with it on my behalf. They would have held a thorough investigation months ago. They would know who did it and exactly what happened. I could rest easy; justice would be done.

〰

I was still travelling to and from Westmead for ongoing surgery, and my empty house back in Geurie was continuing to cause problems – the latest was a burst water pipe in the ceiling which was causing damage and needed urgent repair. More bits and pieces from inside and around the house began to disappear. I thought about all the times I'd helped various

individuals in that tiny community. I thought about my open-door policy:
I fed so many of the locals, babysat neighbours' kids, listened for hours to
the lovelorn, and offered a spare bed for the night to those who needed it.
It was so disappointing.

My major goal was getting my children back and, as the weeks wore
on, I kept in constant contact with Coe and Bodean, as well as Denise. A
couple of weeks into November, Coe told me that his aunt had enrolled
him at one of the local high schools near their home in Parkes, and that
there was no further mention of the boarding school idea. Keeping my
voice calm, I asked Coe to put Denise on the line.

'Coe tells me you've enrolled him at a school near you. I've already
taken him to look at Wingham High School and he said he wouldn't
mind going there next year.'

Denise's voice was placating. 'I only enrolled him in case you weren't
well enough to look after him next year and he had to stay here.' There
was a slight pause. 'Has DOCS been in touch with you yet?'

'No, they haven't.'

'I want them to come and assess you so that the kids can be returned to
you as soon as possible. They're your kids and they should be with you. In
fact, I'll go into DOCS today and see about the boys coming back to you.'

'Right.'

She was getting repetitive. Was she really going to persuade the
Department to return my boys? I doubted it. But the very next day I
received a phone call from Helen Robinson at DOCS, concerning
Denise's visit to their office the previous afternoon.

'I'm afraid it's not that simple,' she told me. 'You can't have the
children back before August next year unless a court says so.'

I kept ringing and writing to the Department, doing whatever I could
to organise access. It had been arranged that both boys would visit for the
next school holidays, but Bodean's third birthday was earlier in December
and I requested that he be able to visit for this special occasion. It seemed
silly, I then pointed out, for Bodean to travel all the way back to Parkes,
only to return a fortnight later with his older brother for the Christmas
holidays. Why not let Bodean stay on for those interim two weeks? I could

give him my undivided attention before Coe joined us. I reminded DOCS yet again about the court's assertion that bonding was important. Denise was not happy, but the Department agreed. Another small triumph.

I had never missed either of my sons' birthdays, and Bodean's celebration was made all the more joyous because at long last I had my baby back, and back for good as far as I was concerned. One down and one to go. Bodean was home now, and I wasn't going to hand him back, despite anything DOCS had to say to the contrary.

As I continued my bid to regain custody of the boys, it was becoming clearer to me that the Bodean who was handed back to me bore little resemblance to the happy child I had raised. Instead I had a wild and woolly monster, a mini tornado who couldn't sit still for a minute. At first I made excuses: he'd been through a lot; he wasn't used to the routine; he was in an exciting new environment and overstimulated. Maybe his glue ear had returned and poor hearing was making him unresponsive to gentle reprimands. I made a mental note to get this checked again. Eventually, I had to face the fact that my little boy had been seriously affected by the previous nine months and it would take a lot of patience and consistent, thoughtful input to bring him back.

By this stage I only had to attend rehab in the mornings, so the afternoons and weekends were focused on Bodean. I couldn't take my eyes off him for a minute. He'd begin at breakfast, twitching and jiggling at the table, snatching and grabbing for any food within reach, as though if he didn't get in quick he'd go without.

'He never used to do that,' I said. 'He always knew he'd be fed. He was secure, happy.'

'He's been through a lot,' Sissy murmured. 'Give him time.'

After 'eat, eat, eat', it was 'go, go, go'!

I tried to engage Bodean in appropriate activities: playdough, painting, story books, craft activities, action songs, nursery rhymes, ball games, tricycles; you name it, we did it. Because I was unable to, Sissy would take him for swims in their pool, and both of us would spend hours walking him around the farm, talking to him and showing him all the growing things. We fed the chooks and collected eggs, picked bunches of flowers, ate from the strawberry patch and picked and cut open ripe passionfruit, letting him taste the juicy pulp.

'We won't touch the green ones though. The green ones aren't ready,' Sissy said.

Bodean responded in his weird new way: he looked blankly past us, then broke free, dashing around the corner and out of sight.

'He was never like that. He always liked to keep the adults in view. He liked to hang around. He *engaged* with people!'

'Give him time. He's just a child.'

'But he never used to do that!'

Apart from time in the pool, which he quite liked, Bodean was initially interested in little but destruction. He ripped flower heads from their stems – not just one or two, and not just once or twice. Again and again, entire beds of blooms were slashed with a golf club or similar weapon. He raided the strawberry patch and the passionfruit vine. Every single piece of fruit, ripe or not, was devoured or smashed. He cracked a piece of exposed PVC pipe with a brick, he chased the chooks, and pulled up an entire bed of carrots. Every day there was something.

'It's okay, Donna,' Sissy would say. 'Just explain to him he's done the wrong thing.'

'But he doesn't listen like he used to,' I'd say, weeping at Bodean's latest escapade. 'He doesn't react.'

Things came to a head with two incidents within a couple of days of each other. The first happened just before lunch one day when Sissy was at work and I was making John a sandwich. I'd been playing with Bodean in the sunroom and had left him happily engrossed in building a block tower.

I'd almost finished making the sandwich when Bodean appeared in the doorway of the kitchen. He was wearing his 'guess what I've been up to' look.

'Uh oh. What have you done?' I asked, putting down the knife.

Without a word he turned and walked out.

I followed him into the garden. 'Where is it?'

He looked up at me, his lips in a half smile. This was his 'you'll find out' look.

It didn't take me long. A swift glance around and my gaze landed on the herb garden and the remains of a once magnificent concrete goanna. It was Sissy's special garden ornament, a birthday gift from John. A golf club lay on the grass nearby.

'Oh my God, what have you done?' I buried my face in my hands. 'Maybe I can fix it, glue it together.' The giant lizard had been decapitated, and the body had great lumps gouged out of it all the way down to the obliterated tail. Who was I kidding? It was totalled.

I knew I had to tell John, and tell him now.

'Come on, Bodean,' I said, taking my son's hand. 'You have done a very naughty thing and now we have to go and see Uncle John. He's going to be very upset.'

Bodean stared back at me blankly.

We found John in the vegetable garden. 'John?'

He hadn't heard us approach, and looked up, his face dripping with sweat. 'What?' He must have known by my facial expression or tone of voice that it was bad news.

'I've got something to tell you.'

He straightened up and leaned on his spade. 'What now?'

'You know that lizard of Kathryn's?'

'Yes.'

'It's all smashed up.'

'You're joking.'

'No, I'm not.'

'I've had just about a gutful of this!' John tossed the spade down and dashed past us towards the house. 'He's annihilated it. It's absolutely stuffed. Have you any idea how difficult it was to find?'

I tried to replace the ornament, taking Bodean with me to the local garden centre to explain to him what we had to do, and why. We chose two fairies, to go with the one Sissy had among the lemongrass. It wasn't the same though. They weren't special like the goanna.

A couple of evenings later, Bodean tried John's patience even further. The weather had turned unusually cold and Sissy suggested I forgo bathing Bodean in the laundry tub, and put him under the shower instead. I was reluctant at first. Bodean's nightly bath was always a challenge, with plenty of kicking and screaming as I struggled to lift him into the water, but I could usually make it fun for him. Unless he had to have his hair washed – he would scream blue murder if so much as a drop of water landed on his head, again, unlike the child I had known. I was afraid a shower spray would cause total meltdown, but the night was cold so I finally agreed.

'You get his gear and I'll watch him,' said Sissy. She and Bodean were in the family room with everyone else.

I returned a few minutes later with an armload of clothes and bath toys. 'Where's Bodean?'

'He's in the bathroom, waiting for you,' Sissy called from the kitchen.

I dashed off in the direction of the shower. God only knew what he'd managed to destroy in the few minutes I'd been gone. Bodean was standing on the bathmat; he watched as I scanned the room for signs of mayhem. Everything seemed to be in place.

'Come on, Bodean,' I said, tugging his T-shirt off. 'You're going to have a shower. That'll be a treat!' I was preoccupied though. He must have touched something. I looked in the toilet, and then over at the hand basin. I noticed John's contact lens container, a shallow dish normally filled with liquid in which John placed his lenses each night when he came in from working. I peered more closely at the container. There was neither liquid nor lenses in it.

Maybe John hadn't taken his contacts out yet, I rationalised. I crept out of the bathroom and peered around the corner into the family room. John was sitting back in his easychair watching telly. He was wearing glasses.

Back in the bathroom I was frantic. I put Bodean's shirt back on and began crawling around the floor on my hands and knees, patting the tiles carefully to try to locate the contacts.

'What did you do, Bodean?'

Bodean shook his head. 'Didn't do it. Didn't do it.'

After a few more minutes of fruitless searching, I approached the family room.

'John, did you put your contact lenses somewhere?'

'What do you mean?' he asked, shooting out of his recliner like he'd been bitten by a snake. He pushed past me to the bathroom, closely followed by Sissy, Jennifer and Patrick.

He seized the empty dish and peered inside before whirling around to face me. 'Where the bloody hell are they?'

Sissy was edged in beside him, her hand on his arm. 'Now, John, he's just a little boy –'

'I'm getting bloody sick of this! Things broken, smashed!'

'Don't worry, John. Perhaps we can find them,' said Sissy.

'I'll replace them,' I said, wishing I'd just put Bodean in the laundry tub.

John was searching around the basin. 'That's not the point!'

Bodean, meanwhile, stood stock-still, his fingers in his mouth, watching the adults with detached interest as we began to scour the bathroom.

We did find one lens, ripped in half. The other never showed up.

I realised I had the best physio on earth in Bodean. I would spend my days glued to him. The property wasn't childproof, so dangerous items like tools and paint were within easy reach. It was too risky to try to contain Bodean around the house so I packed a picnic and we tramped down the hill to the creek.

We would play with stones, dig in the sand and paddle at the water's edge, just like old times in Geurie. I was tired by the time we reached the water, but the uphill climb home was even more of a challenge. Bodean would take off like a hare and I would have to scramble after him as best I could in my burns suit, knowing that the cows, of which he was wary, would inevitably slow him down, forcing him to hang back and wait for me.

After lunch I'd try to get him to lie down. He would fight, kick, roll, scream and cry, all of which I ignored as I lay beside him, pinning him down with one arm and holding a simple picture book with the other. It was usually a book he could join in with: a rhyming text, something with bright, engaging pictures. 'Where's the dog, Bodean? Point to the puppy.' Bit by bit he'd forget his protests and become absorbed in the book.

Gradually, I would loosen my arm and begin to stroke his cheek. His eyelids drooped and I'd stroke them as well. Close, close, open. Close, close, open. It was a game requiring immense patience. Finally, he'd drop off and with relief I'd do the same.

To familiarise Bodean with his family again, Sissy suggested I use my photo albums, which she and John had collected from the house in Geurie. It was a good suggestion, and the photo game became one of the first quiet-time activities in which Bodean would willingly involve himself. We played it daily, sometimes more than once.

I'd sit Bodean on my knee, open an album and start.

'Look,' I'd say, in my 'we're having fun' voice, pointing to the various faces. 'There's Nanna. There's Grandpa. There's Aunty Sissy. Can you find Jennifer on this page?'

'Jennifer!' He pressed a chubby finger over her photograph.

'Good boy! What about Coe? Where's Coe?'

Again he pointed and laughed.

'Well done! Who's this?' I asked, pointing to a picture of himself, sitting on Coe's lap.

'Bodean!' he squealed. 'That's me!'

Holding my breath, I then pointed to a photograph of myself – my old self, when I had a face.

'Who's that, Bodean?'

'Mummy! There's Mummy!' He pointed and pointed, jabbing at the photograph and searching for more. 'There's Mummy!' His eyes lit up as he saw another and another.

I turned the page. 'And is Mummy anywhere here?'

'Yes! There she is! There!'

As he turned to me and smiled over a picture of his long-lost Mummy, I took a breath and said it. 'I'm Mummy.'

He stared darkly at me and the smile vanished. 'No!' He turned back to my photo. 'That's Mummy!' He tapped my paper face emphatically.

It wasn't long before Bodean began to call people by their correct labels. Not just in the photo albums, but to their faces. Jennifer was Jennifer. Nanna was Nanna again. My sister became Aunty Sissy. Uncle John, Grandpa, Grandpop Leonard, Patrick. They all got their names. Every day, I'd wait to get a name too, but Bodean was steadfast in his refusal to call me anything. There had to be something I could do.

After a while I invented another game, similar to the first but based on eyes. I'd point to his beautiful blue eyes in a photograph. 'Look at your eyes, Bodean. They're yours. Look at Coe's eyes in this picture. Where are Nanna's eyes? Find Patrick's eyes.'

He began comparing people's real eyes with their eyes in the album. Sissy would crouch down next to him as he sat on my lap. 'Look at Aunty Sissy's eyes. Now, can you find her eyes in the photo?'

In my album I had one particularly clear photo of myself, a duplicate of the one that the school had sent to the boys all those months ago. It was a head-and-shoulders shot, and in it my eyes were a deep, shining blue. Nothing else about my face was the same anymore. I had a brand new misshapen mouth, a lopped-off nose, and a mass of lumpy purple-red skin grafts. Only my eyes were left.

'Look at Mummy's eyes,' I said casually one day, turning to this photo. He peered at the picture for several seconds, at the eyes of his long-lost Mummy. Without prompting, he turned to look at me, straight at my eyes. Back to the photo, back to me. The photograph, me, the photograph, me. I held my breath as his head swivelled back and forth. He reached up and placed a chubby hand either side of my cheeks, cupping my face in his two tiny palms. His eyes stared harder into mine, peering past the stranger's face. Finally he spoke, his voice amazed and breathless. 'There you are, Mummy! There you are!'

'Yes, my baby, it's me,' I pressed him to my chest and began to cry. 'You clever boy! I knew you'd find me eventually.'

Our long game of hide-and-seek was over. I had a name.

Fourteen

As Christmas approached, my relationship with Bodean continued to improve. He was becoming used to the new me. To help him understand my altered body – why Mummy couldn't run and kick a ball with him – I involved him in the weekend visits from Barbara Hall, the community nurse who attended to my wounds and dressings.

Bodean would sit on the end of my bed, his eyes riveted to the gowned and gloved nurse as she cut open the sterilised packs of cotton balls, disposable tweezers and saline solution. After my wounds were cleaned and dressed, Bodean would help apply moisturising cream and zip me into my burns suit. Long after we left Sissy and John's, he continued his involvement in this ritual and developed a special empathy for anyone who was ill and in pain.

Bodean might have been bonding with me, but Coe was unreachable. In December, he came to stay for the Christmas holidays. Like before, he was uncooperative and surly to the point of rudeness. Normally I would have taken him to task about his behaviour, but instead I let him go to bed late, picked up after him without complaint and bit my tongue when he snapped at me.

My reasoning was simple: where he would like to live the following year would influence future placement of both boys by the Department. Adamant that I would not be handing them back to Denise, I needed to make the option of staying with me as attractive as possible.

In January, though, Coe delivered some bad news. 'I'm not staying with you all holidays, you know. Aunty Denise is taking me to Queensland.'

'Oh, that'll be lovely,' I said, secretly cursing Denise. 'Give me a call when you get there so I know you're okay. And it'd be nice to send Bodean a postcard.'

Fortunately, just a few days after Coe left for Queensland, my friend Deb came to spend some time with me. Apart from my family, I had few visitors in those first months out of hospital. I'd received a couple of phone calls from my old friend Yvonne and her daughter Sue. They missed me, they said. But because they were so closely connected to Garry, I knew my relationship with them could not be sustained. I spoke often to John and Shirley Heller but, like the rest of my friends, they were too far away to make visiting easy. Deb's visit was a rare treat.

I met her at the door wearing cotton pull-up slacks and a baggy T-shirt over my burns suit. I'd left my facemask off for the occasion. She gave me a hug and passed me a bottle of something. 'God, you look so much better! You know, compared to when I saw you in hospital.'

Like all the others who tried to reassure me with comments about 'looking better', Deb meant well. At least she hadn't come out with those other well-worn lines: 'This happened for a reason', and 'It could have been worse'.

I took the bottle and glanced at the label. 'Champagne. Nice touch.'

'Well, you *are* out of hospital. We can celebrate, can't we?'

Sissy and John had a caravan out the back ready for me to move into when I was well enough. Deb and I used it that night to have some privacy for our last glass of Champagne. I had my wallet open on the bed between us and was showing her some pictures of Coe and Bodean. Our heads touched lightly as we bent to examine the photos.

'I guess you haven't got any of him,' she said as I slipped the boys' faces back behind the scratched plastic. 'I'd like to see what he looked like.'

'I could probably find one somewhere, buried in one of my photo albums. Take a look under the bed.'

'I presumed you would have destroyed them,' Deb said, climbing off the mattress. 'I mean, a monster like that. You must hate him.' She reached under the bed and pulled out three or four albums bulging with the past.

'Deb, these people not only worm their way into your life and your photo albums, but they also become embedded in your heart and your memory. The feel of them, the smell of them ...' I glanced down at my hands for a moment and blinked. 'I know you don't get it but it's a grieving process,' I said, raising my head again to look at her. 'As unsavoury as it seems, feelings don't get turned off like a tap. Of course there's hate. But there are lots of other emotions too. He was the man I dreamed of growing old with.'

She shrugged but looked unconvinced. 'Anyway, let's have a look at him.'

The photo I showed Deb had been one of my favourites. It was a shot of Garry sitting on the grass, leaning up against his motorbike. He was wearing a black T-shirt that sagged around the neck. It had AC/DC emblazoned across it in chunky red and yellow graphics; a lightning bolt separated the letters. His jeans were black, his boots Johnny Rebs, also black, with silver studs and a large silver ring over each ankle. He was cradling my cat, Monty, in his arms, squinting straight at the camera, eyebrows raised. He was smiling, his lips pressed together in a wide, self-conscious grin. He looked almost goofy – certainly harmless. Maybe that's why I'd always liked this photo.

'He looks okay. He looks normal.'

'Control freaks do look normal. They don't come with a sign across their foreheads.' I shut the album and pushed it to one side.

'What happened to him?'

'The rumour was that he lost all the fingers on one hand. Months later it was his whole hand. Soon it'll be his arm.' I rolled my eyes. 'I have no idea if any of it's true.'

Deb drained her glass and got up to put it on the sink. 'How does Garry feel about what he's done, do you know?'

'My old neighbour, one of his friends, Sue Ross, rang me a while back. Said Garry has been telling everyone "something just flew through the air and ignited". She was quite shocked when I told her he deliberately pulled out his lighter and lit me up.'

Deb plonked herself down on the bed again. 'And DOCS? What's happening with the boys?'

'I can't believe how sneaky a government department can be. Would you believe they lodged a care application in Parkes on 23 June, then left a phone message at Westmead the next day to say they were going to visit me the following Monday.'

'I don't get it.'

'It was only because of a curious social worker that we were able to intervene. She rang my solicitor because she got suspicious. I mean, this was the Department of Community Services coming to see me. My solicitor rang the Department on the 24th. It was a Friday and they served her with papers by fax. When she rang me, I gave her instructions to ring my sister. Friday afternoon, and this was for court on Monday. How prepared do you think my solicitor would have been? I was lucky I even found out about it and had a solicitor.'

'So the care of your children was going to be decided without your knowledge, and they were going to tell you on Monday?' Deb looked at me, aghast.

'Yes!'

'Isn't that illegal?'

'It *sounds* illegal. Anyway, instead of a done deal it became an interim order for six weeks. At the next hearing the boys were placed in Denise's care for twelve months. Access by my family was blocked.'

'But what about you?'

'Denise was asked to make an undertaking to encourage my access, but I wasn't exactly in a position to organise it. My family couldn't bring them because they didn't have access. The whole thing was a farce. And in court they wouldn't even give my solicitor time to read the affidavit properly. As for my DOCS file, he wasn't allowed to read that either. He wasn't even allowed to submit character references on my behalf.'

'But how could they do that?'

'Who knows? Now I've been told the Department justified the care order by saying there was going to be a difficult custody conflict. But I was okay with the boys being at Denise's. I only nominated my sister as a carer after DOCS interfered. The Department said we couldn't reach consensus in the family conference. They reckon they made the care order to prevent further trauma to Coe and Bodean.'

'But wasn't that done *after* the interim order? After they'd already tried to award care to Denise? It doesn't make sense. Sounds like they were covering themselves.' She flopped back on the pillow and clasped her hands behind her head, staring at the ceiling.

'Anyway, now I have a barrister. Last year he began organising procedures through the Family Court to get joint custody for Sissy and me. He's also looking to get the care orders revoked through the District Court.'

'God, this is serious.'

'It's all such a mess.' I rubbed my eyes and stood up to put the kettle on. 'Denise is now saying she wants me to have the boys permanently, and I'm going to do everything to avoid handing them back to the Blakemores at the end of January. But according to DOCS, to get Coe and Bodean officially back in my care, it has to go through court. It doesn't matter what Denise thinks.'

I could see Deb trying to find something to be optimistic about. We sat in silence for a while.

In the second half of January, Coe returned from Queensland. There had been no phone call, and no postcard either. I wanted to ask him why, but I forced myself not to comment.

Denise, who had been staying nearby with her parents, came over so we could discuss what would happen with the kids now that the holidays were drawing to a close. I knew by this stage Coe was leaning towards staying with me, but I wondered how Denise would take it.

'I had a talk to Coe in Queensland, Donna, and I know he wants to stay here,' Denise said. 'That's right, isn't it, Coe?'

'Yeah,' he said. 'I'll start at Wingham High. I've decided.'

'Right then,' I said, slightly bewildered. Was this a trick? 'That's great news. We'll get your gear sorted tomorrow then. Uniforms and everything.'

'I've already told DOCS Coe wants to stay here. I've told them I've seen the place, how it's all lovely,' said Denise, blinking at me. 'They'll be contacting you.'

I wondered why Denise would have the power to sway DOCS. Perhaps this was just another example of 'Blakemore big talk'. I told myself not to get too excited, as hope flowered in my chest. 'So you're all okay with this?'

The phone began to ring, shrill in the momentary silence. It was Richard Gray from DOCS. He was manager for the Parkes cluster and was ringing to speak to all of us: Coe, Sissy, Denise and me.

'The Department is looking at rescinding the care order,' he said as I came on the line. 'Coe has just told me he wants to start at Wingham High. Denise agrees Coe and Bodean should be with you, and your sister is obviously supportive.'

I was shocked. It seemed too easy. 'What do you mean?'

'The children can stay with you and we'll probably recommend rescinding the order.' He sounded impatient.

'What does "rescind" mean?' I had to be sure.

Richard sighed. 'The children can go back into your care.'

'Just like that?'

'We'll need to send one of our officers out to interview you and the children, check everything is all right. It will be someone from the Taree office.'

'So they'll definitely be staying with me from now on?'

'As I said, you'll need to be assessed by someone from the Department. While that process is taking place, say, over the next four to six weeks, the children will stay with you.'

'That's great! Send out as many officers as you like. What happens next?'

'At the moment, your children are still officially in the custody of Denise Blakemore, even though they're living with you. To change that, your application to vary the order and have the children back in your care will need to go through the courts. It's just a formality. You don't have to be there.'

'I'll be there,' I said. There was no way I was going to be fobbed off this time.

In early February, the Department sent out Neil Wilkins from the Taree office. I heard his car pull up and came out to the gate to welcome him.

Neil was a mild-mannered man with thinning grey hair and an earnest look about him. I ushered him into the family room, offered him a seat at the table and some afternoon tea, and introduced him to Sissy and Bodean. Coe was at school, but due home soon.

Niceties over, I sat down opposite him and got straight to the point. 'Neil, I'm guessing you won't like to hear what I'm about to tell you, but I'm going to let you know anyway. The Department has stuffed up badly.'

'What do you mean?'

I explained the assault and my subsequent time in Westmead. I talked about what DOCS was doing behind my back while I lay in hospital. I laid bare their accusation of self-incineration, their rushed attempts to put procedures in place following the temporary care order, their skewed investigation, and the fact that my family was denied access to the children.

Neil sipped his tea and listened carefully. When I'd finished, he donned a pair of metal-rimmed glasses and read the affidavits, my collection of character references and my solicitor's summary. I was waiting for denials or condescending comments; I did not get the reaction I expected.

Neil wasn't defiant or defensive. Instead he took it all on board. 'This doesn't look good, Donna, I have to admit.' He took his glasses off, folded them and returned them to their case. 'I think the first thing I need to do is get your files transferred from Parkes to Taree. You and your children are here now, so the files need to come to our office.'

For the first time in a year I had met a DOCS official who was prepared to look at all the information with open ears and eyes and, even more importantly, an open mind. He may not have believed me instantly, but he was prepared to listen. If only the Department employed more people like Neil.

Over the next few weeks, Neil became a regular visitor to the house, getting to know my family. We felt comfortable with him and welcomed his visits. I presumed we were still being checked out but he never made it seem that way.

'How are you going with my files?' I asked him one day as we walked around the garden with Bodean. 'Made any progress?'

He shook his head. 'There's definitely something not right. Parkes don't seem to want to hand them over.' He stooped to pick a strawberry. 'Being fobbed off by my own department makes me inclined to believe what you say.'

'I'm over that way soon, for the revoking of the care order. It's happening in Forbes. Can I do anything?'

'Maybe you could call in to the Parkes office. Make some enquiries. It might hurry them along a bit.' He popped the strawberry in his mouth, while I tugged Bodean away from demolishing the remainder of the bed. 'Do you mind?'

'Anything to get to the bottom of this mess.'

The matter of the care order was scheduled for 15 March 1995 at Forbes Courthouse. My sister drove me over the day before, leaving Mum and Clyde in charge of the household. As the Blakemores lived in nearby Parkes, I had contacted Denise and arranged to call in, have a cup of tea and retrieve my sons' possessions before attending court.

Arriving at Denise's at the agreed time, Sissy and I found no one home. I knocked on the door of the bungalow and walked around to the backyard. I winced as the video I'd watched in hospital jumped into my head. There was the trampoline, the swing and the old caravan. A couple of dogs barked half-heartedly in the morning heat, and broken toys and household junk lay about in the dust. A few towels flapped on the clothesline. We walked back to the front and left a note saying that we'd called and would be back later in the afternoon.

I had never been in a courtroom before and as I took my seat my hands were shaking. I was self-conscious about my appearance, steaming in my burns suit, and terrified I was going to get a stress-induced coughing fit. I checked I had my inhaler in my handbag just in case, and tried to ignore the curious glances of those around me.

There was a hushed formality about the room, a little like church. I glanced around and saw a young man in a dark suit with a bunch of papers in front of him. An older man was beside him, also suited up. They were whispering together, their heads bent close. I assumed the younger guy was the solicitor representing the children, and the other was the DOCS solicitor. I'd expected at least one of the Blakemores to attend, but Brian, Denise and Danny were nowhere to be seen.

We all stood as the magistrate entered and took his seat in front of us. He put on a pair of glasses and looked down at the papers in front of him, saying something to the effect that we were here to vary the court order from the previous August. I didn't understand a lot of the legal jargon, but I do remember the young solicitor bounding out of his seat to address the magistrate.

'I don't think revoking the order should be that easy, Your Honour. The mother has a drinking problem.' He darted a look in my direction. 'Surely she needs to undergo some sort of rehab or supervision. I don't see any evidence of that. Before the children are just handed back we need some assurance that the alcoholism is under control.'

Panic rose in my chest. I couldn't believe it! Hadn't these people read my comments about that allegation in the affidavit? Hadn't they read the medical reports?

I noticed the DOCS solicitor whispering frantically to the children's solicitor, frowning and shaking his head. He didn't seem too happy about the outburst. Suddenly the DOCS solicitor jumped up.

'We have no problems with the rescinding of the order,' he told the magistrate.

I could see the children's solicitor was about to protest, but the magistrate interrupted. 'I remember this case.' He nodded and looked back at his papers. 'And if my memory serves me correctly, the mother wasn't the one with the drinking problem. It was the father.'

'I still think she needs to be assessed, Your Honour,' the children's solicitor asserted.

Court was adjourned briefly and I stepped outside, digging around in my bag for my inhaler. Sissy was soon by my side and put an arm around me. 'Just take it easy, Donna.'

'Take it easy?' I sucked in two sharp puffs of Ventolin. 'Thank God the magistrate remembered who the alcoholic is! Anyway, I've just spent six months in hospital, for God's sake. I've had probably three mouthfuls of beer and half a bottle of champagne in the last twelve months.' I wiped away a tear.

I needn't have worried; back inside the courtroom, the children's solicitor stood up, a slow flush creeping over his face. 'I have no queries about the matter, Your Honour,' he said in a subdued tone. 'The children wish to return to their mother and, as their representative, I have no further problem with that.'

This was odd. Had the DOCS solicitor cautioned him about impeding the proceedings? Did DOCS want the whole matter to go away quietly? Did they want *me* to go away quietly?

'What have you got to say about your accusation against the mother?' the magistrate asked.

The children's solicitor gave me an unhappy look. 'I must say I apologise for my insinuation that you had a drinking problem.'

Beside him, the DOCS solicitor nodded, satisfied.

*

Back in Parkes, Denise still wasn't home. She had read the note though, because a green garbage bag had been left on the porch for our collection.

A decrepit plastic push toy leaned against the bag. Mum had given it to Bodean for his second birthday. Now it had a wheel missing and the handle had snapped off. There was a large crack down one side.

I wrote Denise another note. 'We called around again but you weren't here. I'm leaving Bodean's cart. Maybe you can use it?'

Perhaps we also should have left the garbage bag of stained, torn clothing – the sum total of my two sons' possessions. The boys' good leather shoes, new outfits sent by my parents, and decent hand-me-downs that had been taken from Geurie were not included. I found the photo of me that the school had sent, scrunched up and minus the frame.

Before we left, Sissy and I went around to the neighbours. I wanted to speak to Denise and ask her about the missing belongings. Perhaps the neighbours had an idea of when she'd be back.

'Don't know anything about them! Don't want anything to do with them!' was the stern reply through the screen door. 'Now, if you don't mind –'

'Wait!' I called. 'We're not friends of theirs. We were meant to pick up some belongings, and there's quite a bit missing, that's all.'

'Doesn't surprise me. Can't tell you how many times we've complained to the police about the bloody racket over there. The parties, the drinking, the music, the fights. It's a bloody nightmare.'

Great. These 'neighbours from hell' were the DOCS-assigned carers of my children. The Department had insisted on character references for Sissy and John; I wondered if they'd sought the same for the Blakemores.

As I'd promised Neil Wilkins, we called in to the DOCS office in Parkes to enquire about my files – not once, not twice, but three times. I wanted to speak to Richard Gray or Maria Williams, but the first two times I was told they were 'not available' and to 'come back later'. On the third visit to the office they still weren't available so I went through my story again and explained that the care order had been revoked.

'I know that the Taree office has asked for my files. I was wondering if I could see them?'

The woman behind the counter looked me up and down like I was scum. Her department had removed my children; as far as she was concerned, I had 'child abuser' stamped across my forehead.

'You can't see your files. You are not permitted to do that.'

'Neil Wilkins is my caseworker. I know he's requested them to be sent to Taree. He asked me to enquire about the hold up,' I said politely.

The woman raised her eyes. 'We'll send them to the Taree branch when the paperwork's done.'

'It seems to be taking a long time.'

'I told you. They will be sent!'

⁂

Back at Sissy's place, the boys and I had moved into the caravan and its small annex in the backyard. This was a double-edged sword. On the one hand, it gave us much-needed privacy and independence. Apart from using the main bathroom, we were reasonably self-sufficient in our tiny home and could cuddle up in my bed and watch TV, eat and prepare our own meals. We had a few familiar things from our home in Geurie, and the caravan offered some respite from the worry of my boys inadvertently doing the wrong thing in the main house, like Coe helping himself to the fridge or Bodean touching things he shouldn't. In the caravan we had a piece of our own territory. But after owning my own three-bedroom house in Geurie, the caravan was also a reminder of our reduced circumstances.

'As long as we're together, boys, that's what counts,' I'd rally, but I knew it was the start of another long haul.

Although others were marvelling at my progress, I was battling low moods and a variety of other health issues. I spent a lot of time crying. I was also in a lot of physical pain.

'You've always been good at art. Why not take up painting? It might help distract you,' one of my colleagues from Orana Heights suggested.

'There's not enough black paint on the mid-North coast,' I told her flatly.

Several people suggested that keeping a diary would help, including Deb. I had never been much of a writer, but I was willing to try.

In March 1995 I wrote:

I am still in fear of the next needle, dressing change, shower,
doctor's visit. When I wake up in the morning I feel like the old
me. For a few minutes, I lie as still as a post, pretending. As soon as
I move though, the pain brings reality. My arms are the worst. I
can't reach up too far. The splitting sensation in my armpits is
sickening. I know I need more operations. The thought of going
back to hospital terrifies me.

And my face! Sometimes I forget until I have to go out. The
public remind me all the time. Little children stare openly, and
come back for more. It's exhausting, pretending not to notice. Why
did I ever bother to look after myself all these years, when now I'm
stuck with this hideous new look?

It must break Coe's heart when he looks at me. He used to be
so proud of me, especially at school. Even at recess and lunch he'd
come over to me on playground duty with a group of his mates, or
they'd visit me in the classroom if I was working in there. Now I
see the hurt in his eyes. At times he forgets, until he turns to say
something. His look is heartbreaking.

It was obvious Coe was having big problems. Now he was officially back
in my care, I was no longer too scared to say no to him, but my normal
parental limit-setting wasn't working. He continued to be ill-tempered
and disrespectful, a real know-it-all. Once we had been so close; now I
knew a part of him hated me.

Early in the term I paid a visit to his high school. His bad behaviour at
home was being mirrored in the classroom and playground. I looked back
through his primary school reports, all glowing, full of words like
'mature', 'sensible', 'responsible' and 'caring'. His high school teachers had
no such compliments. They saw him as belligerent and uncooperative.

I let his teachers know what had been happening in Coe's life, and
asked them not to be too lenient but to bear in mind the trauma he had
gone through. I told them that if at any time there was a problem, I was

to be contacted. I wanted to know exactly what was happening with regard to his behaviour and his academic progress. I also offered to do voluntary work in the library to become part of the school community.

But my efforts made little difference. Coe would come home each afternoon in a dark mood, stomping around the back to the caravan. He'd chuck his bag into the annex and then go straight to the tiny fridge, ignoring Bodean and me completely.

'How was your day?' I'd ask.

'How do you think it was?' He'd pull out a drink or a piece of fruit and turn towards the door.

'I only asked how your day was, Coe. I can see you're angry and I don't think it's anything to do with school. You might feel better if you talked about what's worrying you.'

'I don't want to talk. Get off my back!'

Everything seemed to turn into an argument. Coe would slam the door behind him, jump on his bike and pedal into the distance. I'd bought the bike so he could let off a bit of steam without having to ask Patrick to borrow his, but when Coe returned he was just as unpleasant.

'How about you wash the vegetables with Bodean while I get his bath ready?' I'd ask.

'No, I'm not doing that. You do it. He's your kid, not mine.'

I thought back to when Coe used to sit beside Bodean's bassinet and wait for him to wake, or hold his little hand while he took a few wobbly steps. Coe had always been so proud of his little brother. Now he seemed to have a chip on his shoulder about him.

When Coe played with Bodean, he was teasing and sarcastic. It was like poking a snake; when Bodean finally snapped, Coe would jeer, 'Look at the little crybaby. Boo hoo!' I winced at his harsh, hectoring voice. He sounded so like his uncle, Danny.

'That's not playing, Coe. That's teasing. Try playing!'

At night, though, with tea over and the lights dimmed, I saw glimpses of the old Coe. The three of us would snuggle up in bed to watch television together and he'd put his arm around Bodean to pull him close, talk to him softly and stroke his cropped blond hair.

I began to tiptoe around Coe's moods. In some ways it was like reliving my time with an abusive partner, modifying my behaviour to keep the ill-temper at bay. It couldn't go on. One day I spoke to my counsellor, Ruth Neil, about getting Coe some help; she suggested I make enquiries through Youth Services, attached to Community Health.

The next week I talked to Marjorie Spence, one of the coordinators, and took in Coe's old school reports as well as an ongoing album, full of achievement awards, work samples, merit cards and sporting ribbons. I also explained what had happened and how Coe was behaving.

She looked carefully through the reports and examined the album. 'I've never seen this done before. You've got every little gold star and merit award here. It's a beautiful thing to do, and certainly not a sign of an uncaring parent.'

She went on to suggest Coe see Julie, one of their youth counsellors, who would be closer in age and perhaps have more success in drawing him out. I made an appointment for him the next afternoon.

Coe protested, but I didn't care. 'You've got an appointment, son, and you're going. If they ask you whether you're there of your own free will, you say yes. You don't have to speak if you don't want to. You can sit there for the whole 50 minutes and say nothing, but you're going to see this counsellor.'

Although Coe disliked going, he stuck with it for some time. We never talked about it as it was confidential, but the counsellor did tell me that he had started to open up. At home his anger subsided; he knew there were boundaries now.

※

Early in 1995, I managed to scrape together enough money to buy a second-hand car, an old Gemini sedan. It was a real bomb, but good enough for my purposes. It gave us a little more independence: we were able to go to the beach for picnics and barbecues, and visit Mum and Clyde in Laurieton, just like old times. I could take care of my own errands and also drive Coe to and from town twice a week for basketball practice. Most parents just dropped their kids off, but I liked watching Coe train. During the breaks he'd bounce the ball to Bodean and chase him up and down the court. It was good to see them getting along better.

Basketball was popular in our little community and it wasn't long before Coe became skilled enough to be included in the competition. A competition with proper matches and proper spectator crowds.

On the afternoon of the first match, Coe came home from school in an odd mood. He was preoccupied as he changed into his shorts and basketball top, filled his drink bottle, found his shoes. His brow was furrowed and he was unusually quiet as he moved about the van.

'Want me to do that for you?' he asked as I began washing potatoes for tea.

'Can I make you a cup of coffee, Mum?'

'How about I read Bodean a story? Would you like that, Bodean?'

His behaviour had improved but this was overattentive! Clearly, he'd been thinking about something at school. I guessed it was to do with the basketball game that afternoon.

Putting the last of the vegetables in the pot, he finally spoke. Here it comes, I thought.

'Mum, by the way ...'

'Yes?' I spoke casually, sipping my coffee at the table as Bodean played on the bed nearby.

'Maybe it's best you just drop me off.' He busied himself wiping the sink, but he looked as guilty as hell. His tough demeanour had vanished. He was a young boy again – blushing, vulnerable, anxious. 'You look pretty tired this afternoon,' he added.

'Is that so?'

'You can come back later and pick me up.' He kept his eyes averted as he went to his sports bag by the door.

I watched him closely. 'Is that the only reason?'

'Yeah, yeah ...' He was crouching down now, re-checking his water bottle. He slipped it away, zipped his bag up, scratched his hair and adjusted a shoelace.

'Are you sure?' I persisted. 'Is there anything else?'

'Oh well ... yeah ...' He began to stumble over his words. His voice quavered. He stood up and tried to eyeball me, to swagger and bring the tough guy back. Instead his skinny shoulders slumped. He hung his head.

'If that's the real reason, that you think I'm tired ... But maybe it's something else.' I kept my gaze on him as once more he shuffled around his bag. 'Whatever's bothering you, it's okay. I won't be upset. You need to start talking to deal with this stuff.'

He looked up at me and a fat tear slid down his cheek. His words tumbled out in an almost incoherent rush, his face crumpling. 'I just – it's – I feel so bad, you know. With how you look, with everybody staring ... wanting to know, like, what happened, and going on and on and gawking, I feel embarrassed being seen with you.' He swung away from me.

I stood up and came towards him. 'Coe, I understand what you're saying and it's so good you can talk about it. Yes, people are going to stare. They're going to say things without thinking. But son, I'm always going to be different. That isn't going to change.'

He turned to face me and nodded, too choked to speak.

'And there's something else that's never going to change.'

'What's that?' he whispered.

'I'll always be here for you and Bodean. I'll always be your mum.'

As I finished speaking, Coe began to cry again. 'I'm sorry, Mum. It must be so awful for you. I'm so sorry, so sorry,' he repeated, pushing his damp face into my shoulder.

I put my arms around him and rested my cheek on his head. 'You've got nothing to be sorry for, Coe,' I said, breathing in the smell of his tears and sweat. 'I understand. I understand and I love you.' I stepped away after a moment, blinked hard and turned to gather up Bodean and find my bag. 'Come on, I'll drop you off.'

'I want you to watch me play, Mum,' Coe blurted out. 'If you can put up with this, so can I.' He snatched a handful of tissues from the box on the table and blew his nose. 'I hate crying,' he said, shaking his head.

'It's okay to cry, mate. Look at me. I haven't stopped!'

The three of us went to basketball that afternoon. Bodean and I sat in the front row and cheered our heads off. When Coe scored his first goal, he glanced around to check we'd seen him, his face pink and sweaty, full of hope. I gave him a thumbs-up and across the crowded court he sent me back a wide, spontaneous grin. I could see it; my child had started to heal. And he was never embarrassed about my appearance again.

Fifteen

It was now April 1995, twelve months since Garry had chosen his birthday surprise for me, his gift of fuel and flame. My 38th birthday, on 31 March, had been no cause for celebration. The following day, the anniversary of the assault, was imbued with a deep sorrow. The cool earth smells, the early evening chill and the leaves shifting from green to muted rusts, golds and clarets all echoed those days, hours and minutes before everything changed.

The French call it 'the time between the dog and the wolf', when the last rays of sunlight fade and dusk slips like gauze over the landscape. I stood in my sister's backyard and stared out at the purple mountain range. One year on and I'm still here, I thought. I've survived.

My boys were in the caravan. I could hear the faint drone of the television through the thin aluminium walls, and Bodean's occasional laughter. Sissy and her children would be preparing tea, with John relaxing in his chair, reading the paper. They had forgotten the gravity of this moment, these minutes.

In my gloved hand I held a single sheet of paper. It was from my time in hospital, a prayer penned by an unknown writer, which Sister Pat had used to comfort me through those dark days. Now I sat in the fading light and said it to myself. I didn't really need the sheet. I knew it by heart.

I asked God for strength that I might achieve;
I was made weak that I might learn humbly to obey.

I asked for help that I might do greater things;
I was given infirmity that I might do better things.

I asked for riches that I might be happy;
I was given poverty that I might be wise.

I asked for all things that I might enjoy life;
I was given life that I might enjoy all things.

I was given nothing that I asked for;
But everything that I had hoped for.

Despite myself my prayers were answered;
I am among all men most richly blessed.

I folded the sheet of paper. I was blessed because I was alive, and fighting back.

⚡

Neil Wilkins, my DOCS officer, still hadn't received my file from the Parkes office, despite continued assurances that it was on its way. By mid-April, Neil was getting suspicious and suggested I speak to my local MP, Wendy Machin. From there I was instructed to ring the Ombudsman and Community Services Commission, and to put a complaint into the Health Department. I rang the Ombudsman and was referred to Community Services, who referred me to the Community Liaison Department.

Perhaps DOCS got wind of my agitation, or maybe it was just coincidence, but on 28 April, my files finally turned up at the Taree office. Neil rang with the news.

'The files are here.' He sounded flat, abrupt. I heard him breathe out: a long, slow sigh. 'Oh, Donna,' he said at last. I was struck by the downward intonation, and imagined him leaning his forehead into the palm of his hand.

'Obviously you've read them,' I said, the heat rising under my pressure suit.

'You'll need to come into the office,' was all he'd say.

Neil took me to an interview room, and offered me a seat at a long table. I was reminded of my police interview back in December. My mouth and throat had suddenly gone dry; I asked for water.

Neil sat down opposite me with the file, a thick wad of papers stuffed into a manila folder. 'I can't let you read directly from your file, Donna. But you're allowed to sight it.'

'That's useful.'

He didn't smile, but sat neatly frozen like a storefront dummy. I had never seen him look so grim before. 'I've read it,' he continued, 'and it's absolutely scandalous.'

My heart began to thud. He blinked back at me from behind his glasses and shook his head slowly.

'What do you suggest I do?'

'Go to the top. This is so serious you need to take it as high as you can.'

'What do you mean?'

'I suggest you use the affidavit you showed me, because you haven't got the files, and I'm not sure there's a way of you accessing them at this point.'

I started to panic and scrambled in my bag for my inhaler. 'I still don't understand what I have to do.'

'You'll need to write a letter to the minister, put your complaint in writing and refer to the information you have in the affidavit. The fact they've accused you of self-incineration for a start. It's all the way through the file. Hasn't your assailant been interviewed? Haven't charges been laid?'

'Yes, the police know he did it. It's going to court.'

Neil thought for a moment. 'What DOCS did, it's outrageous, Donna. If you like, I'll help you draft the letter of complaint, but not here.' He glanced around as though there were spies. 'I can't do it at the office. We'll make a time for me to come out to your place and at least make a start.'

The words 'make a start' stayed with me. It didn't sound like preparing my complaint against DOCS could be done overnight, and I was right. Not only was building the complaint a time-consuming business, but other matters also intervened. Life had become hectic: looking after my boys, attending rehab and counselling, dealing with Social Security and taxation problems, and applying for a Housing Commission home. On 14 May, Mother's Day, I was admitted to Westmead for an operation to gain more arm movement. I was also in the thick of divorce proceedings, including the sale of the Geurie house.

In June I travelled to Sydney for one last meeting with my barrister, Bruce. I told him about Neil's reaction to my DOCS file.

'I'm preparing an official complaint,' I said. 'But perhaps I should be thinking about court action.'

Bruce shook his head. 'You have little hope of winning a claim against the Department, Donna. I know it seems unfair, but just be content with the fact your children have been returned. Some people waste their entire lives trying to right a wrong.'

'So I have to live with the fact that they took my children unjustly?'

'I don't think you've got a choice.'

※

Throughout the first half of 1995 I was also in continual contact with the Department of Public Prosecutions (DPP) over my assault, sending them character references, photographs of my burns and any extra information I felt they needed to know. The Crown Prosecutor handling my case changed at least three times during that year. Every time I received a letter informing me of the change, I sent another wad of information off.

I also rang Frank, the investigating officer, to enquire about progress, and occasionally he rang me. This was how I found out about a court directions hearing in February 1995, and another in March, concerning my case.

As usual, I was bamboozled by the legal jargon and didn't fully understand what these early court dates entailed. I hadn't attended; I'd been informed, 'You don't have to be there. We can do this without you.' All I knew was that these dates were leading up to the day that I would have to appear in court as a witness for the prosecution. The day I would take the stand and see Garry for the first time since the assault. Would I see an apology in his eyes? Remorse or shame? Revulsion at the sight of me? Or perhaps he'd just stare straight ahead: too hard, too long ago, too drunk, too mad; don't remember.

I dreaded seeing Garry, dreaded the whole idea of going to court. My nights were crammed with vivid courtroom dreams, with leering defence lawyers spitting out trick questions like machine-gun fire.

Court had been scheduled for 14 August. Two days before, Mum and Clyde drove Coe and me to Dubbo. It was winter, but the weather was sunny as we made the journey inland through Singleton and Maitland, stopping at a small park in Merriwa for Thermos coffee and chicken sandwiches before travelling out into the flat dusty landscape of the Central West.

It was a long drive, spent mostly in silence, my fear of what lay ahead compounded by the fact that Coe and I were forbidden to speak about the assault. The warm air swirled around the cramped car interior as we chugged along the flat black highway to Dubbo. I was almost passing out with the heat.

The family unit had been booked by Brenda Carrig, my Witness Assistance Scheme (WAS) officer. Brenda was attached to the DPP; her job was to support people like me, who found themselves dragged into the tangle of the legal system. Brenda was a lovely woman, great for a chat whenever I contacted her with questions or concerns, but short on information.

Frank called in briefly the day before court to check we'd settled in. We didn't speak about the case though, and I had little idea of what to expect or where to go when we arrived.

〴〵

Mum, Clyde, Coe and I huddled together on the lawn outside the courthouse with John and Shirley Heller, my old friends from Geurie. There were plenty of others about. Next to us, a couple of blokes were involved in a furtive conversation. One, in jeans and joggers, puffed rapidly on a cigarette. He wore a checked polyester shirt, two vertical crease marks running down the front, fresh from the cardboard packaging. The other was in a neat suit but still looked shifty, and talked out of the side of his mouth. A middle-aged woman stood to the left of us; I caught a glimpse of her face, puffy and careworn as she scanned the crowd for a familiar face, a clue about what to do, where to go. She was just as lost as I was.

Finally Frank found us and led the six of us inside to a long corridor lined with seats. Here there were more people waiting to go into court.

'Where do we wait?' I asked, eyeing the gathering crowd.

'Just take a seat outside the courtroom here.' He indicated one of the vinyl chairs, and Mum made a move to sit down.

'Wait, Mum.' I turned to Frank. 'I'm not sitting outside in the corridor. I've got a young boy here, and neither he nor I feel like coming face to face with the man who assaulted me. Isn't there somewhere else?'

This seemed to throw Frank for a moment. He glanced up and down the corridor and then back at me. 'How about you and your family wait in one of the rooms? The Crown Prosecutor will be along any minute, and you'll need to talk to him and the solicitor anyway.'

Frank left us in a small, tidy office jammed with filing cabinets, several shelves of law books and a large desk. By this time, Brenda had joined us. The seven of us sat in silence. It was like being on death row, waiting for the gallows. I was a witness for the prosecution, the victim of a crime, and yet the anticipation was making me sick. I felt like a criminal.

At last the door swung open and Howard Hamilton, the Crown Prosecutor, bustled in with a soft bag in one hand and a folder in the other. He was followed by Roger Montgomery, the solicitor for the DPP, and a third member of the legal team. They all wore dark suits and someone smelled of aftershave.

'Phew!' the prosecutor said, tossing the bag down. 'Running a bit late.'

Mum and Clyde left at that stage, along with John and Shirl, but Brenda stayed with Coe and me as the Crown Prosecutor slipped on his black gown and took out his wig. He had a conversation with Coe about the wig, told him it was made from horsehair, and let him touch it. Then Coe was sent out to join Mum and Clyde. I wondered when we were going to get to the case conference I'd been told about, as time was obviously running out and I needed court preparation.

The three gentlemen sat behind the desk and began to shuffle papers. I seemed to provoke paper shuffling. The prosecutor let out a sigh and cleared his throat. He looked up from his papers and then over to me. 'I'll be asking you some questions in court, Donna; you just answer them simply.'

'Right.'

'There's one thing.' He glanced at his colleagues. 'We're all having difficulty with why a man would set you on fire.'

I stared at him. 'Well, I ... Pardon?'

'We just don't understand. You must have said something to upset him.'

'I said to him, "No, you are not to take the car."' I did my best to answer the question simply.

'But why would a man set you on fire if he has petrol on himself? What did you say to him?'

I swallowed. Obviously my reply hadn't been simple enough. I gave it another try. '"No, you're not to take the car."'

The prosecutor leaned back in his chair. 'Think about it. You've got petrol on you. He has too. Why would a rational man ignite you knowing full well he's going to catch alight too?'

I sat straighter in my chair and eyeballed the three of them. 'He wasn't a rational man. He was out to get me at all costs. He wasn't thinking, "Hey, I spilt some petrol on myself too." He wasn't thinking like that. He was in a rage!'

'You must have provoked him in some way.'

'No! I said he couldn't take the car, and he went off!' I turned to the solicitor. 'Didn't you get all the things I sent you? You should have this information.'

This brought on another bout of paper shuffling. 'Er, yes,' the solicitor muttered, his head down. 'We have been getting various things ...'

The Crown Prosecutor looked across at the solicitor in surprise. 'What information?' Before the solicitor could answer, he glanced at his watch and stood up, reaching for his wig. 'We're running late. You'll be able to take the stand and explain all this anyway.' He picked up the file and tucked it under his arm as his colleagues gathered their own papers in preparation for court.

Was this the sum total of my case conference? As far as I was concerned, the ship had sunk. If these guys didn't get it, how was I going to convince a courtroom? I turned to Brenda who was still sitting beside me, neat and nice with her pageboy haircut and floral dress. She looked like a fellow kindergarten teacher.

'Why don't they believe me? I tried to explain two or three times.'

'You'll get an opportunity in court, Donna.'

'They just don't get it. What's the matter with them?'

Brenda frowned. 'Donna, they don't understand the dynamics of domestic violence.'

'Domestic! Is that what you call it? What a cosy expression – I thought it was just plain violence.'

As I waited to be called, Coe was brought back in, and then Mum and Clyde. John and Shirl wanted to be there too and were sitting in the public gallery.

Waiting, waiting, waiting: there are no words to describe the awfulness of those moments. I couldn't sit still. I couldn't talk. I stood up and began to pace. Up and down, up and down.

'Donna, sit down!' Mum grumbled. 'You'll wear a bloody hole in that floor.'

By this stage, I had worked myself into a state. I was going to be chewed up and spat out in court, while Garry watched. The people who were meant to be on my side didn't seem to get it, so imagine what the defence lawyer would do. And what about Coe – would he be in for the same treatment?

I'd finally sat down when Frank burst into the room.

'You beauty!' He strutted over and pulled up a chair. He was grinning broadly. 'Good news! He's pleaded guilty.'

'Can you repeat that?' I asked.

'He's pleaded guilty as charged!'

John Heller had come in with Shirl; he was frowning. 'Are you sure? I heard him plead not guilty to something.'

Frank turned to look at John. 'No, mate, he pleaded guilty to maliciously inflicting grievous bodily harm.'

By now I had my pen and pocket diary out. 'What charge was that again?'

'Maliciously inflicting grievous bodily harm,' said Frank.

'I'll just write that down,' I said, flipping over the pages. 'What was it again?'

'Bloody schoolteacher,' said Mum. 'Think she'd be able to spell by now.'

'No, it's not that. I want to get the wording right.'

Frank repeated the charge slowly and I wrote it down. 'So what does that mean, Frank?'

'It means we can all go home.'

John wasn't convinced. 'I'm sure I heard ...'

'No, he pleaded guilty,' Frank assured us. 'There's only the sentencing now. That'll happen some time down the track, but you don't need to be there.'

It was all too easy.

Frank was talking about filling in the forms for witness expenses, but I hadn't finished. 'How is the judge going to know what I look like, what happened to me? He's never seen me. How can he sentence the perpetrator without seeing the victim?'

'Do you want to do a victim's impact statement?' asked Frank.

'What's that?'

'You get doctors' reports, various documentation, to show how this crime has affected your life.'

'I think that's a good idea. The judge hasn't seen me. Garry's guilty plea automatically stops me from being seen in the witness box.'

Frank's face was all smiles again. 'No worries, Donna. I'll get the forms organised for you.'

Although I'd been suspicious initially, it seemed like everything was going to be fine. Garry had pleaded guilty, and I hadn't even had to see him, or his support crew, Adrian and Sue Ross.

'I can't get over it,' Shirl said later. 'After all he's done, the three of them just sat there and waved at us.'

'Never mind, Shirl,' I said. 'At least it's all worked out in the end.'

My relief did not last long. Days after returning to Sissy's place, I received a letter from one of my old work colleagues, Sue Rootes. She'd enclosed a clipping from Dubbo's *Daily Liberal*, reporting that Garry had pleaded guilty to negligently inflicting grievous bodily harm.

I couldn't believe it; it had to be a mistake. It was definitely 'maliciously'. I'd written it down.

I rang the *Daily Liberal* and they put me in touch with the court reporter. No, it wasn't a mistake. According to the court reporter, Garry had pleaded guilty to a lesser charge. Lesser charge, lower sentence. As far as I knew, there had only ever been one charge.

I rang the Dubbo solicitor for the DPP and got short shrift.

'The offender was charged with negligently inflicting grievous bodily harm. That's what he pleaded guilty to, Donna. That's what we accepted. It's over.'

'No, that's not right.'

'I'm telling you again, that's what he was charged with.'

'No, it's not! I've never seen or heard of this charge,' I said. 'It's never been mentioned. Where did it come from? It's not even on the subpoena. Did you just make it up or something?'

'Of course I didn't make it up,' the solicitor snapped. 'That's what he was charged with and that's what we accepted. If you've got a problem with it, perhaps you should speak to the investigating officer.'

I rang Frank, who was now at Castle Hill station.

'I don't know what's happening, Frank. There seems to be some sort of mix-up. I've been told to ring you.'

'What's the problem?'

'What did Garry plead guilty to?'

'Maliciously inflicting grievous bodily harm, Donna.' I could tell he was sick of the question.

'That's what I thought.'

'What do you mean?'

'It's been written up as "negligently" in the paper. I've checked with the solicitor of the DPP and he said Garry pleaded guilty to "negligently" and that's what he was charged with and that's what they accepted and he told me to ring you if I had a problem with it, so now –' I was aware I was rambling and, as I paused for breath, Frank cut me off.

'I was in the courtroom, Donna. I know what I charged him with, I know what he pleaded guilty to and I *know* what I told you afterwards in a room full of people.'

⁂

On 27 August 1995, almost two weeks after Garry's court case, I was back in Westmead for another operation. Further grafting had to be done under both arms, with skin harvested from my better leg. I was working on my victim's impact statement and my complaint against DOCS. I had been gathering more photos, character references and other evidence to bolster my case. Now that Garry had pleaded guilty to *something*, I assumed my DOCS complaint would be cleared up quickly.

I was also trying to track the origin of the suicide story. According to my work colleagues and other locals like John and Shirl, the rumours began flying thick and fast after the assault. The staff at Orana Heights had been so incensed at the gossip mongering that they had publicly declared their support of me through their newsletter the following term. But where had the rumours originated?

Coe's statement, made at Wellington Police Station the morning after the assault, didn't tally with my memories. Although Coe related a struggle over petrol, the roles were reversed, as though I was the aggressor. As for Garry, he was passive, barely referred to, as if someone had whispered, 'Don't mention Garry. He's in enough trouble as it is. Remember, don't mention him, son.'

Garry's past behaviour, his public and private history of drunken violence, did not fit with Coe's account. I know I had petrol deliberately thrown in my face and down the front of me; I wear the scars to prove it. An accidental splash? A negligent act? I don't think so.

From the DOCS affidavit I could see Constable Adderley had been a major player in my character distortion. Had he been partly responsible for the gossip about suicide? Someone had told me about Freedom of Information. Under this act, introduced in 1989, I was able to obtain Matt Adderley's documentation from the night of the assault. I made an application to the New South Wales Police Service for his notes.

Three weeks later, their Freedom of Information Unit sent a one-page submission from Matt Adderley outlining his knowledge of the incident, along with the Wellington Police Station occurrence message. The documents reiterated Coe's assertion that I was the aggressor.

Was that genuinely the way Coe remembered it? Or was he protecting Garry? Maybe he was just plain mad at me. After all, I'd made him stay home and mind Bodean when he'd wanted to visit his mate. He would have been in shock – had that affected his statement?

Before the trial, I hadn't been allowed to speak to Coe about the assault. Now that the trial was over, he wasn't keen on revisiting the trauma of that night. I had to respect that. He did repeat one thing, though.

'I knew Garry did this to you, Mum. I saw it. I would have told them if they'd asked, but nobody asked. I'm sorry, Mum. It's my fault.'

Coe's statement had certainly skewed the events. But he hadn't let me down. Someone else had taken hold of the ball and run with it.

※

Following Neil's advice, I worked mainly from the affidavit to question the Department's case against me. The document had ended abruptly after five pages of rubbish. I wasn't sure if I had been given a copy of the whole affidavit; were there more pages? I needed to find out.

At the front desk of the Taree office, I asked to speak to Neil.

'He's not available,' said the woman behind the counter. She was young, sharp-faced and unfriendly.

'Maybe you can help me then,' I said, putting the affidavit down between us. I introduced myself and gave her a brief rundown of my situation. 'I'm doing some work on my case and I'm not sure if this is the last page of the document,' I said, flipping to the final sheet. 'Could you have a look in my file and tell me if I've got the whole thing?'

'You've already seen your file. Neil showed you when it arrived from Parkes.'

'I saw my file, but I wasn't allowed to read it. Could you take a look at this document and compare it to the copy in my file? I really need to know if I've got all the pages.' I kept my voice calm and reasonable. I even smiled. It made no difference.

'We can't do that,' she said, folding her arms.

Behind her, another officer was watching with mild curiosity.

'All I want is a yes or a no,' I said. 'Could you take a look? It's really important. Please.'

The woman glared at me. 'You've got your kids back, haven't you?'

'Yes,' I told her.

'I wouldn't make waves if I were you.'

Sometimes you can pinpoint a moment in time – a split second when you turn a corner or slide into an abyss. Over the past 18 months I'd experienced a number of life-altering moments. This was another: I was through with being dismissed.

I leaned across the counter until my eyes were centimetres from her powdered complexion.

'Can you see me clearly?' I asked.

She hesitated. 'Yes.'

'I've been on fire. I'm not scared of you, or your threats.' I paused for a moment and, in those few seconds, a vital connection became clear. Freedom of Information! Of course!

I opened my bag and found my purse, chequebook and pen while the officer looked on mutely. I wrote out a cheque for $15 – the concession amount for accessing information from the Government – and snapped it from the book. I slapped it down on the counter with my pension card.

'What are you doing?' she asked.

'I'll have the whole file now.' I slid the payment towards her, keeping my face expressionless. I was through smiling to these people.

'What? The whole thing?' she asked, looking astounded. 'It's huge!'

'You've got 28 days to deliver the whole file. Under the *Freedom of Information Act.*'

'Oh, but –'

'Twenty-eight days,' I repeated before turning on my heel and marching out.

We'll see who can't do this and can't do that. We'll see!

Sixteen

For a year and a half, my sister was unstinting in her support. Sitting by my hospital bed, battling DOCS on my behalf, giving my boys and me a home when we had nowhere else to go. But the increasing messiness of my life had wreaked its own havoc on the lives of those dearest to me, including Sissy and her family.

As I moved into the caravan with my sons and began to claw back my independence, the cracks in my relationship with Sissy began to show. Coe, Bodean and I grew detached from our relatives inside the house. Apart from a nightly shower, the occasional use of the phone, or taking Jennifer and Patrick with us on weekend picnics, our lives became separated by a chasm of delayed stress and resentment. Returning from Garry's trial to hear that the Department of Housing had found a place for us was, therefore, good news for everyone.

At last things seemed to be looking up. I now had a home for my little family, but not in the infamous Housing Commission area of Taree as I'd assumed. Instead, my new home was in the nearby village of Wingham. As soon as the news came through, my boys and I jumped in our car, with Sissy and her family following, eager to see our new home.

Irvine Street was a quiet cul-de-sac across the railway track from the main part of town. There were only about eight houses in the tiny street, which ended in a grassy patch of vacant land complete with a creek and a makeshift bridge. My house was second from the end: a white, fibro cottage with mission-brown trim, a ragged patch of lawn and a circle of white painted rocks surrounding a pine. After living in a caravan for so long, it was like a palace.

While we waited for the house to be cleaned, painted and carpeted, my family made several visits. Mum and Clyde came down from Laurieton, and Dad and Bea travelled up from Sydney to inspect my new premises while the neighbours inspected us, peering out from behind faded curtains and over backyard fences.

Another armpit operation at Westmead had taken place a week before we moved in, allowing me to eventually perform a range of simple tasks I once took for granted: reaching up to higher shelves, pegging laundry without having to stand on a milk crate, brushing my hair and slipping clothes on without help.

John had picked up my furniture from Mum and Clyde's place while Sissy, the kids and I loaded the remainder of my family's possessions into the back of a trailer and made the short trip into Wingham. After dumping the shabby pile of boxes, bags and furniture in the middle of the lounge room, Sissy, Jennifer and Patrick drove back to their farm to resume some sort of normal life.

As I watched the empty trailer turn at the end of the street, I was struck by the feeling that all these years later, I was once again the pesky younger sister.

'Wave goodbye to Aunty Sissy and your cousins,' I said to Bodean, taking hold of his wrist and flapping it in the air.

Although I was elated to have my own place, I was also full of self-doubt. Would I be strong enough to cope by myself, with two boys to care for? According to the medical experts, my recovery was nothing short of miraculous. For someone who was never meant to walk or talk again, who was destined to spend the rest of her life in full-time care, I was aware of just how far I'd come through sheer stubbornness.

I still had my medical needs: Murelax to help me sleep in the face of nightmares and flashbacks, Panadeine Forte for pain management and Ventolin to help me breathe. I was also given Aurorix for depression after I'd implored my local GP to give me something to dry the tears up – I literally couldn't see where I was going. These chemical concoctions were one safety net and, until now, Sissy and John had been another. Now I was on my own.

'Just do what you have to do,' I told myself as I made my way back inside to the mound of possessions spread over the lounge-room floor and up the hallway.

Coe stood beside me and sighed, his adolescent face curled into a pimply scowl. 'How are we going to straighten this out? It'll take us forever.'

'We'll tackle it a box at a time,' I said. 'We should probably get Bodean's and your mattress into your rooms and make the beds up. I'll use the lounge until I can buy another mattress.' I moved over to where the two single mattresses had collapsed in the hallway. 'You take one end, Coe, and I'll take the other. Bodean, you get the pillows.'

'Mum! You're not allowed to lift anything. Remember?' Coe said.

I shrugged. 'We can't live like this waiting for my armpit to heal. Come on. A room to yourself, Coe, like old times.'

The boys and I tried to create some order from the chaos, but it was slow. Even finding the sheets and making the beds took almost an hour. By early afternoon, Bodean was ready for a nap. For once he didn't need too much persuading, keen to lie down in his new bedroom. At three o'clock I heard him stir and poked my head into his room.

He blinked up at me and stretched both arms out. 'Pick me up, Mummy. Pick up!'

I looked down at him and sighed. With my wasted muscles and frequent operations on my arms, it was a rare treat for Bodean to be picked up. It seemed I was constantly refusing him. 'Okay,' I said at last. 'Just this once. Mummy's arms are tired.'

I bent down slowly and reached under his arms to hoist him up. I knew as soon as it happened – as soon as I heard that sickening rip – but didn't let on to Bodean. I staggered across the narrow hallway and into the bathroom with him clinging to my hip and then lowered him gently to the floor.

'Sit on the toilet, Bodean. Mummy just needs to check something.'

Still blurry with sleep, he gave me a grumpy look and yawned. He complied though, and watched silently, pants around his ankles and bare legs dangling from the toilet seat as I stood in front of the mirror. I wriggled out of Mum's shirt and peeled back the dressings.

Perhaps it just needs a bit of patching, a bandaid or two, I thought, momentarily averting my gaze, trying to downplay the sting and throb of my armpit. I lifted my right arm up. A bandaid? Who was I kidding? My new skin graft had ripped, bursting the newly healed edges and leaving a gaping hole, like a vivid slash in a lump of raw steak. If I'd been so inclined I could have inserted a finger or two, right up to my second joints. A faint metallic whiff floated up from my armpit, the smell of blood. The wound hadn't started to seep, but it wouldn't be long.

'Oh Christ,' I whispered. 'Christ, Christ, Christ!' I eased myself down on the cold edge of the bath, feeling suddenly faint. A fat spring blowfly buzzed around the low ceiling as Bodean slipped off the toilet and perched beside me.

'Coe!' I called. 'Can you come here for a minute?'

Coe stuck his head around the door. 'What's up?' His brow creased as he looked down at me, hunched and shaking. 'Are you right, Mum?'

'I'm okay. Just take a look under my arm, will you. Tell me if it's as serious as I think.'

Coe bent his head to check the wound as I lifted my arm up. 'Oh, Mum!'

I clamped my arm back down to stem the blood flow and stood up slowly, steadying myself on the doorjamb. 'Come on, boys. We're going for a drive.'

Dr Pederson, my GP, injected shots of local anaesthetic deep into the fleshy, damaged cave of my underarm, stitched everything back together, placed my arm in a sling and folded it over my chest.

'No more lifting,' he warned as we left the surgery. 'Go home and rest.'

※

The following day, with Coe straightening his room and Bodean following me like a shadow, I decided to tackle the laundry. A load of washing had to be done and would take my mind off the lounge room: it was worse than ever after one-armed hunts for kettles, mugs, toilet paper, clothes and towels.

I loaded the machine with a bundle of the kids' clothes. I soon had a slow, creaky rhythm going: bend down, grab an item, straighten up, drop it in the tub. Bend, grab, straighten, drop.

'Bodean, want to play a game? Help Mummy throw clothes in the washing machine.'

The hot water tap wasn't connected and I didn't have the strength or the tools to rectify this, so cold water was going to have to do. Returning a while later, I discovered the machine hadn't emptied the final lot of rinse water: the clothes lay submerged in several litres of grey liquid. Why did everything have to be so bloody difficult? There was an old margarine container under the sink so I fetched this and proceeded to bail out the water with my free hand.

I'd been going for about ten minutes – bend, dip, straighten, tip – when there was a loud knock on the door.

'What now?' I grumbled, turning the handle.

Mum and a pink-faced Clyde stood on the doorstep. Clyde was mopping his bald head with a handkerchief, murmuring something about it being hot for September. Mum wasn't listening. She was staring at my immobilised arm. 'I knew something was wrong. Told you, Clyde,' she said, clamping her lips together and shaking her head. 'What have you done to your arm? And where's your sister?'

I stepped back to let them in. 'I busted it open. Now the washing machine won't empty. I'm trying to bail the water out.'

Mum followed me into the laundry. I picked up the margarine container and nodded towards the troublesome machine. 'I'll have to empty it somehow.'

'Give me that,' said Mum, snatching the container. 'Why isn't the hot water connected? John should've done that before he left.'

'Oh, Mum, they've done enough. I can't keep relying on them.'

Mum turned and gave me a look before hoisting the sodden mass of clothing into a plastic laundry basket. Clyde, ever the gentleman, offered to wring and hang the clothes out. Mum and I left him to it and headed back to the lounge room to survey the chaos.

'We can't have this bloody mess,' said Mum, pulling her sleeves up and ripping open the nearest garbage bag. 'At least I can make a start.'

'I've got news for you: I haven't stopped.'

Mum waved me away. 'Clear off and go put the kettle on, love. Make us a cuppa.'

Clyde came back inside and he and Mum went to work, unpacking boxes and bags, putting away crockery and cutlery, pots and pans, assembling the bunk beds and moving furniture.

I had a wardrobe, kitchen cupboards and a linen press, but little storage space for the boys. Mum and Clyde returned the next week with a cupboard, and Di Hannigan, an old friend from Orana Heights, sent her husband up with a wardrobe for each of the boys. Dad and Bea came to stay and put up hooks and curtain rods. He bought me new sheets and towels and several boxes of groceries. I tackled one box or bag each day until the last item was finally packed away in its correct cupboard, shelf or wardrobe.

Even with all the help, my household was still lacking many basic necessities. The day John, Sissy and I had packed up the Geurie house, I could only to take what would fit in the small truck, and many things had been left behind and sold. Now, with no money to spare, I had little choice – I had to seek out charity. *Do what you have to do. Do what you have to do to get to the end.* This was my new mantra.

Mum came with me to see a Smith Family representative in Taree. At least I had my mantra; Mum just had her embarrassment.

'You definitely qualify, dear,' the stout, grey-haired lady assured me as she handed back details of my pension. 'What a terrible time you've had, losing everything. And such horrific injuries.' Behind her glasses her eyes brimmed with tears, which she fought to control. It was a nice change to have someone else weeping instead of me. She took a shaky breath and continued. 'You are entitled to two singlets each for your boys, two pairs of socks, two pairs of shoes, two pairs of undies, and two bras for yourself, two jumpers –'

'I think we're probably right for clothes,' I said, smiling across as Mum squirmed beside me.

'But I can see you're very needy, dear. This is what we're here for,' she said, leaning forward. 'And when the weather warms up, you can come back for your summer clothes. Two of everything.' She patted my hand. 'You're also entitled to a Christmas hamper, dear. A tinned ham, pudding, a cake –'

'Really, we don't need food,' I interrupted. 'There are others worse off than me.'

The lady looked disappointed. 'Well, it's up to you ...'

'There are some things you can help me with. I need a single bed for my teenage son and a mattress for me. If you could find us something, I'd be grateful.'

She beamed at me until the corners of her eyes crinkled. 'It would be our pleasure to find you a double bed and a base as well as a bed for your son. We deliver free as well. And I didn't mention before but we can put the phone on for you, and also pay your bond.'

Mum tut-tutted and shook her head. I kicked her under the desk.

'Mum!' I said, as we walked outside. 'You look like you've been sucking on lemons. I'll do what I have to do!'

Mum wouldn't look at me, but stared straight ahead, clutching her shopping basket. 'I never thought I'd see the day when my daughter was reduced to begging. That's not how we brought you up.'

It was true. When Sissy and I were kids, we didn't dare ask for anything, especially from other people. Not even a drink of water. But times had changed.

'If I have to rely on charity, Mum, then so be it.'

'Next thing you'll be rattling a bloody tin on the street corner.'

'Knock it off, Mum.'

She didn't hear me though. She was suddenly glaring at two little girls who'd turned and gawked at my face.

'What are *you* looking at?' she asked.

'They don't mean it, Mum. They're just curious.'

In October, my victim's compensation money came through. I had been awarded the maximum amount at the time: $50,000. People continue to be surprised by this, assuming that with my injuries I'd be worth millions. Not so. I had even met with a compensation lawyer about it.

'Car accident?' he'd asked.

I shook my head.

'House fire?'

'No.'

'Accident at work?'

'No.'

'How did it happen then?'

'My boyfriend did it to me. At home. In my backyard.'

'Has he got any money? Assets?'

'No.'

His shoulders dropped. 'Sorry to say, but you're worthless.'

As a victim of crime, unless my perpetrator was filthy rich, the $50,000 government compensation was the only thing available. Still, this money gave me the start I needed, and I was grateful for it. Apart from much-needed household items, I bought a brand new red Mazda and a lawnmower, as well as a carport and a garden shed in flat packs, both of which Dad erected for me. I bought a computer and a new desk for Coe, to help with his schoolwork, and a bike with trainer wheels for Bodean. I also paid legal fees accrued during my fight to regain my kids, around $10,000 in all. I put money aside in a holiday fund, for my boys to go to the snow the following year. I hadn't forgotten my hospital wish list, and now that I had a decent car there'd be no stopping us. A car meant escape, freedom. My dad had taught me that.

There was another item on my wish list that I didn't need a lot of money for. A handful of coins bought me a large bag of sunflower seeds and, after a determined afternoon clearing an overgrown garden plot at the back of the house, the boys and I planted the entire bag. Being used to dry Geurie, I figured that only a small percentage of the seeds would germinate, so why not sprinkle the small black seeds thickly over the soil?

Every single seed sprouted; I soon had a sunflower jungle in my backyard, a sea of flapping green leaves beneath giant yellow discs. All through that first spring and summer, as each batch of plants sagged and died, we pulled up the shrivelled stalks and replenished the garden bed with fresh seeds, watching the plants' progress. Our cat sneaked through the greenery each evening at dusk, watched by the boys and some neighbourhood kids who, with nothing better to do, gravitated towards our small family.

As we settled into our new life, I waited for news of my DOCS file. Finally, on 18 October 1995, I was able to collect a copy of it from the Taree office.

There were pages missing – cover sheets, duplicate pages, details of the Department's legal costs, and referee information on Sissy and John. The details of the person who'd originally notified DOCS were also removed; I don't know why. I already knew the notifier to be a health official, clearly named on the cover sheet of Maria William's affidavit, the document I had received the previous year from my solicitor, the document I was working from to construct my complaint. So much for the Department's assurances about keeping notifier details a secret.

My file was fat but by page nine I was already convicted. According to DOCS, I was an abusive parent. Not alleged, but stated as fact. The investigation/assessment summary read as follows:

347740 BLAKEMORE, COE
MALE 00/00/1982 PARKES
FOR NOTIFICATION DATE: 02/04/1994 TIME: 18:00
ASSESSMENT DETAILS:
ASSESSMENT COMMENCEMENT DATE: 05/04/1994 TIME: 09:30

ACTUAL ABUSE:

PRIMARY ABUSE CODE: E67 PARENT'S EMOTIONAL STATE
THREATENS CHILD

SECONDARY ABUSE CODE: E79 OTHER EMOTIONAL

ASSESSING STAFF: 9316960 WILLIAMS, MARIA CLARE

ABUSE DETAILS:

N/M AND DEFACTO INCINERATED THEMSELVES IN FRONT OF
COE AND SLOSHED PETROL ON BODINE. COE HAS BEEN
EMOTIONALLY ABUSED OVER A NUMBER OF YEARS AS A RESULT OF
BOTH HIS PARENT'S ALCOHOL ABUSE. COE HAS HAD A MAJOR ROLE
IN CARING FOR BODINE.

It had taken the Department three days and eight pages, or four if you discounted the cover sheets, to find me an abusive parent. How had this happened, this swift condemnation? Where was the investigation?

It appeared Coe's words, sprinkled with inaccuracies, were then distorted by various adults, who put their own spin on his recollections.

During the tussle over the petrol container, fuel had been spilled. Accidentally. Garry had then flung petrol in my face and down my front. Deliberately. This was somehow translated as Garry and I dousing each other. Garry then pulled a lighter out of his back pocket and set me alight. This had been interpreted as mutual, deliberate incineration. We did not 'slosh petrol over' Bodean, deliberately or otherwise. The police had already ascertained that Bodean had no petrol on him.

I remembered that, when Bruce Levet had told me 'DOCS believe you did this to yourself', I had passed it off as a ridiculous misunderstanding that would be cleared up by speaking to the police on the case. How wrong had I been?

Apart from the notifier's inaccurate statement, there had been a few well-chosen comments from Denise, the concerned aunt who wasn't exactly sure how old Bodean was. Coe had lived with his paternal grandparents up until the age of five, she said. Untrue. I was an alcoholic, she said. Untrue. Coe did most of the basic caring for Bodean, Bodean had no speech, Bodean had not asked for his mother, she said. All untrue.

In the file, it was recorded that Denise expressed concerns about the boys' futures. She was worried that when I was well, the children would automatically be returned to my care. The Department assured her that this would not necessarily be the case.

Denise's simpering words rang in my head, over and over. 'They're your kids, Donna. I never wanted to keep them. I'm just looking after them until you're okay.'

So a few wildly inaccurate comments from Denise, and a traumatised 12-year-old's statement interpreted by a health worker had led to me being labelled abusive? Shouldn't there be a mound of paperwork leading up to such a conclusion? Not as far as DOCS were concerned. They did things differently, it seemed, back to front.

After they'd already convicted me, they decided to interview a small collection of biased individuals. Convict me *then* selectively gather comments to fit a faulty conclusion. Did they interview my boss or my work colleagues? No. Did they interview any of the 800-odd parents of the kids I'd taught over a decade and a half? No. Did they speak to Coe's teachers or Bodean's day-care mother? The family doctor? No, no and no. Did they speak to the investigating police officer, Frank Kuiters? Family friends? The general Geurie community? Did they even speak to the bar staff at the bowling club to ask about my drinking on the day in question? No. Did they interview my parents, stepparents or sister? Not then, not before I was convicted. And when Mum, Dad and Sissy separately informed DOCS that I didn't incinerate myself, did DOCS investigate? No – why record anything contrary to the decision already made?

Even if they didn't bother with my character references, did they seek character references for Denise? How suitable a carer was she? What about the neighbours' stories of drunken parties and police visits? When my sister was interviewed *after* the original care order went to court, she had to submit references, affidavits, house plans and photographs of every room in their house in an effort to convince DOCS of her suitability as a carer. Interesting, considering that at Denise's place, my sons ended up sharing a bedroom with two other boys and, on some weekends, three grandchildren, making seven children in all.

As in the affidavit, Denise Blakemore had been the main informant, with a few nods from Ann Blakemore, my mother-in-law. Brian didn't say anything for or against me, but this had been dismissed by the Department as his being protective of me. Constable Adderley, who had seen me once in the car with Garry and had been phoned twice for assistance with Brian, had plenty to say 'off the record'. The man didn't even know I was a teacher. The Fords, relatives of the offender, also put in their two cents' worth. My life and those of my children had been in the hands of these five biased, ill-informed individuals. It was extraordinary.

Throughout the great wad of forms and notes, I had been labelled an abusive mother over and over. I suddenly realised all the people who had been told, incorrectly, that I had incinerated myself: Dr Mulcahy, who had examined Bodean on behalf of DOCS; psychologist Janet Webster; the Parkes Children's Court and Magistrate; my solicitor, Ann Kinghan, and barrister, Bruce Levet; Westmead Hospital staff; various DOCS officers, members of my family. The list seemed endless.

As thick as it was, there were many pages photocopied and inserted more than once in the file, giving the initial impression of a thorough investigation. I noted also that there were documents missing from the records: letters from my sister requesting access visits; my written complaint about Bodean calling Denise Mummy; another complaint about Coe being rebaptised without my consent; the report to the DOCS hotline of Brian snatching the boys back in the latter part of 1994; and my phone calls about access requests.

Now armed with my entire file, apart from half a dozen or so pages, I continued to work on my complaint to the minister, gathering hospital records, affidavits, newspaper clippings containing police statements, and photographs of my scarring. I also included character references, sending additional ones as I gathered them over the long months to come.

DOCS had collected their thin package of poison. I, in turn, gathered dozens and dozens of endorsements from the people that the Department failed to interview.

There were comments on my drinking habits:

I have never seen this lady intoxicated or out of control.

She has never been called before the Board of Directors, or asked to leave the club's premises because of misconduct or from intoxication.

I have, on occasion, shared some champagne with Donna and have observed her use of alcohol to be moderate and appropriate, with no adverse personality or behavioural effects.

On my parenting:

To accuse Donna of child abuse is ridiculous. I have seldom seen anyone who gives more, or better quality, to their children than Donna. She is fiercely protective of her boys – and they are really well behaved children who have been raised to understand and appreciate values. Her boys have been taught practical household skills and organisation and they competently share the chores ... They are really nice boys – raised with love, expectations and consequences.

As a mother she has always put her children first. The children were always well dressed, very well mannered and never did I see her children out roaming the streets unsupervised as were some children in Geurie.

Her love, devotion and caring of her sons Coe and Bodean was always her first priority.

On my general character:

She is a very community-minded person, always the first to offer assistance to anyone in need and always participating in community events.

She always has the welfare of others as a priority, whether it be children or adults.

I feel that if there were more people with the character that Donna has, our small village of Geurie could only thrive and benefit.

I knew, as did my referees, that the Department had got it wrong. And they continued to get it wrong, even after they were informed of their mistake. I was well aware that, if I had died, my children would have been brought up to believe I had never loved them.

At the time of being deemed an alcoholic, abusive mother, I lay in hospital, with no chance of defending myself. Now, I had to set the record straight. I wanted an apology. I wanted procedures to be improved and my files to be corrected. I wanted the workers involved to be reprimanded. I wanted financial assistance for the legal fees I had accrued due to the Department's erroneous investigation. What happened to me should never happen to another victim and their family.

On 31 October 1995, I sent my 25-page complaint to the Minister for Community Services, Mr Dyer. I included another 20-odd pages of evidence to support my concerns.

I knew I had a choice. With my children back, I could let it go or I could push on. It wasn't in my nature or my upbringing to accept such injustice.

I'd been in training for this my whole life. I decided to push on.

Seventeen

Dubbo's Courthouse, Police Station and Department of Public Prosecutions sat in a neat official cluster, three corners of an administrative Bermuda Triangle. I stood in the centre of it. I was back in the Central West for a reason: to sort out the reduction in Garry's charge, the casual swapping of the words 'maliciously' and 'negligently'. Seeing as no one could give me a straight answer over the phone, I decided to front up to the DPP in person. I also had an appointment to speak to Constable Matt Adderley, now based in Dubbo, about his part in the DOCS disaster.

I hadn't wanted to make this trip. I knew the drive would be interminably long, with frequent stopping to relieve the rubbing and jarring of my new skin, and the aching of my joints, cramped behind the wheel. Travelling for 12 hours in February, dressed in my burns suit and without sweat glands, was like being locked in a pressure cooker.

Apart from the journey itself, there was also the prospect of having to deal with officialdom. For days before I left, I argued with myself:

'Just let it go, Donna. Why put yourself through it?'

'But it's not right. I need answers.'

'Don't bother. Who's going to listen to you?'

'I'll be sorry if I don't go. After the sentencing it'll be too late.'

'It's already too late.'

'Get up! Get dressed! Stop whingeing. Just do what you have to do.'

I wasn't angry – I'd been angry too many times since hospital and the anger sucked all my energy. Nowadays I needed what little energy I had just to force myself out of bed each morning. The change in Garry's charge made me feel betrayed rather than angry; disappointed by a system that was there to protect the victims and punish the perpetrators.

Large towns like Dubbo have their own DPP with a solicitor and crown prosecutor, and a particular pecking order. Roger Montgomery, the solicitor for the DPP, had been handling my case, and was one of the three suits I had spoken to on the day of Garry's trial.

The solicitor for the DPP gave me an impatient look as he took a seat behind his polished desk. Shirl sat next to me for moral support.

'What can I do for you, Donna?' He stooped over a heap of paperwork.

'I want some answers about the downgrading of Garry's charge from "maliciously" to "negligently".'

He sighed, leaned back in his chair and clasped his hands behind his neck. 'As I told you on the phone, the charge was never changed. That's what he was charged with, and that's what he pleaded guilty to.'

'But he was charged with "maliciously inflicting grievous bodily harm".' I could feel my heart beginning to race. Shirl was sitting still as a post, even more out of her depth than I was.

'No,' Roger said sharply. 'He was charged with, and pleaded guilty to, "negligently inflicting grievous bodily harm" and that's the charge we accepted.'

'But that's not right,' I insisted. 'Even my court subpoena had "maliciously". Was there some sort of deal struck?'

'I'm telling you straight out that there was no "deal".'

'All the way through, I've been informed that it was "maliciously". Frank even said "maliciously". He said he knew what he'd charged Garry with.'

'That's right,' Shirl piped up. 'I was there after the hearing. Frank said "maliciously".'

Roger folded his arms. 'You must have misheard.'

'I didn't mishear. I wrote it down. I'd never heard of the charge "negligently". The first I knew of it was when it appeared in the newspaper.'

'He was charged with "negligently inflicting grievous bodily harm". That's what he pleaded guilty to, and that's what we accepted,' Roger repeated.

I stared back at him dumbly. There was no way I was getting past his brick wall.

'If you've got any problems,' he continued, 'Frank's in town on a case. He's across the road at the courthouse. Go and have it out with him.'

'Well, it's just …' I faltered and looked down at my lap.

'You've misunderstood. Your offender pleaded guilty as charged.' He was leaning forward now, enunciating each word with exaggerated clarity like I was an imbecile.

'Okay, I'll go and see Frank then.' I reached for my bag. Why had I bothered to make this trip?

'Oh, by the way, we received those inclusions you sent us – the extra documents for your victim's impact statement.'

I leaned back in my seat again. 'Good. I thought it was important for the judge to see photos of how I used to look as well as how I look now, and I put in some character references for him to read. I know I didn't need to write a formal letter to him, but I decided it was a good way of really explaining how the crime changed my life and my children's lives, giving him specific examples –'

Roger interrupted with a wave of his hand. 'That stuff's all irrelevant, unnecessary and unqualified. It won't be given to the judge, and neither will the victim's impact statement. The case doesn't warrant it.'

I was stunned. 'But how will he know how I've been affected? I've lost everything!'

'He's got medical records.'

'How will that tell him about the career I've lost, about not being able to return to my home, with the offender living across the road, about my –'

'It's all irrelevant,' he repeated bluntly. 'The court's not interested in knowing you as a person.'

'I can't believe this!'

Roger seemed unaffected. 'If that upsets you, you'd better prepare yourself. The offender will probably get a good behaviour bond.' He shrugged.

It was then that I snapped.

'If my victim's impact statement isn't going to be passed on, I want the judge to look into my eyes before he gives the man who did this a good behaviour bond.'

Roger snorted. 'That's not going to happen. The judge won't be seeing you.'

'What? I'm not allowed to go to court?'

'I suppose you can sit in the public gallery.'

'You're saying I can sit in the back of the court? That's so insulting.'

'The judge may see you from there. Then again, he may not.'

'This isn't good enough,' I said. 'I want to be seen and heard. I want to take the stand.'

Roger stood up, putting an end to the meeting. 'Victims do not ask to be seen and heard. Victims certainly do not request to take the stand. They go *away* and get counselling.'

'I thought you were meant to be on Donna's side,' Shirl muttered.

I realised later that Roger's refusal to take my document to the judge was actually lucky. If my victim's impact statement had been accepted, I would have left Roger's office and gone home satisfied that the judge would get to know my side of things. But the judge was not going to read what I had to say.

Shirl and I found Frank across the road in the courthouse. He was standing in the long corridor where victims and perpetrators were meant to wait. It brought back sharp memories of the previous August, when I had refused to sit there, feeling like a criminal, waiting for Garry to appear.

Frank, dressed smartly in a dark grey suit, looked burly and self-assured, but his face lit up when he saw me. 'Donna! Geez, you're looking good.' He patted me on the arm. 'It's great to see the improvement. I can't believe you're the same person who came hobbling into the police station to make a statement all those months ago.'

I felt immediately relieved to be face to face with someone so supportive but professional. I trusted Frank; surely he could get to the bottom of this mess.

'What brings you here, anyway?' he asked.

I launched into my explanation. 'I tried to have it out with Roger, but he just kept repeating the same old line – that's what he was charged with, that's what he pleaded guilty to, that's what we accepted.'

Frank looked grave. 'To tell you the truth, I'm surprised he pleaded guilty to anything, considering the lack of evidence.'

My jaw dropped. 'Lack of evidence? You're kidding me?'

'You were both fighting over the petrol, Donna.'

'I was fighting all right, but not for the petrol. I was fighting for my life.'

'I took Coe's statement and I talked to you. Even after your interview I wasn't sure we had enough to charge Garry.'

'Coe was trying to protect Garry; the police were informed of that. As for my statement, I know it was lousy. I'm not an expert in giving statements!'

'That's normal, Donna. I know that.'

'Anyway, you would have had information from other witnesses. Neighbours, people in Geurie, the ones at the club that day – they saw the beginnings of Garry's temper. And the ambulance driver, George Harper. I told him who did it. I really struggled to tell people. I screamed out to the nurses too; it's in my hospital records. They informed the police.'

Frank did not comment on this. 'Don't forget, Garry was seriously wounded as well.'

'He caused his own injuries. I didn't have a choice over mine.' I waved my hand in front of my face and chest. 'I think I win the scarring competition, Frank.'

'Anyway, as far as the change in charge goes, this happens all the time. We investigate, do our brief, play our role in the whole thing, then we hand it over to the DPP and it's out of our control.'

'What do you mean?'

'The DPP can take bits out, cull it, reduce our investigation. If they think any part of our evidence is irrelevant, out it goes. We get fed up with it. We chase these criminals, get a case against them, hand it to the DPP, thinking, "Great, it's gone to court, the offender will be found guilty, put behind bars." Then three months down the track we're in the middle of another investigation only to find we're chasing the same offender.'

'How does that happen?' Shirl asked.

'Things go on after we hand the brief over to the DPP.'

'Was there some sort of charge bargain?' I asked. 'Because if there was, Roger's denying it.'

Frank shrugged. 'They say it doesn't happen. I'll tell you one thing, though. I'll stand by what I said to you and your family that day after court. It was "maliciously". You even wrote it down.'

'Roger reckons I misheard you.'

'You didn't mishear.'

'You haven't heard the worst of it yet,' I said. 'They're not going to accept my victim's impact statement.'

'Again, I'm not surprised. Anyway, if it is "negligently", it only carries a maximum of a two-year jail sentence, victim's impact statement or not.'

I stared at him. 'You've got to be joking.'

Frank pulled a face. 'I know, it doesn't seem right. I mean, look at you.'

'Thanks.'

'Well, you know what I mean ...' He cleared his throat and fiddled with his tie.

'Roger reckons Garry could get off with a good behaviour bond.'

'That's possible.'

'I really believe that the judge would think twice about a good behaviour bond if he saw me. For him to see me, I have to take the stand. How do I do that?'

Frank looked stunned. 'I don't know. A victim is only called as a witness if the offender doesn't plead guilty. I've never heard of a victim requesting to take the stand when they don't need to.' He scratched his head. 'I don't know how you arrange to take the stand. But that doesn't mean it can't be done.'

But that doesn't mean it can't be done. If Frank hadn't said those eight words, I would have gone home satisfied I'd done my best. But these words changed my thinking. I *could* take the stand; I just had to find the correct procedure. I had to find the right person to ask.

'Donna, before you go, everyone knew he did it to you, despite the lack of concrete evidence. It was a shitty thing to happen. I wish you didn't have to go through all this.'

Was it lack of evidence that eroded the case or was it charge bargaining? Or a bit of both? Whatever the answer was, there was little I could do at this stage to change things. My last hope for any sort of justice lay in fighting to be seen and heard in court.

I called a friend with legal expertise.

'I've got a problem.' I ran through the whole story.

'You can't change the acceptance of a guilty plea,' he said.

'I know that, but perhaps I can give the judge something to think about. My victim's impact statement isn't going to be handed over, so I need to physically be in court. And not up the back. I need to take the stand. What do I have to do?'

'That's easy,' my advisor said.

'Really? Nothing's been easy so far.'

'Put your request in writing and present it to the DPP. Make sure they date-stamp it, and make sure you get a copy. And don't say I told you.'

'Why didn't Roger tell me what to do?'

'He probably has his own reasons, Donna. I'm sure you can work it out.'

I could work it out all right. If Garry had not pleaded guilty and I had walked into court as a witness for the prosecution, a jury would have been horrified. It's likely they would have hung, drawn and quartered him. The defence knew that the best thing for their client was to keep me out of court. They could do this by getting Garry to plead guilty to something.

A guilty plea was also very convenient for the DPP. The alleged offender pleading guilty would save them time and taxpayers' money. A guilty plea for a lesser charge – a fair swap and no one will have to see the victim. Everyone wins.

I was about to put a spanner in the works.

If I appeared in court at the sentencing, and especially if I took the stand, the judge was bound to wonder why the charge was only "negligently", and why it was accepted by the DPP. His suspicions would be aroused. Were the defence and the DPP in cahoots?

With my written request to take the stand, I returned to the office of the DPP with Shirl in tow. Roger came out to the reception desk, looked at me then at the paper I was holding. His eyes narrowed.

He held up his hand. 'I don't want that. You don't want to do this.'

'I'm requesting to take the stand. Here's my letter.' I placed the paper on the counter between us. 'I want it date-stamped and I want a copy.' I gave him a stony look; I would not smile at this man.

'No! You don't want to do this. Do you realise you'll be subjecting yourself to cross-examination?' He sounded as if I'd be subjecting myself to pack rape, he was so vehement. 'You'll be ripped to shreds!'

I would not be sidelined. 'I want it date-stamped,' I repeated. 'Now, please.'

'But they'll be able to cross-examine you over every part of this. I'm warning you, you don't want to go through that.'

'Is it any worse than being set on fire?'

Roger gave a heavy sigh, leaned across the counter and took the request.

How fortunate that I had blundered along the right path! Like finding out about the victim's impact statement, I had stumbled onto the fact that I could request to take the stand. Asking questions and being persistent were qualities I had always encouraged in the classroom, but they shouldn't be required as a victim in the legal system. We have the right to be informed about options and processes; we shouldn't have to blunder.

I had finished with Roger for the moment. Constable Matt Adderley was next on my list.

'Can I help you, madam?'

'My name's Donna Blakemore. I'm here to see Matt Adderley. I have an appointment.'

The police officer consulted the book in front of him. 'Ah, yes. Take a seat, madam. Constable Adderley won't be long.'

He soon appeared and led us into the bowels of the station to an interview room. The room was small and stuffy; there was no desk. Matt wore his uniform and sat with his legs apart, his elbows on his knees and his hands clasped in front of him. He leaned forward slightly. He was just as I'd remembered him: tall, blond, clean-cut. Today he seemed vaguely defensive. He certainly didn't look compassionate or sorry.

'I've come to see you about what you said to Maria Williams, the DOCS officer.'

'Yes, I got your correspondence, and it's been dealt with as a letter of complaint. I think you outlined your concerns pretty thoroughly.' His face remained expressionless.

'I wanted to see you face to face, to get some answers and make sure you understood what you did.'

'Yes, go on.'

'I have Maria Williams' affidavit here.' I pulled the document out of my bag. 'I don't know you that well, Matt, and I don't think you know me very well either.'

He was cocky. 'I don't know about that.'

'You'd been in Geurie for around three years before the assault? During those years, the only contact I had with you was when I was parked in the car with Garry; when I called you and you came around because Brian was throwing bottles through the window; when I phoned you after Brian gave me a black eye; and the following morning, when I called around to apologise for waking you. You said something like, "Don't worry, Donna. That's what I'm here for." You asked me what I was going to do. I told you Brian was leaving, and you replied that it was a good thing.'

'Yes, I remember.'

'Besides that, you didn't know me. You didn't socialise at the club; you didn't play bowls or cricket or attend other community functions. You had no other contact with me. I doubt if you even knew what I did for a living.'

The constable shifted in his seat and looked away.

'You weren't on the case, and you shouldn't have been talking to anyone about it, whether you were part of the investigating team or not.'

I was referring to Maria Williams, but I was also aware that Matt had been gossiping with some of the Geurie locals about the case. 'Matt keeps us informed,' someone had said to Shirley. I had passed this on to Frank, who was furious. Sometime later, Matt transferred to Dubbo.

'Yeah, well, if you mean Maria Williams, I was allowed to talk to her,' he said. 'She was a DOCS officer, after all, and I was concerned about Coe's wellbeing.'

'She rang and told you she was Maria Williams from the Department of Community Services. But how did you know?'

'What do you mean?'

'It could have been anyone. It could have been a journalist.'

'Yeah, but she was who she said she was.'

'In this case.' I looked at him and he averted his eyes. 'Anyway, what makes you such an authority on my life?'

'I used to see you with that Yvonne Ford, in the car, on weekends.'

'Yes?'

'With all those kids.'

'Did you know where we were going? I had my two boys; she had her grandchildren. We used to take them on picnics – yabbying, fishing – that sort of thing. I spent a lot of time with my kids, you know. Did you ever see them out roaming the streets?'

'No, I can't recall seeing them.'

I looked down at the affidavit. 'You told Maria Williams that on the day of the assault, "Garry and Donna were drinking most of the day." How would you know that?'

'I don't remember saying that.'

'Well, here's another. You also said, "Donna and Brian Blakemore were always drunk and fighting." When did you see me drunk?'

'When I was called out to your place the night Brian was going berserk. You were drunk.'

'I was sober! I'd been home looking after the children and was fast asleep. I was in my pyjamas if you remember. I rang you for help.'

Matt glared at me and said nothing.

'And the night Brian gave me a black eye, I was sober then as well.' I checked the affidavit. 'Here's another quote: "Coe did most of the caring for Bodean, not too much responsibility on the part of the parents. On past performance, neither parent would be capable of caring for the kids." Do you remember that one?'

At this point, Matt's shoulders sagged, a tide of pink crept up his neck, and he began to stutter. 'But, but, oh, I thought – I thought, I suppose ...'

'Yes, you thought, but did you actually know?'

He hung his head. 'When I read all those references you sent, I was quite surprised.'

'You didn't know me. You got on the phone and made out you were an expert on my character, my parenting, my life with my children.'

He looked up at me, his face bright red. 'Look, I did say those things, Donna. I said them and I shouldn't have said them. I kept on telling her over and over that she should be asking other people. I also said a lot of things that aren't in that document. For instance, I suggested she contact your workplace, Coe's teachers, neighbours. I told her they'd be able to give her more information than I could.'

'You said the other things, though? The things I read out?'

'Yes, I did, and I'm sorry.' He shifted in his seat. 'I have to admit, I could never work out why you took up with Garry. He was a time bomb waiting to go off: aggressive and dangerous. He'd caused havoc in Wellington – removed from pubs, involved in high-speed chases on his bike. Up for indecent exposure too.'

I was taken aback. 'Really? I didn't know that.' I looked at Shirl. 'Had you heard that one?'

'News to me,' she said.

I turned back to Matt. 'Yes, for various reasons, I made a big mistake, and I have to go forward living with that.' Matt looked pleased at my admission. I hadn't finished though. 'However, I was the victim here, not the criminal. And I was *never* an abusive mother. And the thing is, Matt, you played a huge part in DOCS taking my children. It's true; they were deeply traumatised by the actions of a man I'd invited into our lives. I made a dreadful error of judgement. But their trauma was greatly compounded by the Department's care order, and I'm not going to let that one go. What you need to realise is that if my complaint to DOCS ends up in court, they'll be looking for someone to blame.'

The police officer drew himself up to his full height. 'I'm not scared of going to court. I'll stand by what I said.'

'That's good. They'll be looking for a scapegoat.' I tucked the affidavit in my bag and stood up. 'But I accept your apology.'

'As I said, it won't worry me if this ends up in court. By the way, because your complaint was sent to the powers that be, don't be surprised if you find a senior police sergeant on your doorstep about it.'

If this was another attempt by an official to scare me, he could take a ticket and expect a long wait. 'That would probably be Sergeant Barry Johnson. I've met him before. He's a nice man. Very professional.'

Eighteen

Garry's sentencing was scheduled for Friday, 8 March 1996, International Women's Day. With only one week to go, the DPP still couldn't tell me if my request to take the stand would be presented to the judge. On Monday I rang Brenda, my Witness Assistant Scheme Officer.

'I need to know.'

'Just a moment, Donna. Howard's in his office; I'll ask him.'

She came back after a few minutes, placating and slightly nervous. 'He's going to read over your file and let you know.'

Was I being fobbed off again? With the sentencing day looming, I needed a back-up plan in case my request was stymied. In desperation, I had two headshots of myself blown up to poster-size. One was from the year before the assault: smile lines fanned the corners of my eyes. The other, taken many months after, showed the same eyes set in a bewildered, scarred face. If I was unable to take the stand, my idea was to wave these pictures from the public gallery, creating a disturbance. Back in 1996, victims were not encouraged to attend sentencing, let alone draw attention to themselves.

With no further word from the DPP, I began ringing a variety of victim care services, some of which Brenda had told me about. One was Victims of Crime Assistance League, or VOCAL, which offered some interesting advice.

Just before the sentencing day, I rang the DPP once again.

'This is the last time I'm asking, Brenda. I need to know today, before I leave for Sydney.'

AUSTRALIA POST

WELLINGTON PO. 2820

COPY/DUPLICATE RECEIPT

MyPost Account $
New account
Registration date: 16-06-2015
MyPost number: 1006954030
Digital Receipt Requested.
TOTAL
Payment Not Required $0.00

Please retain this receipt until
you've received your MyPost card.

'I think they're wondering what you'll do if your request to take the stand isn't passed on, Donna.'

I took a deep breath. 'Tell them they'll be reading about themselves in the newspaper. They'll be hearing about it on the radio and seeing me on national television.'

Brenda went to pass my message on.

'Yes. The answer is yes. Howard is going to submit your request, Donna. But he said to tell you that, on the day, the judge could still refuse to see you. It's up to the judge.'

It's up to the judge. These words nagged at me as I headed towards Dad's place in Redfern. It was Thursday afternoon, the day before sentencing. My bluff about the media had brought an instant reaction. Perhaps media involvement was the way to go.

With the boys safely delivered to Dad, I eased myself back behind the wheel, already bone-tired and sore from the day's drive, and jangling with nerves over the thought of my first court appearance. At Surry Hills I walked into the *Daily Telegraph* office feeling at least a hundred. I was nervous. I'd never dealt with the media before and I'd heard how ruthless the press could be.

I asked to speak to a journalist. A young bloke appeared, his sleeves rolled up, his tie loosened. He exuded a crumpled sort of eagerness.

'Hi, I'm Andrew Burke. What can I do for you?'

I talked to him for what seemed like hours. He listened patiently, scribbling notes, nodding, sometimes shaking his head, occasionally clarifying. At one stage he brought out a packet of supermarket biscuits and coffee.

'I'm hoping this would make a good story,' I said when I'd finished.

'Yes!' He nodded enthusiastically, slapping his notebook down on the table.

'Seeing as I've given you a story, I was wondering if you could do something for me in return.' I looked at him over the top of my mug. Was this how one dealt with the media? I plunged on. 'If I'm *not* allowed to take the stand, I'd like you to write something about how the legal system treats victims, keeps them invisible. Future victims need to know, and the public needs to be aware of how it really is. And if Garry gets a good behaviour bond, perhaps something about lenient sentencing.'

'Sounds feasible,' Andrew said. 'And if you do take the stand?'

'If I'm allowed to take the stand, you could write a "well done" sort of thing, how good it is to see victims of crime being given a voice and a face. And if the judge gives the offender a jail term, congratulate the system for taking a stand against violence. I was a schoolteacher once. Sometimes, when you reward those doing the right thing, it can be more powerful than constant criticism.'

Andrew arranged for some photographs to be taken, and by the time I got back to Dad's place, a clear plan had formed in my head. If the judge said no, I would wave my photos from the public gallery, causing a scene. And I'd expose the bastards through the media. If I was allowed to speak, I'd simply read out my victim's impact statement.

The next morning, Dad drove Coe, Bodean, Mum and me to Penrith Courthouse. Roger Montgomery met us in the corridor outside the courtroom. He wore a pinstriped suit and carried a bunch of folders under his arm. His shoes gleamed.

'There you are, Donna!' he said, grinning. 'We've been looking for you. Howard's here too. We've come all the way from Dubbo especially for you. We don't usually do that, you know.' He waggled a finger at me. 'Usually we leave it up to the local guys, but we wanted to be here just for you.'

My relief must have been obvious. At last I was being looked after, and I wouldn't have an unfamiliar solicitor and prosecutor from Penrith dealing with my case.

'That's nice of you.'

Roger snapped into business mode. 'We need to go over a few points. On your behalf, Howard will mention your request to the judge in court. I received your last letter about the medication you're on now. We'll submit that, along with your retirement certificate showing your years of service, your loss of career, your loss of ability to earn income.'

'That's great. So it's all organised?'

'It's still up to the judge, Donna, but there are some things I need to reiterate to you if you *are* allowed to take the stand.'

'Oh good. This is all new to me. I've got no idea about court proceedings. I've got a plan though.' I fished around in my bag and pulled out a copy of my victim's impact statement. 'I'm going to read this letter.'

Roger's eyebrows shot up. He shook his head until I thought it was going to fall off. 'Oh no. No, no, no. You can't do that. You can't take that letter and read it. You can't take any paper whatsoever into the witness box.'

'Right then,' I said flatly. 'So I have to remember everything? Just talk on, without any props, about how my life has changed?'

Roger glanced at the courtroom before answering. 'Let's just say, the most important rule is only speak when spoken to. If someone asks you a question, you may answer it, but don't speak unless spoken to.' His eyes narrowed and he gave me a hard stare.

Once more, I could feel myself shrinking. I was a kid again – do as you're told; don't make trouble; they're the experts, not you.

'And by the way,' he added, 'don't go waving those photos around. That's not allowed either.'

Feeling stupid, I folded up my letter and tucked it back inside my handbag. I took a seat in the public gallery with my parents and the boys. Andrew Burke sat with us. By this stage I was trembling and overheated. My throat itched. I could feel the onset of a coughing fit. Why had I pushed to stand up and make a spectacle of myself? Dumb, dumb, dumb! To still my nerves, I focused on the fact that Roger and Howard had come all the way from Dubbo. They would set things right. They knew what they were doing. For a moment it seemed ridiculous that I had ever questioned them.

There were a lot of matters before the court that day, and the cavernous room was filled with all sorts of people waiting for their matters to be called before the judge. A sour hint of body odour wafted around me. I pressed my face into Bodean's hair and breathed in apple shampoo. As I straightened up, I noticed a man sketching, looking at me and then back at his pad, his pencil moving rapidly across the page. My face must have caught his attention.

Bodean had begun to wriggle and squirm. I took out my pen and began to draw, firstly to amuse him, and secondly to distract myself from the prospect of facing Garry for the first time in almost two years.

'You draw something,' I whispered, passing Bodean the pen.

He took the biro from me, thought for a moment then began to scrawl violent squiggles across the page. Andrew looked on.

'Do you want me to write a story with your picture?' I asked when Bodean was finished.

'Yes, please, Mum.'

'Okay. What is it then?'

'Fire, Mum. It's lots of fire.'

Andrew and I stared at each other over the top of Bodean's head. I had not spoken about the attack in front of my boys. I was under strict instructions not to, but Bodean knew. He knew.

Our matter was called early. As Garry had not yet appeared, the matter was stood down in the list to give him time to arrive, and my family and I stepped outside for a break. Andrew came with us.

Garry walked up the road towards the courthouse. He didn't see me but I saw him. I was struck by how well he looked. I had half-expected him to appear pale and gaunt, worn down by ongoing stress or remorse. But this wasn't the case. He walked jauntily, his shoulders back, bronzed face relaxed, like he was heading downtown to the pub on his day off. His hair was pulled back in a ponytail. He wore blue jeans, black boots and a black, long-sleeved shirt. The only sign of his injuries was the empty end of one sleeve, tucked neatly into the top of his jeans.

Garry's eyes were focused ahead as he walked along the footpath, squinting against the glare. I was glad he hadn't noticed me. Once again I was scared of him, and overwhelmed with shame. How stupid to get myself entangled with the likes of him, I thought.

With Garry now present, the matter of Regina versus Clynes was once again called. There was a flurry of movement and a flap of black gowns at the bar as people changed places. A murder of crows. Howard

Hamilton and Roger Montgomery had moved forward, along with the defence and their client.

I sneaked a look at Garry. He was staring straight ahead, poker-faced.

This change of DPP personnel was unusual and caught the judge's eye as he presided over the courtroom. 'What are you lot doing here? Who's running Dubbo Court?' He gave a small smile but his tone was not altogether friendly.

Was it unusual for Howard and Roger to be here? Should I be suspicious? Don't be ridiculous, I told myself. They know what they're doing. You're out of your depth.

Howard put forward my certificate of retirement from teaching and mentioned that I had requested to take the stand.

The judge's brow rippled. 'Really, I don't understand the reason for this request. I've got mountainous medical records pertaining to the victim.'

The defence jumped in eagerly. 'Yes, yes, I agree with your worship. The records are all there, for both parties.'

The judge peered down at Garry's legal team. 'I hope you're not implying that the victim doesn't have the right to request to take the stand?'

The defence lawyer back-pedalled. 'Oh no, your worship, I wasn't implying that at all.'

Damage done, the room lay silent. 'Call the witness,' the judge said at last.

The court officer appeared, and motioned for me to come forward. I focused on the judge, who stared back from his eyrie, his eyes growing wider as I approached.

I knew Garry was probably watching me, staring at the person I'd become. I faced him, searching for a sign of remorse. There was none. Instead he looked away.

I took the oath and sat down, feeling everyone's eyes on me. And I was hot, so hot. The judge was still watching. The microphone sat centimetres from my lips. My voice, in danger of complete collapse, would soon be booming around the entire courtroom. I waited. Speak when spoken to.

Howard stood before me, all bushy brows and florid cheeks. The wig made his face look fat, jowly. In the voice of a Shakespearean actor, he asked me to state my name and where I lived. He waved the certificate I had sent him and asked if this was a correct account of my years of service. He checked my current medication, and verified that I would have another operation on the 18th of that month, with a series to go. His questioning was closed, rapid and precise. He left me no opening to talk. When he said he had nothing further to ask, I felt something was not right.

It was the defence's turn now. I held my breath for the gruelling cross-examination. None came. They had no questions. I sat in the witness box with my mouth closed as instructed and my brain screaming. I could hear the rattle of my lungs. Someone in the gallery coughed. No one spoke. I felt as foolish as anyone could ever be made to feel.

Finally the judge broke the awful silence. 'Why did it take you nearly two years to resign from teaching?'

At the time I considered this a stupid question. Didn't he know I'd been otherwise occupied?

He moved on. 'I noticed your voice is very gravelly and breaks down easily. I suppose that would affect your ability to teach?'

'Yes, it does. My voice comes and goes. I have vocal cord damage. Sometimes I can talk, sometimes it fails me.'

'I can hear your breathing is laboured.'

'Yes, I have permanent lung damage; my trachea is narrowed because of the scarring.'

'So you wouldn't be able to project your voice in the classroom?'

'Not at this stage. To read stories and sing songs would be just about impossible. Sometimes I don't even have enough breath to get through a simple nursery rhyme for my son. I'm still having speech therapy. I used to take the grade for daily fitness too. I can no longer run, play or exercise due to airway damage and body restrictions.'

Through these questions the judge was allowing me to talk about the injuries.

'With my sweat glands burnt away, I can't cool down,' I added. 'I overheat easily, even without the body suit.' What else was in my statement? I didn't know it, but I *could* have requested to read my letter. I could have said I'd wanted to add something. I could have asked for a drink of water. I could have asked for a break. I could have done lots of things.

The judge asked me about further surgery. He enquired about my face.

'This is it, I'm afraid. I might be able to get a nose further down the track, but I'm not sure.'

His next comment was unexpected. 'It's noted that you were intoxicated on the day.'

'I went to the club to have a few birthday drinks. I wasn't rolling drunk. I'm a responsible drinker.' I felt blamed by his remarks. Did the judge think that if I hadn't been drinking, Garry would have behaved?

'Your birthday?' The judge was sifting through his papers. He looked up. 'I also note that you are a much older woman.'

'Yes, I am.' What else could I say?

With the brief questioning over, I made an impulsive decision. I *would* speak without being spoken to, and too bad if I got in trouble. I cleared my throat and plunged in. 'I just wanted to thank you for allowing a victim of crime to be seen and heard. It was good of you to give *this* victim of *this* crime such an opportunity.'

The judge was impassive. 'You may step down.'

Despite my little speech, I left the witness box angry and disappointed. I felt I had done very badly. I had not said all I'd needed to say. I had tried but failed.

The defence was now putting forward reasons why their client should qualify for a discount:

His mother and father were both deceased.

He had addressed his alcohol problem and seen a counsellor.

He had shown remorse by pleading guilty, sparing the victim undue stress and trauma.

He had suffered injuries himself.

He had no real 'Ned Kelly' record. (I presumed this meant he hadn't actually murdered anyone.)

He had no jail experience.

Being so young and defenceless, his safety in jail couldn't be guaranteed.

The defence continued, wringing sympathy for this poor naive man who had been taken advantage of by an older drunken woman.

My family and I listened, appalled, waiting for the DPP to charge forward and champion my own good character and reiterate my losses. But perhaps that only happened in the movies.

It was the judge who spoke next. He called the case 'a tragedy of enormous proportions' and the public would find it difficult to comprehend a two-year maximum sentence in this case. He said he needed more time to consider his decision, and court would adjourn until the following Thursday. 'But you,' he said, nodding towards Garry, 'You'll be a guest of Her Majesty's pleasure for the week.'

In the Crown Prosecutor's office, Howard and Roger were chuffed. They were strutting about, congratulating each other.

'That went really well!' Howard said, pulling off his wig and scratching his head.

'Really?' I said. 'You think it went well, did you? Why didn't you jump up and put *my* good character forward? The fact that I'm a respected citizen with no police record. And what about my losses, and my children's losses?'

Taking off his gown, Howard turned to me. 'Oh good God, Donna. We're not here to defend you or represent you in any way.'

'What are you here to do then?'

'We're here to represent the crime against society.'

'Wasn't I part of society once?'

He began shovelling papers into his briefcase.

Roger responded for him. 'The law's a funny thing. You'll never understand it. You ought to think yourself lucky he received a week in jail.'

'Lucky! I'll think of that every time I look in the mirror.' I turned on my heel.

※

Because the sentencing had not been finalised, Andrew Burke was unable to print the story we'd envisaged. 'Do you mind if I contact a colleague of mine about it?' he asked. 'Her name's Sandra Lee. She has a column in Saturday's paper.'

On Saturday, 9 March 1996, an article entitled 'Courage prevails, justice fails' was printed in the *Daily Telegraph*. The article included before and after photos of my face.

> Yesterday in Penrith District Court, Ms Blakemore, 39, stood a few metres away from Garry Clynes, the man who caused the hideous scarring when he splashed her with petrol on Good Friday, 1994. Guts.
>
> In the quieted courtroom with her 14-year-old son sitting in the public gallery ... Ms Blakemore spoke about wanting to be seen and heard. As a victim. She looked at Clynes – the first time in two years – but he looked away.
>
> 'I just want the judge to see me and see the damage that has been done to me,' she said.
>
> Her appearance was about victims' rights and justice. She wanted to be known and it is important to know her, like we should know all victims of horrific crimes. It makes them real.
>
> 'It went from a push to a shove to incineration,' Ms Blakemore said yesterday after her court appearance.
>
> '... Women sometimes feel it's their fault; it's women's lot. I advise women if they are abused, tell their friends, tell their family ... and seek support.'

The article went on to say that the initial charge of maliciously inflicting grievous bodily harm carried a maximum penalty of ten years in jail. It explained that Garry's charge had been reduced to negligently inflicting grievous bodily harm, the maximum sentence being a jail term of two years.

This same Saturday, I had taken my parents and Coe to a matinee performance of *Miss Saigon*. Do something hard, then do something nice, I figured. I left Bodean with Aunty Dassie and Uncle Ronnie. When it was time to pick him up, Uncle Ronnie met us at the door, his affable manner replaced by both irritation and excitement.

'The phone hasn't stopped ringing,' he said, throwing up his hands.

We followed him inside. 'What do you mean?'

'They've tracked you down. Ray Martin, Helen Wellings, someone from a radio station. You're in the paper you know.'

Bewildered, I sat down. Aunty Dassie stood behind me, one arm around my shoulders. She placed the article in front of me and the family crowded around to read over my shoulder.

'You're famous, Mum,' grinned Coe.

Back at Dad's place, it was no different. The phone wouldn't stop ringing. Suddenly everyone wanted me: radio programs, women's magazines, television stations. I had been dubbed 'the victim with attitude'. Perhaps I hadn't done so badly after all.

There are some men I like and some I love, but after the 'boy's club' of the legal system, I'd had a gutful of blokes. I made the decision to go with Channel Seven's *Today Tonight* and its female anchor, Helen Wellings.

The following day, I went to Balmain to meet with Helen and her assistant, Laura Sparkes. I explained that I wanted the plight of victims of crime to be made public. I wanted the opportunity to get the message out there, loud and clear: anyone suffering abuse should take action immediately, before it was too late. The crew would come to my place the next morning to begin filming.

I drove back to Wingham with Mum and the boys. We arrived to the sound of the telephone. It was Laura from *Today Tonight*.

'We're here,' she said, her voice low, conspiratorial.

'What do you mean, "here"?'

'We're here in Wingham.'

I resisted the temptation to draw back the curtain and take a peek into the darkened cul-de-sac. 'You beat us home? Did you come by helicopter?'

'You've got no idea what it's like, Donna. We've had jobs lined up and turn up only to find our opposition's been and gone, with our story. If you think the legal system is bad, the world of media is dog eat dog, take my word for it.'

'You're not out the front are you?'

'No, but we'll be there at six o'clock tomorrow morning.'

⁙

True to their word, the crew was on my doorstep bright and early the next day.

'We'd like to follow you around, film what you usually do during the day,' Laura said.

Simple. Or was it?

Coe emerged from his room, wearing his school uniform and an adolescent lip-curl. Laura managed to interview him briefly before he fled like a fugitive, backpack slung over his shoulder, baseball cap pulled low over his brow.

Breakfast with Bodean was next. We all jammed into the tiny kitchen: Laura, the soundman, cameraman, lighting man, equipment, Bodean and me. Bodean had cereal; I had toast. Once, twice, three times.

'Can you eat breakfast again while we stand behind you?'

'And again so we can shoot from this angle?'

'And while we film from over here?'

Breakfast took almost an hour.

'There's a basketball ring out the back,' said Laura brightly. 'Could we film you playing a game with Bodean?'

'Are you kidding?'

'Right. What about walking Bodean to pre-school?'

The walk was like breakfast. The cat came with us, for the first three or four times at least. Out the front door, down to the vacant lot, over the creek and back again. Over the creek and back again. Over the creek, up the hill and back again. I was beginning to empathise with film stars.

'Donna, the cat's gone home. We need the cat in all the shots.'

'I can't make the cat do that. It's a cat. Besides, it's deaf.'

We filmed all day and into Tuesday.

'There have been times when we nearly lost her,' said Mum, face to the camera. 'There have been times when I questioned, "God, why have you let her live?" … I don't think there's words to describe Donna. As one of her colleagues wrote in one of the letters, "You're a gutsy lady". And if that's words, that's Donna.'

They filmed me helping out at pre-school.

'These are little kids, guys,' I warned them. 'Don't bother asking for a repeat. You'll just have to catch them as best you can.'

After lunch, Laura took me aside apologetically. 'Donna, we'd like to film more of your scarring.'

I gave her a look. 'I'm not getting in a swimming costume, if that's what you mean.'

'Oh no! I didn't mean that.'

'Good.'

'Would you mind getting in the bath with the towel around you?'

'I don't think so! I used to be a schoolteacher. You can't have me running around half-naked.'

'Please, Donna. Get the biggest towel you've got. We'll do it with dignity, I promise.'

And so with the soundman perched on the toilet bowl, the cameraman almost in the hand basin, and Laura and the lighting technician squeezed in the doorway, I prepared to show the nation a sight I was sure many would never forget. My legs, my arms, my neck, my shoulders – all exposed like a weird lunar landscape, a lumpy twisted mass of purples, reds, pinks and creams.

I suppose some would think it exploitative television. But I wanted the country to see what damage could come from the crime we call 'domestic' violence. Domestic? How I wished we could drop that cosy little adjective. Violence was violence.

Late on Tuesday, Helen Wellings flew in to complete the interview.

'You loved him?'

'Yes, I did. And I trusted him.'

'So how does it feel that he's done that? In fact, he wanted control to end your life in a sense, didn't he?'

I couldn't answer her. I looked away. I blinked. I looked back at the camera.

'It's a bit hard for you to talk about.'

I nodded. The camera kept rolling. Soon the tears came.

'I'm really sorry,' I said afterwards. 'I didn't want to cry on national television.'

'Please don't worry. It'll all be okay,' Helen said.

I didn't feel so bad when I noticed the cameraman had been crying too.

※

The following Thursday, Penrith District Court was crawling with media. Helen Jackson from *Today Tonight* ushered me through a mob of camera crews, microphones and reporters. I recognised Andrew Burke from the *Telegraph* and gave him a wave.

'Donna, can I talk to you?' he yelled.

'We don't want you talking to anyone,' said Helen firmly, taking my arm and guiding me towards the courthouse.

'But he was the one who first listened to me, believed me.'

'You're signed to us, Donna. I'll speak to him if it'll make you feel better.'

Inside the courtroom, the judge gave his summing-up. Once again he brought up the age difference between Garry and me. He also noted that both parties had been drinking, and that Garry's drinking was excessive. I was stung by his comments. So what if I was older? As for my drinking, I had a right to have a drink whether it was my birthday or not. I enjoyed a drink. I enjoyed eating a steak too but it didn't mean I wanted to consume the whole cow.

The judge did admit that I had sustained horrendous burns. 'The injuries that she suffered beggar description and the pain she has suffered, and will suffer, defies imagination,' he said. 'If this is not the worst offence of this kind, then I don't know what is. It is difficult to imagine any greater degree of hurt being visited upon anybody than in this case. That you would flick a lighter in the presence of yourself and another person doused in petrol has to be regarded as one of the most negligent acts imaginable.'

The judge made the point that there was an element of doubt over the exact circumstances of the assault, and that this was why the charge had been reduced from 'maliciously' to 'negligently'. I suppose he had to explain it somehow.

'I expressed some surprise last time you were here and I am still surprised that this offence has a maximum sentence of two years,' he said to Garry. 'Although the circumstances of this matter call for a sentence far greater than that allowed, it would be unjust of me to sentence you to two years.'

The judge sentenced Garry to a 15-month jail term, with nine months' parole. Despite the judge's misgivings, Garry had qualified for a discount.

On 21 March 1996, Jean Lennon was shot dead outside the family court in Parramatta by Hoss Majdalawi, her estranged husband. She was attending court to determine custody issues over their four children. Jean had suffered extraordinary domestic violence for years, but every time she went into hiding with her children, her husband pursued her. It had been alleged she was terrified of him killing her and her children.

One week after her murder, 150 people congregated outside Parramatta's family court dressed in black to protest ongoing violence against women, and the legal system's failure to deal with it. I was desperate to attend the protest but was now back in Westmead for more surgery under both arms. My right elbow was also operated on, with skin pleats inserted to allow me to straighten my limb. Channel Seven filmed the operation.

My segment on *Today Tonight* aired only days after my operation, when I was still in the Plastics Ward at Westmead. There were other patients and their visitors already watching the television in the ward common room, and I didn't like to barge in and take over. I'd kept the news of my TV debut quiet, unsure of how it would turn out.

'Dad, do you know where there's another television around, one that's likely to be free?' I asked.

He grinned. 'That's easy. The waiting room near the ICU. Speaking from experience, no one is in the mood to concentrate on television in that department. It's turned off most of the time.'

Sure enough, the waiting room was empty except for a lone middle-aged couple whose loved one had had a heart attack. We chatted to them for a bit and then asked if we could watch *Today Tonight*.

I hadn't realised, but the crew had gone to Geurie, filming the outside of the bowling club and the front of my house. They had recreated the fire, the camera tracking a flaming path into my backyard. I stared at the television screen; I was back there, running blindly, caught in that rolling, tumbling gush of fire. Dad put his arm around me and squeezed my shoulders as we watched.

Several minutes in, the older couple must have realised they were sitting next to the subject of the program. They gaped at me in amazement.

'That's you, isn't it?' breathed the woman. 'Tom, it's her.'

'Yes, I can see that, love.'

I wiped my eyes and smiled. I'd never made anyone star-struck before.

After the program I returned to the Plastics Ward. The nurses and patients had all been watching. They were waiting for me. As Dad and I entered, they clapped and cheered.

'Donna, we saw it!' said one of the nurses, wiping her eyes. 'It was wonderful. Why weren't you here?'

I smiled at the small crowd, embarrassed by the attention. 'They did a great job.'

After the program, the Westmead switchboard was flooded with calls from well-wishers, one lady even offering to donate skin, bless her heart. If only it were that simple.

In a matter of days, my life had once again turned upside down. My first appearance on television had shown me that, despite its reputation for trouble-making, the media could be a powerful ally.

To be thrust into the limelight in such an unexpected way was the start of much bigger things for me. I was forced to become a victim but I'd regained control and given myself a new label – 'survivor'. I had survived lethal burns. I had survived having my children unjustly wrenched from me. Now I had survived the legal system.

I did not want anyone else to go through what I'd endured, of that much I was sure. My way forward was now becoming clear.

Nineteen

Throughout 1996, my battle with the Department of Community Services continued. Back in February I had received a letter from The Hon. Ron Dyer, Minister for Community Services, referring my complaint to the Department's Liaison Unit. They would advise me of the outcome – another investigation that excluded the victim. I rang Jenny Carney, the officer assigned to my matter, and explained my concerns.

By the end of March, my complaint had been handed over to another officer, who had referred it to the Assistant Director General for review. As my documents went from desk to desk, I sent more and more information to support my stance. The complaint was now well over 60 pages. I was getting tired.

Although Coe remained secretive about his time in Parkes, feeding me snippets now and again, I sensed more than ever that the Department's placement decision had not only pushed me to the brink but had also compounded both my sons' fragile emotional states. I knew the Blakemores. My instincts told me that as carers they had not been the best choice for my boys. An official psychological assessment was done for both Coe and Bodean. Although Bodean was too young to be formally interviewed, Coe opened up to the psychologist and confirmed my worst fears.

The Department had recommended trauma counselling for both boys, yet the Blakemores had not followed through with it and the Department had not enforced the recommendation. It's doubtful that a 12-year-old boy would, without adult insistence, elect to see a counsellor. So Coe went without ongoing counselling during which he could have confided details of the assault and of his relationship with me prior to the assault. Why?

'Brian said he felt Coe did not need counselling,' Maria Williams had stated in her affidavit back in 1994. The psychological assessment suggested otherwise:

> Coe says that previously he would continually wake up with nightmares about the assault ... Coe says for a long time he was extremely sad about what had occurred, and that he used to cry a lot ... It is difficult to imagine the trauma which anyone, let alone a child of 12, would go through watching his own mother being set on fire. Not only did Coe have to deal with this event but he was further traumatised by being removed from his home and community, to live in another town with relatives who were virtual strangers to him.
>
> Additionally, he was led to believe his mother would die and that his future now lay in his new foster family. Not surprisingly, Coe appears to have dealt with these events with a mixture of denial, regression, anxiety, anger and depression.

Maria Williams had quoted Denise in the DOCS file and again in her affidavit as saying: 'Coe was pretty upset after seeing his mother, but he's been able to talk about it since, and seems better now.'

The psychologist's report again differed:

> Coe says that on his return to Parkes [from Westmead], he was discouraged from discussing anything to do with his mother, and that as a result he gave up asking for information. Coe has very clear recollections of considerable anxiety and fear not only about what would happen to his mother but also what the future held for him and his brother.

Denise's words kept coming back to me: 'They're your kids, Donna. I never wanted to keep them. I'm just looking after them until you're okay.'

I went back to the psychologist's report:

Coe is also obviously very well aware of what occurred with regards to the Community Services investigation into his mother. He says quite openly that his aunt and uncle tried to convince him that his mother had attempted suicide, and that she was emotionally unstable. Coe says that in the beginning, he resisted this, as he knew the truth of what had happened. He says however, that as the months went by, he began to doubt his own recollection of events, and to wonder what was real and what was fantasy. Coe says that now he has had time to think about what had occurred, he is extremely angry at his aunt and uncle, and that he says he never wishes to see these people again ...

The history of this matter would suggest that Coe and his brother became embroiled in a [paternal] family conspiracy, and it appears that efforts were made by various people to try and convince Coe in particular, that the events he witnessed had a different interpretation.

As I continued to push for the Department to acknowledge its negligence and overhaul its procedures, I received my first invitation to speak publicly. The Domestic Violence Advocacy Service asked me to talk at Circular Quay in Sydney on National Stop Violence Against Women Day. Their coordinator had seen me on *Today Tonight* and had read some newspaper articles about my assault and the subsequent court case. She was impressed that a victim of domestic violence was actually going public.

One of the ironies of it all was that DOCS were the major sponsor of the event. They had dubbed me an abusive mother but were also hailing me as a remarkable victim, willing to speak out and be visible. I found this darkly humorous, but I accepted their invitation, believing in the existence of services to protect children.

'I'm Donna and I'm a survivor of a crime labelled "domestic violence".' I told the audience. 'There is no excuse for violence. As a society, let's recognise where the blame, the guilt, the responsibility for the crime should fall – onto the offender, not the victim.'

I hadn't done too badly for my first public speaking engagement, I thought, despite the nerves. Other opportunities for speaking out publicly arose, many from Ken Marslew from the Enough is Enough organisation. I travelled around with Ken, speaking at community rallies, high schools and even Parliament House in Sydney, where I attended a forum on Criminal Law – the System and the Community.

Audiences like these, full of high-profile service providers – retired judges, DPP solicitors and crowns, and state politicians – were not always open to hearing what I had to say. They were part of the legal system, after all, and may have felt the need to defend it. But I wondered how many had walked in a victim's shoes.

※

That year was memorable for more than just my public speaking debut; 1996 was also what I call the Year of the Nose.

I organised an appointment with a reconstructive surgeon who had a reputation for rebuilding facial features. One option for a new nose involved lopping off a chunk of my good ear; another was to flap a piece of skin down from above the bridge of my nose. This would mean scooping out a sizeable piece of my forehead, which had healed up quite nicely, but it seemed a shame to put a crater in the centre of my brow. The third option was a prosthetic nose. To find out more, I was referred to Sydney's Dental Hospital.

'This is weird,' I said as I settled myself in the dentist's chair. 'You do realise there's nothing wrong with my teeth?'

The dentist smiled. 'We do all sorts of things here. We do ears too.'

'Just the nose will do.'

He leaned over and peered intently at what was left of my nose. 'Now you know there'll be surgery? You're going to have to have studs implanted either side of where the base of your new nose will be. The nose will clip on and off.'

I was disappointed. 'So it still involves an operation?'

He nodded. 'But then again …' He straightened up and stared into space for a moment. 'Do you wear glasses?'

'My vision is fine at present. I don't wear glasses. Is that bad? Do I have to wear glasses before I get a nose?'

'No, no.' The dentist shook his head. 'It's just that, if you wore glasses, we could attach a new nose to your glasses.'

I looked at him and laughed. 'If that's the case, I could pop down to the newsagent and buy a Groucho Marx mask – get the eyebrows I need as well.'

The dentist reddened. 'Yes, it does seem a bit silly, and anyway, you don't wear glasses, so that's out. The disadvantage with studs is you'll need surgery. The other thing is, no matter how much make-up you wear, there will be a very obvious ridge across the bridge of your nose.' He ran his index finger gently across the space between my eyes. 'Just here.'

'Any other good news?'

'You'd have to wear your nose every day, because without it the studs are exposed. You need to be careful when you're swimming too. The prosthetic noses have a tendency to – er – float away,' he added, with a small, self-conscious laugh.

I closed my eyes and for a moment imagined my nose drifting past an unsuspecting group of bathers. Could you grab that for me please?

The dentist continued. 'And you'd need to get a new nose every year. They deteriorate. Oh, and one more thing. You've got to be sure to clean it regularly.'

'I see.'

'How old are you?'

'Thirty-nine.'

'Frankly, I think you're too young for all this. We build a lot of prosthetic noses for older people who've lost their noses through skin cancer.'

'I have to admit, waking up each day and seeing my nose on the bedside table – it could be a bit much. And at 80 years old, who'd be willing to clean my nose out for me?' I pulled a face.

'You don't want 40 years of that,' he agreed.

I made another appointment to see my reconstructive surgeon.

'So the prosthetic nose isn't an option?' he asked, after I told him about my trip to the dental hospital.

'I don't think so! And I have to say, the idea of lopping an ear off or scooping a hole in my forehead isn't too appealing either. Isn't there another way?'

'We could do less damage to your forehead if we had some excess skin to work with.'

'Couldn't you stretch it somehow from the inside out?'

His face lit up. 'Wait a minute. We could do what we do in breast implants.'

'A boob? On my forehead?'

'What happens is we put a balloon under the skin of your forehead and inject it with saline solution. Inject it regularly and slowly blow it up.'

'Sounds feasible.'

The surgeon clapped his hands together. 'That's what we'll do then. When it's big enough, we'll take the balloon out and we'll have a decent flap of skin to flip over, keeping it connected for the blood circulation. We'll need to grind a little of your original nose back, but by the time we've finished you should just have one fine scar down your forehead where we've pulled the skin back together.' He was really looking enthused now. 'You'll need two tubes up your nose for breathing, and six to 12 operations to form the nostrils.'

I blinked at him and gripped the side of my chair. Was this going to be worth it?

'There are risks, of course,' he said. 'Once we've flipped the skin over, there's a chance, like any other graft, that we might lose it.'

'Right,' I said faintly. 'So what with the grinding of my original nose, I could actually end up with less nose than I have now?'

'Yes, that's right.'

I was silent for a moment, digesting this possibility before asking more questions. 'Timewise, what are we looking at?'

'You'll have to be in hospital for three months.'

'Why? I won't be sick.'

'We can't have you walking around the streets scaring people. You'll look like the Elephant Man.'

'Then I'll stay home. I can't just disappear into hospital for three months. Who do you think is going to look after my two boys?'

'Have you got family?'

'Listen, my sister is barely speaking to me, and my mum and stepfather do enough minding already. I'll just stay home.'

He shrugged. 'It's up to you. But one of your local doctors would have to inject the saline solution on a regular basis. Could you find someone who's willing?'

'Dr Pederson would enjoy doing that, I'm sure.'

'Before we get started on the procedure though, I'll have to cut your throat.' He went on to explain that because my neck was so tight, it pulled my chin down and distorted my face. This dragging down needed to be corrected by slitting my throat and inserting a skin graft. 'We need a big, thick graft to use for a skin pleat to release your neck.'

I looked at him. 'I always hate "big" and "thick" when they're used to describe the skin you're going to harvest. "Big" and "thick" means "deep and painful" as far as I'm concerned.'

'I'm afraid so. We'll take the graft from your right thigh. You've still got some good skin there.'

I'd planned to take Coe and Bodean to the snow after my operation, so before the anaesthetic kicked in, I scrawled a brief note to the guy in charge of the harvesting device. I fixed the note to my donor site:

Take care when harvesting skin. I need this leg for skiing in two months' time.

I had painful memories of staff trying to dig dozens of crooked staples out of my grafts after surgery. So I posted another message at the base of my neck, hidden under my surgical gown. This note was specifically for the medico wielding the staple gun:

To the guy who's got the automatic:
1. Are you licenced?
2. Shoot straight.
3. Less is best.

Following that operation, I had another check-up with the plastic surgeon about my nose reconstruction.

'My office will ring when a bed becomes available,' he told me, 'and then we can start proceedings.'

Call it fate, but his office never did ring. And I never pursued it. I felt my body had had enough. Time to let it rest.

〽

The months rolled past, and life was becoming increasingly busy. My divorce had been finalised the previous December but the Geurie house still needed to be sold. I was dealing with Brian's demands over access and property settlement issues, his uninvited appearances in Irvine Street and his no-shows when he was meant to spend time with the boys.

Coe and Bodean needed my ongoing time and attention too; in the winter of 1996 I crossed off another item on my wish list when we went to the snow. Over five days I bum-ploughed my way across the Thredbo snowfields while Coe and Bodean quickly mastered the basics of skiing. For the first time in two years I was sleeping long and deep each night, without medication and without nightmares.

Despite all that was going on, I was suffering a deep loneliness. My Geurie friendships were severed. I had friends from school and college, but contact was mainly by phone and letter. There was my family, but I needed to connect with others in my new area. Where did one go to do that?

I located a women's support group in Foster, but it folded soon after I joined. I attended the playgroup at the local refuge and found myself sitting with a collection of chain-smoking, depressed women. This wasn't what I was looking for. I became a soccer mum and worked as a volunteer at my boys' schools. I also began to attend Taree Local Court, offering support to any victims of crime who seemed lost and alone.

One day my counsellor told me about the Domestic Violence Monitoring Committee which met once a month in the community health centre in Taree. It was open to anyone who was interested, but mainly consisted of professional people representing various local services: Children's Services, Women's Health, the refuge and Centrelink. There was the local chamber magistrate and a police officer, a trauma counsellor and a social worker. And then there was me. It was clear that I wasn't one of them.

But I persisted. It was a good way to find out what was going on in the community with regards to combating domestic violence, and perhaps an opportunity to offer some of my own thoughts, ideas and energy. For a while I had been researching the dynamics of abusive relationships, educating myself about controlling partners. This knowledge was an important tool to analyse my past relationships, and to heal myself.

I recognised now that there were early warning signs. Garry's emotional abuse caused me to tiptoe around his moods, to feel stupid and doubt my own judgement. Then there was the social isolation, which I'd mistaken for love. 'You don't need to have coffee with your friends. You've got me now.' Why hadn't I recognised this for what it was? Why hadn't I seen past the charm?

I stumbled upon bits and pieces in my search for information, but everything was so disjointed. Yet family violence appeared to be everywhere; I was just one of many. Every time I watched the news or picked up a newspaper I was confronted with stories about someone, usually a female – an estranged lover, an ex-girlfriend, someone's wife or de facto – getting bashed, shot, stabbed, in a 'domestic'. I cut out articles and kept them in a box.

'Pregnant girlfriend kicked because she was nagging.'
'I had to kill her – I loved her so much!'
'He tormented his stepson to death.'
'Man stabbed wife 17 times.'

My collection grew daily, as did my understanding – not only about family violence itself, but also about how the wider community viewed it. Society had embedded misconceptions about such atrocities. And it was not unusual for these misconceptions to be reinforced by a media bias that often trivialised the perpetrator's actions or pushed blame onto the victim. Re-education was definitely needed.

It was around this time that I was forced to deal with Brian. After a number of abusive phone calls and drunken drive-bys, I'd had enough, and went to Taree Police Station. The conversation was unnervingly familiar, taking me back to my police interview with Frank after my release from hospital.

'Did he try to run you over?'

'Well, no.'

'Did he say he was going to kill you?'

'No.'

'Did he physically hurt you in any way?'

'Well, no, not since ... not since our marriage broke up.'

The police were unwilling to issue an Apprehended Violence Order or AVO, but suggested I do it myself, through the chamber magistrate. When I met with him to apply for an AVO, he asked me only one question.

'Is he going to leave you alone?'

'No,' I said. 'Not without an AVO.'

A fortnight later, I turned up to court with a churning stomach. I went alone, but at least I was familiar with the court system. There were several women around me who looked totally lost. Most were by themselves; a few had children with them.

Brian turned up to court in clean jeans, a checked shirt and his usual joggers. His mother was with him. Having nowhere else to go, I waited on the front lawn, just metres away from the pair, putting up with Mrs Blakemore's black looks while Brian chain-smoked and faced the other way.

Monday was largely reserved for dealing with AVOs and the courtroom was full. Our matter was one of the first, and it was over quickly as Brian agreed to the order. As I left the courtroom, my path intersected with Mrs Blakemore's. Perhaps she had timed it deliberately, because she sidled up to me and leaned into my ear. I could feel her warm breath and a spray of spittle against my cheek.

'You're nothing but a bitch!' she spat, before pushing ahead of me towards the exit.

Once outside I burst into tears.

'I saw that. Are you okay?' a plain-clothed policewoman asked, placing a hand on my back.

'Yes, thank you,' I said, wiping my eyes. 'I had no choice but to go for an AVO. He had to be stopped.'

She smiled at me. 'Well, you did it.'

'Yes, I did. And I'm not going to have anyone bully me again.'

With growing knowledge of the legal system, I continued to attend Taree Local Court each Monday to offer court support for victims of crime, mainly women and children who were going through the legal processes of addressing violence in their lives. It was not enough to travel around the country addressing audiences about the issues of domestic violence. I wanted to help my community at a grassroots level, providing a service that had not been there for me when I'd needed it.

Back in 1996 there was no support offered at the courthouse. Fortunately, a host of paid workers were introduced in the following years to fill the void. Leonie McGuire, the manager of the women's refuge in Taree, was often at court, accompanying one or more of her clients. A tiny, bird-like woman, dynamic and progressive, she was greatly respected for her work involving the support of abused women and children through emergency accommodation. She became a staunch ally of mine, and later wrote a reference about those early days at court:

One day I noticed a severely scarred woman – a pretty woman,
lovely bone structure, eyes, hair, slender – but startlingly marked by

some trauma, particularly to her face. She moved among frightened, tense-looking women, clearly soothing, informing, guiding and making a difference. It was a while before I realised what an enormous difference Donna was making to probably hundreds of terrorised women and children.

I would arrive before 9 am most Mondays and stand on the front lawn outside the courthouse, observing. Even honest people are terrified of court, mainly due to inexperience. This inexperience places them at an immediate disadvantage when dealing with the legal system. I knew what it was like to expect assistance and not be able to locate it.

I noticed Carolyn immediately. She was dressed in a smart knee-length skirt and jacket. She was in her mid-thirties, slim, pretty, with shoulder-length chestnut hair and a sweet, unhappy face. She was alone, standing on the front lawn, glancing around uncertainly. I approached her tentatively.

'Hello, I'm Donna. I'm not a solicitor. I'm a volunteer who may be able to help you. Are you going to court today?'

'Yes.' She gave a small smile of relief. I noticed her eyes were puffy underneath her make-up. 'I'm Carolyn. I don't know what to do, where to go.'

'Have you had your name marked off?'

'Was I meant to?'

'Yes. It's like a rollcall – to see who's here and who's not.'

'Oh, right. I didn't know. I was in the toilets.'

I could hear a slight panic in her voice and I put a hand on her arm. 'That's okay. I'll help you with that. Is your matter an AVO?'

'Yes,' said Carolyn, with an embarrassed grimace.

'Did the police take out an AVO on your behalf?'

'No. They told me to go through the magistrate.'

'Why I ask is because if it's a police matter, the police prosecutor would put your case forward for you. Do you have a solicitor?'

'No, I can't afford one. I mean, we have money, but my husband ...' Carolyn's voice trailed off.

'That's okay.'

Her brow furrowed. 'I've never been to court though. What will happen?'

'Who did you take the AVO out against?'

'My husband.'

'Is he here?'

She glanced around nervously. 'I saw him earlier, with his solicitor.'

'If he agrees to the AVO, it can be settled today. Do you think there's a possibility of him agreeing to the order?'

'No, I don't think so,' she said.

'Okay. If he has a solicitor, you're probably right. Do you know that you can tailor-make the AVO to your circumstances? For instance, you might still want to live together, but your order could say he can't approach the family home for 12 hours after consuming drink.'

She held up a hand. 'No. I don't want anything to do with him.'

'If he isn't going to agree to the AVO then it won't be heard today. It will have to go to a full hearing on another day. Do you understand?'

'Yes, I see.' She sighed. 'What will happen then?'

'On that day the magistrate will listen to your side of the story and then your husband's side, and any other witnesses involved. Then it will be up to the magistrate to decide whether an AVO will be granted.'

'Right.'

'When it goes to a hearing, be aware you'll be asked to take the stand to give evidence. Seeing as you haven't got a solicitor to assist with the details of the incident, you'll be doing that yourself.'

'How can I?'

'It'll be okay,' I reassured her. 'Just think of the magistrate as a blank chalkboard. You have to fill in that blank chalkboard – like drawing a picture, but use your words. Be graphic. Tell him exactly what your husband did, exactly what he said and how he made you feel.'

'Well, he just said what he usually says,' Carolyn murmured.

'What's that?'

She blinked rapidly. 'Oh, like he didn't like his evening meal.'

'AVOs are not about the defendant disliking your cooking.'

'Well, you know ... he was pretty angry ... and said things.' She was blushing now.

'What sort of things?' I persisted.

'Calling me names, swearing. You know, things like that.'

'I know what you mean, but you need to tell the magistrate exactly what was said.'

She looked surprised. 'Can I repeat those swear words in court?'

'Yes, you can. If that's what he said, you must tell the magistrate. He needs to hear these words. Some women like to clean it up. That doesn't help at all. Now, you said he was pretty angry. What did you mean by that?'

'He ... sort of ... grabbed me.'

'Did that leave marks? Wounds?'

'Yes, I still have the bruising.' Tears welled up in her eyes.

I gave her a tissue from my bag and put an arm around her shoulders for a moment. 'We'll need to photograph the bruising immediately. Have you suffered any other injuries in the past?'

'Yes. A few times.'

'Like what?'

'A fractured cheekbone. And one time he broke my wrist.' She stared down at her shoes.

'You need to mention this history too,' I said gently.

She spoke in a rushed whisper. 'I never reported it, though. I was too scared.'

'That's exactly what you have to say to the magistrate if he asks you why you didn't report it. The magistrate needs the whole picture. Draw it for him. Are there other words to describe your feelings during these times?'

'Terrified. Threatened. Unsafe in my own home.'

I squeezed her hand. 'Okay. I can't tell you what to say or put words in your mouth. That's called coaching. But the magistrate needs to hear your words in order to justify an AVO.'

'Right.'

'When you say what happened, be prepared for the other side to ask you questions. Their job is to get the best deal for their client, who happens to be your husband. His solicitor may try to suggest things happened another way.'

'What do you mean?' She looked at me, startled.

'He may suggest you didn't get your story right. Maybe you exaggerated, maybe you have a mental illness, or you drink.'

'But I don't.'

'Just remember, the solicitor isn't on your side. He's working for his client. When he questions you, listen carefully. If you don't understand the question, say so. Don't commit yourself to a yes or no answer if you're not sure.'

'Is anyone going to help me?'

'The magistrate will know you're by yourself. Look at him when you answer. Don't look at the solicitor or your husband if it's intimidating. It's the magistrate who decides, after all.'

She took a deep breath, wiped her eyes and gathered herself once more. 'Will I have to question my husband?'

'You can. It might be an idea to jot down some questions beforehand, and any that occur to you in court. Sometimes things come up.'

'What do you mean?'

'If your husband says you have a mental illness for instance, you can go back to that point later in your questioning and ask him about that – if he's got any medical evidence, for instance.'

'Of course he wouldn't, would he?'

'You know he doesn't. The golden rule is: never ask a question unless you already know the answer. Now, have you got witnesses for this last assault?'

'Everyone knows,' she said.

'But the incident you cited. Did anyone see or hear?'

'One woman. My neighbour.'

'You might have to approach her carefully. Most people don't want to get involved.'

Carolyn shook her head. 'She has work commitments.'

'Ask her anyway,' I urged. 'She probably knows a lot of what's been going on. She may even be an ally for you.'

Every case was different. Sometimes, for example, the offender didn't turn up. This was how it was for Wendy, a stout, silver-haired woman in her late fifties who was dealing with court for the first time and was obviously out of her depth.

'Can you see the offender anywhere?' I asked her.

She turned to scan the lawn and courthouse verandah. 'No, I don't think ...'

'They may not have been able to serve the papers on him.'

'What does that mean?'

'It means that the police haven't been able to serve papers about it going to court today. If he doesn't know about it, he won't turn up,' I said slowly. 'But you can ask the magistrate for an interim order.'

'What's that?'

'It's like a temporary AVO, to tide you over from when the papers are served until the next court date. It may mean taking the stand and answering more questions put to you by the magistrate.'

Later in court, Wendy stood before the magistrate and asked him, 'Can I have one of those things to, you know, tide me over?'

'What, an interim order?' The magistrate asked, clearly surprised. An unrepresented person asking for an interim order? It was unfamiliar terrain.

Sometimes a 'PINOP' – person in need of protection – would be approached before court by the offender's solicitor. I saw it a fair bit:

'I'm a solicitor,' they'd say.

The woman would look relieved – an official to help her!

'This is a serious matter. Are you sure you want to go to court?'

'I just want some peace!'

'There's another option. It's just like an AVO. It's called an undertaking.'

'What's that?'

'It's made in court in front of the magistrate, and states that your ex will leave you alone. It uses the same wording as the AVO.'

The woman would then say something like, 'That sounds great. So I don't have to do anything?'

'Absolutely not,' the solicitor would say. 'I'll speak to the magistrate and explain that it's all sorted out and that both parties have agreed to undertakings.'

I'd approach the woman afterwards and explain. 'That solicitor is employed by the offender. Agreeing to undertakings benefits his client, not you. By all means listen, but just remember that that solicitor's working for the other party.'

'What's wrong with an undertaking?'

'It's not an AVO. It's a promise before the court but it's not legally binding. Breaking a promise isn't a criminal offence.'

'So if my ex is banging on my door in the middle of the night and I call the police?'

'They'll ask you if you've got an AVO. You'll say you've got undertakings, to which they'll answer, "Sorry madam, maybe he just wants to talk to you. But give us a ring if anything happens." In a lot of cases an AVO nips further harassment in the bud. It sends a clear message to the bully in your life – you're not taking it anymore. And if the defendant is banging on the door in the middle of the night and you call the police and say you have an AVO, it gives the police permission to arrest and charge that person because breaching an AVO is a criminal offence.'

'But you read about those madmen that hunt the woman down, shoot the family. The AVO was useless.'

'AVOs don't stop bullets and knives, and in such extreme cases the violence has usually been allowed to go unchecked for too long. These are the cases that hit the headlines. We don't get to read about the thousands of times AVOs have actually worked.'

As well as moral support and information, I would take my briefcase with me each week, filled with pamphlets from various local service providers, the majority of which I'd used myself. I knew first-hand about the help the Smith Family offered to people in need; I also had information on the Department of Housing, emergency accommodation, Centrelink, trauma counselling and free dental and medical health. I knew where to source second-hand furniture and cheap groceries. I could help with house repairs, if necessary, using the skills Dad had taught me. I even knew how to hang security doors and fit deadlocks.

From my meetings with the Domestic Violence Monitoring Committee, I learned of a room that had been set aside at the courthouse for victims of crime to wait, away from the offenders. Unfortunately, the use of the room had not been enforced and it was filled with a jumble of office furniture. Solicitors and barristers often used it to have conferences with their clients before court.

I cleared the room out and began chasing the lawyers away. With the assistance of the local magistrate, Paul Couch, we had the room refurbished more appropriately and fitted a sign to the door: Women's and Children's Safety Room. I pushed for it to be available to male victims of crime too, though, as well as supportive males accompanying female victims to court.

I brought videos, toys, activity books, magazines and pencils. I provided tissues, chalk and a duster. I sourced some cheerful framed prints and brought my drill along to hang them. I also attached a second-hand pamphlet holder to the wall and filled it with local information, which saved me dragging my briefcase along each week.

On Mondays I would give the room a quick once-over, emptying the garbage, replacing used activity books and broken toys and pencils, filling up the tea and coffee jars, replenishing pamphlets and checking the milk supply.

At least other victims of crime now had a safe, private place to wait. In 1996 there were no other rooms like this. They've now been introduced at other courthouses but many still expect victims to wait alongside their offenders.

When I first began making an appearance around court, the court staff were curious. Who was I? What business did I have around here? I wanted to show them I was there to help. I was an outsider, but one who was on the same side.

One morning I witnessed one of the new court officers, Michael Healy, approaching people who looked lost, asking if they needed assistance. I was so impressed I went home and wrote a letter to Lyn

Baker, Director of Local Courts. Congratulations filtered back to Taree Court from higher up.

Bernie Stenchion, another court officer, was also making a difference. Not only was he courteous and efficient but he actually went out of his way to volunteer information, gathering together those going for an AVO and taking the time to explain to them the difference between a personal AVO and a Domestic Violence AVO. I wrote another letter. Again the court was congratulated and went on to win two monthly awards. The whole place was uplifted and the court staff began to realise that I wasn't the enemy.

✳

Meanwhile, I was still dealing with the NSW Police Department over my own matters. On 11 April 1996, I received one small piece of justice. I was given an official written apology on behalf of the NSW Police Department for the role Matt Adderley had played in the DOCS bungle.

I also received a copy of the police brief of the investigation into my assault, which I'd applied for under Freedom of Information. 'Brief' was an apt word to describe it for much important information had been left out and key witnesses not interviewed. I rang Frank.

'I realise you were relying on other officers to do their job here, but do you understand there are huge holes in this investigation?'

'What do you mean?' he asked.

'Why didn't anyone get a statement from my neighbour, Trevor Dunn, or Dave, Trevor's neighbour?

'Why would that be necessary?'

'They were the first two people to attend the scene of the crime. I was speaking to them. I told them who did it. And besides, Trevor would have probably heard Garry going off before the assault.'

'I didn't know that.'

'And there was the hospital staff. I told them three times in the first week who'd done this to me. I know they informed the police, but I don't see all the records in the brief.'

'I only had one witness. The documentation could have been useful.'

'Then there was my phone – disconnected, stashed in the unregistered car, with the cord wrapped neatly around it before the crime was committed. How come the police missed that? They seemed to have turned everything else inside out.'

'How is the phone relevant?'

'Think about it – why would someone want to remove my only form of communication? No phone made it hard if help was needed.'

'Maybe he was going to the pub and he didn't want you calling him there.'

'Oh, Frank, really! And another thing, the people behind the bar at the club were never approached. The bar staff knew how much each of us had had to drink. They knew I was a responsible drinker. And the clientele there that day saw Garry's jealous behaviour.'

'Fair point.'

'And to have Adrian and Sue Ross as witnesses for the prosecution!'

Frank groaned. 'Don't tell me they're known to the offender.'

'Adrian was Garry's close friend, and Sue's sister Sandra was married to Garry's brother. He's Uncle Garry to her kids. And these two people were meant to be vouching for me in court?'

Frank sighed. 'I can't believe this.'

'One more thing. My boys spent the night at the Fords' place, with Adrian and Sue and a collection of other people who had a vested interest in protecting the offender. Coe had to give a statement the next morning. They were at him all night – "Remember, that's your story and you stick to it. Garry's in enough trouble as it is." I have a witness who overheard this. He told my family and they reported it at Wellington Police Station. There doesn't seem to be any record of this. But you'll notice Coe's statement avoids talking about the offender.'

'Donna, I can't bear to hear any more.'

'If only you'd involved me in the procedures, Frank. I could have told you these things when it mattered.'

'You had enough on your plate just surviving.'

'Yes, but I survived only to find that the system I believed in had failed me.'

٨٨٨

I was still quietly obsessing over the change of Garry's charge and decided I'd pursue it as far as possible. I had applied for transcripts of the court hearings, writing to the appropriate department with details of the case, Regina v Clynes:

> The case was heard in the Dubbo Courthouse 14 August 1995 and
> 5 September 1995, and Penrith Courthouse 8 March 1996 and
> 14 March 1996. The judge was Judge Terence Christie.

The reply was swift and to the point: there was no record of the case involving that particular judge on those particular days, apart from the judge's summing-up after Garry's sentencing. No record. Now the transcripts had vanished.

Years later, when a researcher for SBS's *Insight* program tried to obtain these same court transcripts, she was given the same reply.

'Donna, just between you and me,' she said, 'you've been shafted.'

My suspicions were further aroused after a visit to the DPP Court of Criminal Appeal in Sydney. I'd arranged the meeting after discovering that Garry was going to appeal against the severity of his sentence. (The appeal was later withdrawn.)

The DPP officer had Garry's file in front of her, which listed the charge as 'maliciously inflicting grievous bodily harm'. I repeated my saga to her and she asked why the DPP in Dubbo had accepted a lesser charge, and why the police department hadn't been informed, or the victim for that matter. She admitted that it looked like something had happened between the DPP and the defence.

'So, in other words, charge bargaining occurred,' I said.

'I'm not saying that exactly but it certainly doesn't look right. All the way through the file it says "maliciously". Leave it with me, Donna.'

But by our next meeting, the tune had definitely changed. The officer informed me that the change in charge should have been altered in the files. It was just an oversight, she assured me.

Armed with the Charter of Victims' Rights, my next idea was to write to the Director of Public Prosecutions, Nicholas Cowdery QC, outlining my case and the DPP's handling of it. In a letter dated 25 July 1996, I suggested charge bargaining may have occurred. From his response on 5 November, it was obvious Mr Cowdery was having none of that.

> I have been advised by the Crown Prosecutor that his decision to accept the plea of guilty to negligently causing grievous bodily harm was made after detailed discussion with you, during which he explained the difficulties in proving the more serious charge.

To my recollection, there was no detailed discussion.
Then there was their favourite defence:

> The decision to accept the plea of guilty also relieved you of the burden of giving evidence and being cross-examined.

I wrote back immediately, asserting that the 'detailed discussion' was a myth. On 20 November, Mr Cowdery returned my letter, although this time his reply was somewhat briefer:

> What has been done cannot be undone.

Anyone would have thought I was asking for my face back.

On 29 January 1997, I wrote a third letter expressing my disappointment at his avoidance. I referred to the Charter of Victims' Rights, most particularly the part that states:

> A victim should, on request, be informed of the following:
> a) the charges laid against the accused or the reasons for not laying charges,
> b) any decision of the prosecution to modify or not to proceed with charges laid against the accused, including any decision for the

accused to accept a plea of guilty to a less serious charge in return
for a full discharge with respect to the other charges,

d) the outcome of the criminal proceedings against the accused.

The Director's third reply wasn't even half a page:

Your recollection of being told that the guilty plea was entered to
the charge of maliciously inflicting grievous bodily harm does not
accord with the recollection of others.

I knew then that if I were to persist in taking on the DPP, I'd need others
to confirm my story. Not Mum or Clyde, or John and Shirl. They would
be discounted as family and friends, and therefore obviously biased. I
needed officials. I decided to start with Brenda, my WAS officer.

I asked about her recollections of the 'case conference' prior to Garry
pleading guilty. I needed her to verify that I was not informed of the lesser
charge at this stage, and that there was no 'detailed discussion' about the
difficulties of proving a higher charge, as Nicholas Cowdery had outlined
in his letter. In fact, the Crown was running late and had to slip his gown
and wig on in front of me.

'I'm afraid I can't remember,' Brenda told me. 'I was in and out of the
room. I wasn't party to the whole discussion.'

I reminded her that she had been present during the entire case
conference. 'In fact, you were beside me the whole time. You were the one
who comforted me when I broke down after they left the room.'

There was a brief silence before Brenda responded. 'You've got a
great memory, Donna. I *was* there. But I can't remember the discussion
between you and the DPP.'

'You work for them, don't you, Brenda?'

She didn't answer.

My last hope was Frank. He wasn't present during the case
conference, but he had always insisted that the charge was 'maliciously'. I
rang him and told him about my communications with Nicholas
Cowdery.

'I'm taking on the DPP,' I assured him, 'not the police force. You're not in trouble.'

He sighed. 'What do you need, Donna?'

'Nicholas Cowdery is saying my memory isn't in accordance with other's. He's not going to admit to charge bargaining. I was wondering if you could put in writing what you told me, in a room full of people, about the guilty plea.'

There was a long silence. 'Leave it with me, Donna.'

Frank's reply did not match his previous statements.

On the matter coming to the District Court, 14 August 1995, I recall that I was the person who advised you that the offender had pleaded guilty to the charge. I do not recall if in fact I told you that it was maliciously inflict grievous bodily harm or negligently inflict grievous bodily harm. I do recall being the person who told you that a plea had been accepted. Again I recall that a number of persons were in the room at the time ...

I stared at Frank's letter. 'I do not recall ...' Of all things, I was not expecting this response. After asserting over and over, 'I know what I told you in a room full of people,' Frank, like Brenda, had suddenly been struck down with amnesia. I grabbed the phone. Frank picked up on the second ring.

'It's Donna Blakemore. I got your letter. What happened?' I spoke in a steady tone. I wasn't indignant or tearful or shaky. I felt instead a weary disappointment.

'It was very difficult for me to write what I did. I hope you understand. I have to say, I really can't recall.'

I continued to press him for some sort of admission.

'Donna, I've thought about this and I have to say once again, I can't recall.'

'My friends and family know what you said, but they'll have no credibility. I want the DPP to be accountable like anyone else. You told me once that this happens all the time. I'm willing to do something about it, but I need you to help me.'

'I'm terribly sorry, Donna. I have to say, I can't remember.'

It struck me then that these were the same words Garry had used in his statement. 'I can't remember. I don't know what happened actually.'

I turned my attention back to Frank, on the other end of the phone. 'There's no point in flogging a dead horse. Thanks for talking to me, Frank. I wish you all the best.'

I pushed the letter into the filing cabinet I'd bought to house all the paperwork I'd collected. If I pursued this with the DPP there was a good chance the whole thing would be buck-passed down to the investigating officer. Frank was a good man, but he was not going to put his neck on the chopping block by siding with a victim against the system. After all, he was a part of the system, being promoted by it. He owed his livelihood to it.

After Frank's letter, I stopped trying to prove that a deal had been struck behind my back, and I stopped corresponding with Nicholas Cowdery.

Still, I wasn't finished with the legal system yet.

Twenty

'We've got another patient who really needs to see someone like you, if you've got the time.'

I had been working with burns survivors since 1995 and was at Westmead Hospital visiting yet another when I'd run into Donna Knapp, my OT. She stood in the corridor outside the Burns Unit, running her fingers through her hair.

'What's the story?'

'His name's Alan. A big, burly bloke from out west. He received burns in an accident on his property. Torso, arms, hands, legs. He's thrown in the towel and has resigned himself to being in a wheelchair forever.'

'I'll bet he loves your visits.'

She rolled her eyes. 'He's become so difficult, Donna. He just ignores us. He won't do anything.'

'I can understand that. I remember wishing you'd all vanish too.'

'Yes, I know,' Donna said, her forehead creasing. 'I probably sound unsympathetic, but he's not going to walk if he refuses to help himself. Could you have a word with him?'

'You'll have to ask the burns manager and staff, then Alan and his family. I don't just go bowling in, you know that. Has he got any family?'

'A long-suffering wife who spends most of her day hunched in a corner of his room hoping for a miracle.'

A couple of afternoons later, Dad and I made our way up to the Burns Unit. Each time I visited, memories came rolling back from the darkest corners of my subconscious. A waft of rotting flesh, a clang of stainless steel, an alarm from a machine, a scream. The hushed, rushed footfalls down the linoleum corridor.

'We can smell you, Donna.'
'You know what that means, Donna.'
'This is going to hurt, Donna.'
'You know the drill, Donna, after three.'

I stopped just inside the entranceway to the unit, took a deep breath and blinked. Exorcising demons. We made our way to the nurses' station. I enjoyed seeing them, thanking them, showing off their handiwork. I'd brought my usual reinforcements: a giant pack of mixed lollies for the staff sugar jar.

Alan's room was one of my old rooms. The nurse announced my arrival to Alan, who was expecting me. In the dim light I could see his bulky form, slumped in a wheelchair like a lump of clay. Over in the corner his wife sat silent, arms crossed, her face obscured by the shadows.

I tapped on the door and walked in. 'Hello, I'm Donna. This is my dad, Mick.'

Alan looked up. His face, bare and momentarily hostile, jerked in surprise at the sight of me. His wife gazed warily in my direction from her grey space, but said nothing.

I plunged right in. 'Oh, mate, hope you don't mind, but I'm buggered. I've just got to sit down.' I pulled up a chair.

He nodded. His mouth hung open. My appearance or my approach, or maybe both, had thrown him.

I chirped on, ignoring the silence. 'I've just been chasing my younger son all over Taronga Zoo today. I'm so tired! And my legs and feet are killing me.' I managed to flick one shoe off, then started on the other.

'I'm Alan,' he finally offered. 'And this is my wife, June.'

'Hello June. You and Dad would have a lot in common.'

She nodded, watching me suspiciously.

'Anyway, Alan, I heard your legs are giving you some trouble.'

His head bobbed up and down. I waited for him to say something.

'Were your legs burnt too?' he asked at last.

'Yes.'

He hesitated. 'Do you think I could have a look?'

I hadn't worn my burns suit because patients often wanted to examine my scarring, to see how theirs might look a year or two down the track. 'Sure you can.' I stood up and moved over to his chair, hitching my dress up to mid-thigh level.

He spent several seconds looking at my scarring, his eyes bulging. He looked up at my face and I saw there were tears rolling down his cheeks. A sob erupted from somewhere deep in his chest.

'What's the matter?'

The words burst from his mouth. 'Just look at you! You're a woman, a slip of a thing. Look at your face, look at your legs. I feel so ashamed.' He buried his head in his bandaged hands. June and Dad had been talking quietly, but now subsided into awkward silence.

I waited. 'Ashamed of giving up?'

He nodded, his head still lowered.

'Well, that's a relief! I thought it was the sight of my legs that had made a grown man cry.'

He gave a small chuckle, looked up, pushed past his tears and smiled. Out of the corner of my eye I could see his wife straighten in her seat. I felt her surprise at the sound of Alan's laughter. Was there hope here? June pulled her chair out of the dark corner and into the light. She had plenty to ask Dad.

Alan was full of questions too. How long was I in hospital? How did I cope? How did I fill in the time? What about the grafts? I told him about my wish list, the list I'd concocted to try to drag myself up by the bootstraps in those dark times. I told him about the sunflowers, about using a whole big bag of them in my tiny garden plot.

'Every single one of those things sprouted – in a two by one metre patch of soil.'

'A one-kilo packet? You didn't, did you? They grow like weeds!'

'Yeah, well, I know that now.'

It was late when Dad and I drove back to Redfern, but when we'd left, Alan was in high spirits, vowing, 'If a bloody woman can beat this, so can I!'

Over the following months, I sent many letters to Alan, and on one of my visits I brought him a big bunch of silk sunflowers. True to his word, he did end up getting out of his wheelchair and went on to reclaim his life. He never forgot me though. 'Whenever I see a sunflower, I think of you,' he said.

Through meeting people like Alan, I knew I was making a difference. I was living proof that burns could not only be endured but that a life could be regained, and that shared experience was something few medical professionals, counsellors, friends or relatives could provide.

The importance of ongoing support for burns survivors was obvious, and I continued to search for information and services. There was the Phoenix Society in America, but at first I could find nothing in Australia. I finally heard about the Burns Support Foundation when I was in Westmead Hospital having contractures released and further grafting. The foundation's president, Cherie Templeton, happened to be a physiotherapist next door at the children's hospital. I was so excited I walked over in my slippers and dressing-gown to meet her.

The foundation was run more-or-less on a voluntary basis and a shoestring budget, but I was thrilled nonetheless. It seemed I'd come home.

I requested a number of posters advertising the Foundation, and I began to send them to all the major city and metropolitan hospitals in Sydney. I also got hold of their latest newsletter; I was hungry for contact with other burns survivors who had made it through the initial survival stage.

'We're holding a camp in a few months, at Milson Island,' Cherie told me.

'Great! Can I come?'

'Sure. I mean, it's mainly for kids, with some of the parents volunteering to run the camp because I don't actually stay for the whole time. You're welcome to join us. May as well enjoy it while you can.'

'What do you mean?'

'Basically, we need money. This could be our last camp.'

'I just found you and now you're folding?' I thought for a moment. 'Maybe some media attention would help.' The embryo of an idea formed in my mind. 'I know some great people, like Laura Sparks from *Today Tonight*. They may be able to help.'

'That would be fantastic! Invite them along.'

About two dozen people attended the camp, mainly young burns survivors and their immediate families. I'd brought Mum, Coe and Bodean along. As we waited for the ferry to take us over to the island, a large man in a straw hat and baggy khaki trousers, with a fishing rod over his shoulder, sauntered over.

'G'day Donna! You don't recognise me, do you?'

'Is that you, Alan? You look great,' I said, smiling up at his beaming face. I'd been expecting Alan and June; I'd told them about the camp in one of my letters but I didn't know whether they'd come. 'Who would have thought you'd be walking around like this, fishing rod and all, looking so normal. Well done!'

It was a good beginning, seeing Alan up and about, but things went downhill once we got to the island. The steep terrain made it difficult to walk anywhere without a struggle. I soon became overheated and breathless. Once inside the cabin with our luggage, I made another disturbing discovery. Bunks. Not the ideal sleeping arrangement for burns survivors, especially ones who'd brought their elderly mothers, I thought, watching Mum heave her bag onto the bottom bunk.

'You're not getting me up there,' she huffed, eyeing the metal ladder that ran up one side of the bed. I followed her gaze to the mattress above hers. I knew where I'd be sleeping.

We had a range of activities to choose from, including archery, abseiling, rock climbing, canoeing and bushwalking. Although I wondered how survivors with breathing difficulties, mobility issues and damaged limbs would cope, I was still optimistic.

A counsellor had been organised to work with groups and individuals, and there was a collection of dedicated, hard-working parents. The burns survivors, most of them children, enjoyed the freedom of being with other survivors. Channel 7 were coming to film, and I'd also arranged for two women who specialised in camouflage make-up to see Cherie before the camp. I thought she'd be able to persuade them to demonstrate their products. Perhaps they could even join up with Burns Support Foundation to assist young girls and women to 'look good, feel better' – that type of plan.

As we gathered in the recreation room to listen to Cherie, my heart sank slowly into my shoes. She dragged a chair out the front and heaved herself up so she towered above us. Almost from the start, she began bellowing. I was the first one in trouble, although she didn't go so far as to name names.

'And before I forget, a couple of make-up girls came to see me a month or so back. I had to shoo them away. No more directing people to me, thank you. I'm far too busy to be dealing with Avon ladies.'

She continued in this vein for a while. Somehow the subject of funding came up, or lack thereof. Les Anger, one of the adult burns survivors, offered to speak to a solicitor friend of his, to see if the foundation could be registered as a charity. The suggestion was waved away. 'No thanks, Les. We can't have any old solicitor throwing advice at us. We need someone who specialises in this type of thing, otherwise we're going to end up in all sorts of trouble.'

Les turned to me and pulled a face. I was still smarting over the 'Avon ladies' comment. They happened to be two highly qualified professionals, attached to a reconstructive surgeon in Victoria. They had contacted me to request support for a client after seeing me on television; I was sure they would have been willing to help the foundation, but now the opportunity was lost.

Another organiser was out the front, reading her own riot act. I tuned out. All I could think of was that I was on an island with no means of escape. And I had a camera crew arriving the next day. If I could have stretched my arms far enough to attempt freestyle, I would have struck out for the mainland that very minute.

True to their word, the crew from *Today Tonight* turned up the next day. Alan was furious. He'd had a bad experience with the media, and was having nothing to do with them. 'If I see my face on national television, I'll sue!' he told Laura.

Like Alan, several other attendees made themselves scarce, more out of nerves than anger. Others reacted differently. One woman, well-endowed and waving her arms in the air like some Benny Hill skit, shrieked, 'Look at me, look at me!' as she dashed past the camera in bikini bottoms and a wet, translucent T-shirt.

'Oh God,' I said, rubbing my forehead. 'One burns survivor threatening litigation, the others overcome with shyness, and an impromptu wet T-shirt competition from one of the organisers. Just what we need to promote the camp. I'm so sorry.'

'Don't worry, Donna,' Laura grinned. 'It's amazing what a bit of editing can do.'

'Have you got enough here to make the show?'

'We've interviewed you, a few of the children, the counsellor and also Cherie, but ...'

'But what?'

She gave me a sly look. 'We could do with a bit more.'

'Oh yes? What did you have in mind?'

'See that wall?'

'What, the climbing wall?'

'That's the one.'

'What about it?'

'Can you climb it?'

'Laura, come on! I've got no muscles in my arms to pull myself up. I've got legs like a chicken. And those little bits of rock jutting out of the wall – I can't turn my feet sideways to balance on them.'

Laura's eyes widened. 'Donna, we really need you to do this for the story.'

'You're kidding.'

'No,' she said. 'I'm not.'

Years later, when I watched the scene from *Bridget Jones's Diary* in which Bridget is filmed sliding up and down a fireman's pole, I was reminded of my 'burns survivor tackles climbing wall' version, which was every bit as unflattering. But to hell with it. After what I'd been through, it wasn't that much to ask. Besides, the foundation was a brilliant concept, and if this media intervention helped keep it alive, why not?

Before filming, I had to be trussed up in a special climbing harness, a sort of nappy arrangement which was attached to a pulley. This would be used to haul me up the wall, making it look as though I was climbing when in fact I was being dragged skyward by five men heaving on the end of a rope. A frizz of orange hair fanned out beneath my safety helmet like Bozo the clown. To complete the picture, I wore a T-shirt emblazoned with a large 'S' – Superwoman. It was either that or Sucker, I couldn't be sure.

As the camera started rolling, I squinted at the footholds jutting out from the wall. 'They're not very big rocks.'

The men began to pull on the rope as I did my best to stay attached to the wall, pretending to climb and have fun. Every now and then I'd swing out into the air and dangle helplessly, like a windblown spider from its web.

'Just get back to the wall and pretend,' Laura shouted. 'You've got to make it to the top.'

Make it to the top I did, finally. I was so relieved, I managed to abseil back to the base of the wall with relative ease. I just wanted to get down! I was jelly-legged and shaking by the time I reached terra firma. I pulled off my helmet and turned to the laughing cameraman. 'I hope you got that, because I'm not doing it a second time.'

'No, Donna, that was good.'

The show aired nationally, six months after my first appearance on *Today Tonight*. The foundation's importance and need for funding didn't fall on deaf ears.

Susie O'Neill, a young, dynamic teacher who had initiated the KIDS (Kids in Dangerous Situations) Foundation, happened to see the show. From the television coverage she could see the Burns Support Foundation was in dire straits. She wanted to help. Her help would end up revolutionising the notion of burns survivor support in this country.

After a few fractious years working with the Burns Support Foundation, Susie, with the help of staff, volunteers and survivors, created the Burn Survivors Network as part of the KIDS Foundation. As one of its founding members, I became a guest speaker and continued my work with survivors both in and out of hospital.

Susie pioneered Camp Phoenix, a luxury holiday in an appropriate setting, with appropriate activities and a variety of support services attached, attended by more than 180 burns survivors and their families. This would never have happened if it were not for media intervention.

I was now even more convinced that the media could be a powerful tool to educate and inform, not only regarding burns survivors, but also victims' rights and domestic violence – the most common form of assault in Australia.

Throughout 1997, I continued to speak out, introducing the term 'survivor' rather than 'victim', encouraging the public not to be silent or invisible or weighted down by misguided guilt. I continued to work at exposing domestic violence for what it was – a criminal act – appearing on television, in newspapers and magazines and at various speaking engagements. I was kept busy but not busy enough to ignore one concern: Garry had been released from jail on 7 June 1997.

I was aware of his release date well before then though, through the Victims' Register. As the date grew closer, the fear grew, but I was comforted by the idea that because he would be on nine months' parole, he would have to report to the police frequently and probably wouldn't be allowed to contact me after such a serious assault. I rang the Victims'

Register and Serious Offender Review Board to check if my assumptions were correct.

'Parole conditions vary for each case,' the officer told me. 'The offender may have to report to his parole officer once a day or once a week or once a month, depending on the degree of risk he poses to the community, and the terms of his release.'

'Once a month? That doesn't seem like much of a monitoring system.'

'That's the way it works.'

'Is there something in place to protect me then – a sort of built-in AVO to inform him he's not allowed to approach or contact me?'

'This man has paid his dues. He's got rights too. He can approach anyone he likes.'

'But wouldn't he forfeit his rights after committing a crime, at least while on parole?'

'I told you, he's free to see anyone he wants. But if anything *does* happen, go and see the police.'

I had hesitated too long last time. I wasn't going to live in fear, waiting for him to finish me off.

By this stage my insomnia had returned with a vengeance. I thought I was on the road to recovery; I thought I was handling life again, but now it seemed I was back to square one, haunted by night terrors, struck with fear at the slightest sound – a branch against a window, a possum scuttling across the roof, an unexpected knock on the door. 'Don't whinge about unfairness – do something.' This was what I'd preached, and now I needed to practise it. I would not live in fear. I had to take steps to feel safe, to regain control.

I had already changed my surname; I was now Donna Carson.

I fitted a spy hole to my front door.

I informed neighbours of my situation.

I informed Wingham police of Garry's release.

I took out an AVO.

'This is the man who assaulted me. I want an AVO for life,' I told the chamber magistrate.

'Life? Don't be ridiculous. They don't give out life AVOs. Five years should do you.'

Garry did not attend court, but the AVO was served on him. The magistrate had a letter from his solicitor stating that his client agreed to an AVO, but only for two years.

'But I asked for five years,' I explained to the police prosecutor.

'He's agreed to two. If you need to top it up after that, come back.'

After court I went around to the office and asked to see the solicitor's letter.

'You can't see it. It's addressed to the magistrate,' I was told.

'But the contents concern me. I'd like the solicitor's address.'

'Well ...'

'Can I see the letter, just for a moment?'

The court worker sighed. 'Oh, okay, Donna, but be quick.'

I took the paper and made a note of the address. I also scanned the body of the letter, which implied that I was a thorn in the side of his client, Garry Clynes, who never wished to lay eyes on 'that woman' again. In order to keep the peace though, Mr Clynes would agree to a two-year AVO.

I wrote to his solicitor:

Dear Sir,

I applied for a five-year AVO against your client, Garry Clynes, so I could reclaim my safety. He offered two years through your representation. After viewing the enclosed photographs, you may understand why I requested five years.

It's reassuring to know that you can guarantee that your client has no desire to contact me or my family. It's reassuring to know that you can guarantee that I have nothing to fear from your client.

Yours sincerely,

Donna Blakemore

I may have lost my case for a five-year AVO against Garry, but my fighting spirit was not diminished. This was lucky because in the months ahead I would face my greatest challenge since my release from hospital. I'd take on that bureaucratic giant, the Department of Community Services. We'd go head to head – right down to the wire.

Twenty-one

It was September 1997. DOCS continued to toss my complaint about from one person to the next. Back in May of the previous year, Maureen Irvine from the Orange office had rung me. I told her I had recently handed everything over to my Taree solicitor, Annette Nicholson. I had decided to sue DOCS.

'I got tired of being given the run-around. The Department left me no choice,' I'd said.

'I'd still like to meet to discuss your request for help with legal fees you accrued to regain custody of your children.'

'What, so nothing about the injustice of the whole case?'

'I've only been sent to discuss the financial side of things.'

I agreed to meet with Maureen at my solicitor's office, but the day before the meeting, Annette rang me.

'As your legal advisor, I'm telling you now not to meet with this woman,' she said.

'But you agreed we'd listen to what she had to say. She's travelling all this way as we speak. Now you expect me to go back on my promise?'

'Why should you worry, after all they've done to you?'

'That's not how I work, Annette. You should have told me sooner. If you want the meeting cancelled, you'll have to explain to Maureen it was you who decided it shouldn't go ahead. And make sure that this doesn't come back to bite me. Make sure they don't accuse me of going back on my word.'

'I'll make it clear, Donna,' she said tightly.

It was now over a year later and DOCS were still avoiding negotiations with Annette. Despite knowing I had little in the way of finances, Annette was working long and hard for me. But DOCS continued to deny they were negligent. Annette pulled in a barrister.

Judith Mundey reminded me of a stick of TNT: neat, compact and full of energy, potentially explosive under a barrister's demeanour. Her husband, Jack Mundey, had taken on the government in the Green Bans of the 1970s, proving that ordinary people had the power to force those in power to change their ways. With this in mind I sensed that Judith would be sympathetic to my fight.

As I sat in her chambers in Sydney, surrounded by a sobering collection of leather-bound law books and gleaming wooden furniture, I was glad she was part of my team. That's not to say I was confident; although I was pushing on with my claim against the Department, a deep and pervasive fear continued to nag at me. Bruce Levet's words often returned to me: 'Don't even think about taking the Department on, Donna. They're just too powerful.'

His warning was not without substance. My legal team claimed that the Department had failed to follow their own procedures. They also asserted that the Department's negligence, including failure to investigate properly and failure to include me adequately in decisions affecting my children, had caused me to suffer 'injury, loss and damage'. However, this latter allegation highlighted one of the major stumbling blocks to my case. The Department could not be held responsible for the adverse effects their placement decisions had on other family members. DOCS, to all intents and purposes, seemed fireproof.

Even though both Judith and Annette held doubts about the successful outcome of my claim, they had decided to take it up. They were appalled at the Department's treatment of me and my children and decided that if I could fight, so could they.

Judith and I were almost at the end of our first brief meeting.

'One final thing, Donna. As a mother, what did you do for your boys?'

'Everything – I cooked, cleaned, shopped, worked, nurtured my boys. I did everything.'

'Did you arrange doctor's appointments for your children?'

'Yes, whenever they needed them. And all their immunisations were up to date.'

'Did you organise childcare?'

'Yes.'

'Birthday celebrations?'

'Yes.'

'School functions?'

'Yes, of course.'

'I'd like you to make a list. Be as specific as you can. Include all those sorts of things, as many as you can think of.'

I nodded and dug my diary out of my bag to make a note of it. As I wrote, I could see Judith was making a move to stand up and usher me to the door. I shifted in my seat, wondering how to tell her what was on my mind.

'Before I go, I need to tell you something,' I said, my voice cracking.

Judith shut the folder and looked across at me. 'Go on.'

'Garry's pleaded guilty. I've told the Department. So ... they obviously have something else on me.' I fingered the gold heart around my neck.

'You need to tell me everything,' Judith said sternly. 'We don't want any surprises.'

'I had affairs, when I was married. And I had an affair with Garry. I was still with Brian at the time.'

Judith looked visibly relieved. 'Donna, let me assure you, that doesn't give the Department a reason to do what they did. It's irrelevant.'

I looked her in the eye, steeling myself for the worst part. I was hoping to make a positive impression on her, to show her I was a good person, worthy of her defence. Instead I was blurting out my most embarrassing secrets.

'One more thing,' I said, speaking quickly, desperate to spit the words out. 'I fell pregnant to Garry when I had the affair with him, and I had an abortion.'

Judith didn't even look mildly shocked. She shrugged. 'Again, so what? You're allowed to choose a termination. That's your right. Your case has nothing to do with this.'

Judith's reassurances were comforting, but as I left her chambers I felt exposed, my transgressions finally laid bare.

On 20 October 1997, I had another appointment in Sydney. In order to examine the damage the Department had caused me by removing my children, I needed psychiatric assessments – one from a psychiatrist of my legal team's choosing, and one from a specialist picked by the Department. According to DOCS, I was already traumatised by my burns. How could losing my children traumatise me further?

'It's rather extraordinary.' Dr Robertson, the psychiatrist nominated by my legal team, pushed the box of tissues towards me and placed his fingertips together in a steeple. 'You don't know me, but I know a great deal about you.'

I dabbed at my eyes and blew my nose. 'What do you mean?'

'Do you remember Chris Basten?'

'My psychologist in Westmead?' A vision of an immaculate suit and polished shoes flashed across my mind. 'The well-dressed one.'

The doctor nodded. 'He was a colleague of mine in 1994. I knew your case through his debriefing sessions, and what you just recalled for me was like listening to Chris. You had the opportunity just now to embellish, but you didn't.'

'I don't think it needs embellishment, do you?'

'Most people embellish over time, colour or exaggerate, forget details. Years later, their story is often far removed from the original tale. Not in your case though.'

I went on to explain the sudden court order from the Department, the last-minute intervention by my Dubbo solicitor, and the horrendous family conference.

'What was it like, knowing you could lose your children?'

'It was the worst moment for me,' I said, beginning to cry again. 'I'm sorry.'

The doctor pushed the tissues closer. 'It's all right. Take your time.'

'Back then I was engulfed in darkness, except for the single flame of my children.' The emotion swelled once more, contracting my throat and chest. I began blinking frantically to stem the tears. I blew my nose again and dabbed at my cheeks. The doctor waited. 'When it became known to me that my boys were being taken, the flame went out, just like that.' I snapped my fingers. 'There was nothing. My children were my reason for hanging on. Without them, what was the point?'

Weeks after my appointment, Dr Robertson sent his findings to Annette Nicholson. It was a favourable report, Annette said, supporting the fact that my trauma was real. In his summary, the doctor wrote:

> I find it medically quite credible that her sudden physical
> deterioration after speaking to her solicitor on 24 June 1994 may
> have been caused or worsened by emotional shock.

He was also of the opinion that I had a 'strong and almost obsessional preoccupation with a sense of injustice in relation to DOCS'. He stated that this was 'likely to persist until a successful conclusion of litigation'.

I was uncomfortable with the term 'obsessional'. It made me sound a bit crazy, I thought. Wild, frenzied. But maybe he was right; maybe I was obsessed. Why wouldn't I be?

※

In June 1998 I took time off from everything to achieve another goal on my wish list. I went to the Red Centre, the heart of Australia, with Mum, Clyde, Shirl and Bodean. Coe didn't join us, much to my disappointment. He had decided to move in with his father. It seemed Coe had inherited a hefty dose of my determination. He wanted his dad to be a dad and, although I knew he was setting himself up for disappointment, I could do nothing to dissuade him.

I'd been planning the trip for 12 months and had informed Annette Nicholson of the dates we would be away. I had no mobile phone but would be ringing Sissy regularly. If Annette needed to tell me anything, she would have to contact Sissy and let her know.

I stopped at a phone box in Alice Springs to make yet another call to Sissy to give a progress report. I didn't have a chance to tell her about our trip though. She had news of her own, and blurted it out as soon as she heard my voice.

'Your solicitor's been trying to contact you, Donna. She says it's urgent.'

What now? I wondered, dialling Annette's number and feeding more coins into the slot.

The phone rang several times before the secretary picked up.

'Donna! Annette's out at present, but she's desperate to speak with you. I don't know what it's about. Can you ring back tomorrow?'

'I'm in the middle of the desert,' I said. 'But I'll do my best.'

Finally, in the dry, red heat of Uluru, I got onto Annette.

'You missed an appointment with Dr Phillips!' She was clearly ropeable.

My heart dropped. This sounded serious. 'What appointment?'

'You had an appointment with a DOCS psychiatrist. It's so unlike you, Donna. You're normally so reliable.'

I jammed the receiver between my ear and shoulder while I dug in my purse for more change. 'Annette, I didn't know anything about an appointment.'

'You missed it and we've had to arrange another which you *must* attend. Unfortunately, your trip is taking place at the time when very necessary procedures connected with your case are occurring. And your failure to attend the original appointment is going to hold everything up. You need to get yourself back here.'

'I'm standing in a phone box looking at Uluru and you're telling me I've got to cancel a trip I've been planning for 12 months? You knew about this trip! I saw you the day before we left. If you'd told me about the appointment, I could have postponed the holiday, but I'm not a mind reader. I don't accept blame anymore when I'm not to blame. I'll deal with it when I get back.'

And deal with it I did. On my return, I wrote Annette a letter. It was, I admit, sharp in tone, and sprayed with words and phrases in upper case. Several days later, I made an appointment to see her.

Her demeanour was one of controlled fury.

'Did you get my letter?' I asked, quite unnecessarily.

'Yes, I did,' she said. 'And I found it very offensive.'

'How do you think I felt, being in the middle of Australia and getting harangued for something I knew nothing about?'

'We sent you a letter.' She marched over to her desk and snatched up a sheet of paper. 'Here's a copy,' she said, thrusting the paper at me.

'Sent to an empty house. That's handy.' I scanned the letter and jabbed a finger at the top corner. 'It's even the wrong address, Annette.' I turned the letter around and held it in front of her face. 'This says number 13. I'm number three.'

She glared at the copy and pressed her lips together.

I waited a moment and then continued. 'I don't want to have this thrown back in my face in court, about how *I* failed to attend. You'd better explain to DOCS just how this happened. I'm not accepting the responsibility. This is what this whole thing's about. Plenty of people getting it wrong, and at the end of the day turning it around to be my fault.'

'All right, Donna. You've made your point.'

I took a step towards the door. 'And by the way, I'm not jumping in my car again to drive all the way to Sydney. If they want me down there, they can get me there and sort out my accommodation. I don't see why this has to come out of my pocket all the time. It's inconvenient enough to ask my mum yet again to look after Bodean while I'm running around attending DOCS appointments caused by their negligence.'

As I drove home, I tried to calm myself but was still shaking with anger as I pulled in. Once upon a time, in another life, I would have allowed myself to be pushed into a corner. But that was the old me – the one who'd died in my backyard. Along with my skin, I'd shed those layers of passivity and self-doubt. I'd stopped thinking, 'They know better'.

I was still polite and professional, but if anyone dared push their responsibilities onto me, I pushed them right back.

〳〵

My new appointment with the Department's chosen psychiatrist, Dr Phillips, was on 9 September 1998. The day before, Mum, Clyde and Bodean had taken me to Taree airport and waved me off. When they arrived back at my house, the phone was ringing. It was Annette.

'Where's Donna?' Her voice was high with stress.

'We've just put her on the plane,' Mum replied.

'I've had a phone call that she's not on the plane!'

'I'm telling you, we put her on the damned plane and waved her off.'

'But I've received word that she failed to board.'

'We saw her take off.'

Oblivious to all this, I rang Mum from the Hyde Park Inn, where the Department had organised my accommodation. Mum, indignant as hell, told me about Annette's phone call.

'It's like the woman wouldn't believe me,' she finished. 'Made me feel like a liar or something.'

'Don't worry about it, Mum.' Disquiet slipped over me as I perched on the bed. 'The Department's spies are obviously alive and well, and stuffing up as usual. I'm here, anyway. That's the main thing. Everything's fine now.'

But things were about to get worse. And even stranger.

My appointment was scheduled for ten o'clock the following morning. I set off with plenty of time to spare, wheeling my suitcase behind me through Hyde Park, past the Archibald Fountain, and across into Macquarie Street. Outside 237 Macquarie Street, at the Criminal Court of Appeals, I stopped to check the address on my paperwork: Suite 45, 9th Floor, 93 Macquarie Street. I began to pick up the pace, dragging my bag downhill, checking numbers as I went.

Number 197, St Stephen's Church. Number 149, Dorchester House. Number 145, The Royal Australasian College of Physicians. Christ, it was further away than I'd thought. Just as well I started out early, I thought, fighting to control my ragged breathing as my suitcase clattered and bumped over the worn paving. At least it was downhill.

Finally, down the far end of the street, I reached number 93, and stood panting for a moment outside the glass doors, trying to regain my composure. I checked my watch. I'd made it, with 20 minutes to spare.

A doorman in coat-tails and a top hat stood out the front watching me. As I noticed him, the first hint of panic curdled in my stomach.

'Can I help you, madam?'

I took out my letter once again. 'Is this 93 Macquarie Street?'

'That's correct, madam.'

'Would there be a doctor's suite here?'

'This is the Ritz-Carlton, madam. No doctors' rooms here.'

I showed him the letter and he perused it for a moment. 'This is the address, but we only have accommodation I'm afraid.'

'I don't believe this.'

'The doctors are all that way, as far as I know.' He nodded back up the hill, then handed me my letter. 'I'm sorry.'

I didn't have a mobile. I didn't have Annette's number with me. I couldn't see a phone box, and certainly not one with the Yellow Pages. I had 15 minutes to comb the length of Macquarie Street and find the elusive Dr Phillips.

I started back the way I'd come, dragging my luggage behind me. As I crossed back over Bridge Street I tried to hurry, puffing in the September warmth. I was beginning to overheat. Soon I was wheezing. I couldn't find the address. I was going to miss the appointment – again. I was going to fall down dead if I kept going.

I stopped in my tracks, leaning on the handle of my suitcase, doubled over, with lungs screaming and throat contracting. Think, Donna, think. Maybe they'd left a number off. Maybe it was 193 instead of 93? I forced myself to look up, scan the building in front of me for a number. Miraculously, there it was: 193. But that wasn't all. Beside the entrance, there was a brass plaque: Dr J. Phillips.

Thank God!

Stumbling into his waiting room, I rushed up to the receptionist. 'I'm really sorry.' I slumped across the counter, trying to expel air from my bursting lungs.

The receptionist looked panicked. 'Are you all right?'

'Am I late?' I couldn't get my voice above a whisper.

'It's fine,' she said. 'Sit down and I'll get you a glass of water.' She disappeared through a door behind the counter, appearing several seconds later with a large mug of water.

Dr Phillips appeared, suited and all business, and frowned at me from the doorway. 'What happened?'

'I was given the wrong address,' I was already close to tears, but angry now too. 'Is this deliberate?'

'Deliberate? That sounds a bit far-fetched; you probably got it wrong. Just calm down. You've got a breathing problem?'

I nodded and took another sip of water. The wheezing filled the silence. 'It's worse when I'm stressed,' I finally managed to say. I grasped the handle of my suitcase.

'You can leave that out here if you like,' Dr Phillips said.

'I need to bring it in. I've brought references, police files, other documents.'

'Very well, but they won't be necessary.'

Dr Phillips offered me a chair, and sat down across from me. He leaned back, turned slightly and patted one of a number of ring binders sitting on the desk.

'I've got your whole life here.'

He was going to wade through that biased investigation and end up believing their lies.

'But before I read that information, sit down and tell me your story. Start with your childhood.'

He listened, stone-faced, as I described my life. Once I'd covered my childhood, assured him I'd never been molested, explained I hadn't been through any traumas at a young age or been depressed or suicidal, I moved on to my marriage and my relationship with Garry. Once again

I related the assault, the hospital treatment, the conviction by the Department. By this time I was bawling my eyes out.

'I just wanted help with the legal fees to get my children back, and I wanted them to apologise – to me, to my family, to all the people they wrongly informed.' I was aware that I was beginning to rant and rave, but I couldn't stop. 'I wanted them to apologise for the shame and guilt I felt, for the problems I had to deal with when I finally got my damaged children back, for the lack of trauma counselling for my boys ...'

As I paused to wipe my eyes and take a breath, Dr Phillips took the opportunity to interject: 'I'm absolutely gobsmacked! I've just had another case in here very similar to yours. Not the burns, of course, but a situation where children were removed, possibly unfairly.' He shook his head. 'Just horrific.'

As I stepped back into Macquarie Street, I thought it hadn't gone so badly. After all, Dr Phillips was selected by DOCS to prepare a report, but he was supportive of what I had to say.

When I finally received a copy of his report from Annette, it seemed that the doctor had changed his mind. He'd read all those folders, whatever they were, whatever they said, and decided I was a liar after all. Or perhaps he'd never believed me in the first place. Whatever the case, his report was well and truly supportive of the Department.

> On balance, it seems unlikely that DOCS had acted in the manner alleged by Ms Carson ... Giving Ms Carson the benefit of the doubt, I believe her ongoing psychological symptoms may, in very small measure, link with the way DOCS officers handled the issue of care of her children ...
>
> If this was proved to be the case, then Ms Carson may have suffered some but relatively minor psychological damage as a consequence. I state this noting her vulnerable psychological state at the time and her then major depressive disorder ...
>
> Whilst I dislike giving percentage estimates, it would be reasonable to attribute 5% of Ms Carson's psychological symptoms

as resulting from the possible action of DOCS officers and 95% as resulting from the action of Clynes and her substantial physical injuries.

Whatever Dr Phillips' abilities as a psychiatrist, his reading comprehension needed work. In his report, he quoted from Dr Robertson's report. However, he quoted incorrectly:

> He noted her history of having deteriorated physically after speaking with her solicitor on 24 June 1994 in relation to her children, but stated that it was 'quite incredible' that such an event may have caused her sudden deterioration.

Dr Robertson had written nothing of the sort. He had stated it was 'quite credible', not 'incredible'.

Dr Robertson responded to Dr Phillips' claims in his final report:

> On page 9 of his report, I think that Doctor Phillips is often dealing with matters of fact which are a matter for the court to determine; eg, in the final paragraph on this page, he states 'On balance it seems unlikely that DOCS had acted in the manner alleged by Ms Carson.' Ms Carson believes firstly that DOCS accepted the story that her burns were the result of a suicide attempt or a suicide pact; they accepted the history that she was drinking excessively; and they failed to look to her mother as a person who would be more suitable to care for her children than her ex-husband's brother's wife.

My legal team also sought a report from my psychiatrist in Taree, Dr Mike Richardson, whom I had seen on a number of occasions. He described me as 'an authentic and internally consistent historian', pointing out that I often supported my accounts 'with documents, newspaper clippings and photographs'. His summary was as follows:

Donna Carson survived an attempted murder, horrific injuries, dreadful persistent pain, multiple plastic operations, protracted hospitalisation and has been left with hideous facial and body deformities. She will, for the rest of her life, be socially and sexually isolated because of her repellent scarring.

Her psychological approach to these burdens has been one of acceptance and stoicism. She has adjusted to her predicament in an heroic way, even with a sense of humour. Her voluntary work with victims, carers and the police attest to her willingness to confront these issues head on. In essence she has transcended the consequences of her injuries without rancour.

Her treatment at the hands of DOCS was iniquitous. DOCS failed to verify their original hopelessly incorrect assessment of Donna as a mother and a victim of assault. They persisted for many months in seeing her as the perpetrator of child abuse. They brought all their bureaucratic powers to mete heavily against Donna by effectively excommunicating her from her two children at a time when she was near death.

As a direct result of DOCS actions Donna suffered severe grief which became a major depressive illness. It was a serious and protracted illness which was to further erode her wellbeing, her quality of life and ability to persevere despite all. Yet she has survived. Her depressive illness has been successfully treated with medications and supportive psychotherapy. Her prognosis must be guarded and will ultimately depend on the response she receives within the court system. To date she has received neither explanation nor even an apology from DOCS.

By the end of 1998, a hearing date had been set for 5 February 1999, at the District Court in Sydney. My emotions were in overdrive. This was the big showdown – DOCS and me at ten paces.

Twenty-two

It's 4 February 1998, just before dawn in inner-western Sydney. Twenty-seven-year-old Gabriella Mazzali is a nurse, out from Britain on a working visa. It's been a warm night and she's sleeping fitfully in her Ashfield flat, spread-eagled on top of the sheets in a pair of boxer shorts.

She is jolted awake by a loud thump, followed by another and another. There is a crack. Her front door is being smashed in. It's not the first time.

Seconds later, he's in her room. She turns in alarm and half heaves herself out of bed. She smells the petrol and inhales in shock as the cold fuel hits her skin.

She is running now, out of the apartment, dripping with fuel.

She makes it past the splintered door and out onto the landing. She hears his footsteps behind her, hears him shouting. She begins to pound on a neighbour's door; her ex-boyfriend just a few metres behind. He's closing in. There is no answer to her banging. And there is no time to wait.

She stumbles to the next door, falls against it, batters it with her fist. The door flies open. The landlord reaches out. He goes to grab her, to drag her inside to safety.

Another neighbour, Steve Swain, appears. He's heard the screaming and thumping.

There's the landlord about to pull Gabby inside. There's Gabby, hysterical, her hands over her face, her dripping arms pushed in close over her bare breasts. And there's her ex; he's right behind her now.

Steve jams himself against the back of Gabby's ex, clamps his arms around him and holds him in a vice. The ex struggles to bend his wrist, to worm his fingers into his pocket.

I imagine the scene again and again. It flashes in my head like a bizarre strobe.

The lighter is flicked.

A bang like thunder, and up she goes, engulfed in orange flame. With the force of the explosion, the neighbour, Steve, is catapulted back into a plate-glass window. It cracks and splinters. Shards of glass lodge in his skin.

Gabby's ex's clothes are on fire and he's careering back to Gabby's flat, setting the puddles of fuel alight as he goes.

But Gabby is a screaming human fireball. Her skin is disintegrating in the flames. She's running too, away from her flat, towards the stairwell. She's throwing herself down the steps, rolling and bumping to the landing below, trying to put herself out.

Steve picks himself up and stumbles into his kitchen. He grabs a jug of iced water from his fridge, leaps down the stairs and tosses it over Gabby. Her skin sizzles. Within seconds there are more people with water. Gabby lies smouldering at the foot of the stairs.

I first read about Gabby Mazzali in the newspaper, and immediately began sending messages of support to her and to Sandra and Terry, her mother and stepfather, who had flown out from England to be by her side. The month after the assault I offered to visit them on my next trip to Sydney.

Sandra and Terry were already at breaking point. Unable to move into Gabby's flat because of fire damage, they were sharing a single room at Concord Hospital.

We spoke for hours, but I refused to see Gabby. 'No, not at this point,' I said when her parents asked if I would visit her. Gabby had burns to over 90 per cent of her body, but along with the top of her head, palms and soles of her feet, Gabby had saved her face.

I knew what massive doses of morphine could do to your head – I'd seen imaginary rats galloping across my hospital room and nursing staff morphing into inhabitants from *Planet of the Apes*. The imagination could be a scary thing, especially clouded with drugs. I didn't want Gabby to see my face and somehow think that this was how she was going to look. She didn't need that.

But a week later, I received a phone call that changed my mind. It was Gabby's mum, Sandra. She was crying.

'Please come quickly, Donna. Gabby's fighting another infection. They don't think she's going to make it. And she's asking for you.'

I went back to Sydney and the next morning Dad drove me out to Concord.

All burns units are different. To enter this one you had to buzz. Inside, just along the corridor, I noticed a sink. Above it hung a sign suggesting people wash their hands; there was no insistence though and most would assume this was for staff use. There were no gowns for visitors either. That's odd, I thought.

Gabby shared a room with three others. A woman with a bandaged leg lay across from her. She had visitors who were neither gowned nor scrubbed. There was a man in stubbies and a T-shirt, with thongs and dirty feet, and a child with a hacking cough. Next to Gabby was a burns patient who'd just come back from having a smoke.

In this shared ward, Gabby was on display. Oh, she was a show! The other patients, as well as their visitors, kept glancing sideways at her and her bank of machines. Her injuries were so extensive, so shocking, she could have died right there. She was swathed in bandages, with just her small pink face, the tips of her fingers and the tops of her toes exposed. She was dripping with sweat, blood and ooze, which would soon harden and dry, making her skin bleed when the staff removed the old dressings.

Discarded tissues, stained pink and yellow from wiping away the seepage, were strewn across her table. A nurse came with medication to be injected into her mainline, and placed it on the table among the tissues.

I stood at the foot of her bed and closed my eyes against the horror of it. Jesus, she's going to die in here, I thought. If the burns don't get her, the infections will.

Gabby opened her eyes. 'Donna?'

I nodded. 'I'm here, Gabby.'

'Make the pain go away.'

Terry and Sandra moved aside to let me get closer.

'Gabby, I can't make the pain go away. No one can.' I kept my words precise to push through the morphine.

She groaned.

'But I know one thing. You're beating this.'

'I'm not.'

'What do you mean, you're not? You're beating this every second of every minute of every day.'

Gabby continued to cry and I gently stroked her arm. 'Look at your beautiful face, your beautiful eyes. You're doing so well, you've come so far. You're amazing.'

A wounded adult was no different to a wounded child. Old or young, it hurt just as badly. Whatever the age, someone in deep physical and psychological pain needed words of encouragement. Tough talks had their place, but this wasn't the time for one.

I waited in silence for a little while, standing by her bed, stroking her cheek. We talked about my boys, her cat, her family and friends, my life in Wingham. Ordinary, everyday things. Relieved to see their daughter responding, Terry and Sandra left us alone and went to speak to Dad.

When we left the hospital, Dad noticed my face was dark as thunder. 'What's up?' he asked.

'Let's put it this way, Dad. When I flew overhead that night in the Care Flight helicopter, thank heavens this inn was full. She's a Concord nurse. Up until two months ago, she was working in this place. This is the best they can do for one of their own? If that's true, I'd have left in a body bag.'

I hadn't said anything to Gabby's parents because I didn't want to alarm them any further, but I was furious. It was true, she was receiving state-of-the-art treatment. She had Peter Haertsch, one of the best burns specialists in the country, treating her, and a new artificial skin had been flown into Australia especially to rebuild her body. But these efforts would amount to nothing if she died. To give her the best chance of survival, she needed a germ-free environment. And privacy.

On the way back up the coast, I stopped at Newcastle to visit with Robyn Cotterell-Jones, the coordinator of Victims of Crime Assistance League, or VOCAL. Robyn had become a friend and colleague.

'You know about lobbying, Donna,' she said sternly, as I finished describing Gabby's situation. 'Go home and write a letter. No more than a page or it won't be read.'

'Yeah, yeah, all right,' I said. Robyn knew I had a tendency to get carried away when I was writing about something that upset me. For someone who claimed to dislike writing, I still wrote letters the size of telephone directories when pushed.

'When you've finished, fax it to me. I'll attach a VOCAL cover letter and get it off to everyone.'

'Everyone?'

'Politicians and the like – those in power.'

Within 48 hours, Gabby's mother was on the phone.

'Donna! Gabby has been moved to a private room.'

'Fantastic!'

'That's not all. This man called Bob Carr contacted us.'

'That's the Premier of New South Wales.'

'He's arranging accommodation and a car, extending our visas indefinitely and giving us financial assistance. I suspect, my dear, you had something to do with this.'

I smiled. I knew now that Gabby would have a fighting chance.

※

Gradually, Gabby got stronger. I visited her regularly and continued to send presents, beach posters and Bodean's artwork to help decorate her room.

'Look, you can pick up a cup and drink,' I said to her one visit. 'It took me much longer than you to learn that.'

'Really? How long did it take you to walk?'

'I could barely stand this far down the track. I know you can already take a few steps. I'm so proud of you, Gab!'

'They say my hair won't grow back.'

'We'll see. They told me that too. I've got hair in places where I thought I'd never see it again, believe me.'

She smiled.

I continued to chat with Sandra and Terry almost daily and urged them to keep an eye on the police investigation.

'What can we do?' asked Sandra.

'I know it's hard to think about the court process with Gab in hospital, but you must keep tabs on things. VOCAL's legal advisor, Howard Brown, will help you out. Take photos of Gabby as soon as possible. Even videos when all her dressings are down. As the police haven't taken any photos, invite them to take photographs with you. This case could take two years to get to court, and by then Gab's going to be walking around, looking fine in comparison to how she is now. You want everyone involved to see what your daughter is going through now.'

'Is that what you did?'

'Photographs of my initial injuries were never thought of, never taken. Not until the investigating officer requested them almost 12 months after the assault. That isn't good enough. I'm campaigning for police procedures to include immediate photographs of victims' injuries. You *must* get photos of Gabby organised.'

Sandra was red-eyed and puffy-faced. I imagine she'd once had a cheerful, easy-going demeanour. But dealing with all this had given her that bewildered, dishevelled look I'd seen on dozens of people supporting loved ones, trying not to fall apart themselves.

'The police haven't come near us,' said Sandra. 'I'm waiting to tell them about that bastard's behaviour before the assault. Gabby was ringing me every week, telling me about the stalking, the phone calls. She spoke to me the day after he broke in and threw red wine over her. I knew something awful was going to happen. I told her to put the police number on speed dial and get the locks changed. I rang her daily, I was so worried for her.' Sandra shook her head.

'You need to speak to the investigating officers, and they need to talk to Gabby – more than once. They need to make her part of the whole process. There are some things they aren't allowed to show or tell her, but there's still plenty of information they can check through her.'

'Terry and I should probably contact the police, see what's happening,' she said.

'Absolutely. Contact the police. Contact VOCAL. Take photographs.'

Around this time, I was involved in a police campaign in Sydney targeting domestic violence. I was touted as their 'face of domestic violence', and my photo was plastered over newspapers and television screens. My police media officer knew of Gabby's case and lined me up to speak with one of the officers involved in the investigation.

The officer was dismissive when I called. I launched into an explanation of the work I'd been doing for the police on their campaign.

'Yes, I know all about domestic violence,' he huffed. 'I've been a victim myself.'

'Really?'

'That's right. I had a girlfriend who used to lay into me. I'll never forget it.'

'Yes, it can certainly happen to men.' I stepped carefully. 'That's why, if you'd ever heard me speak, you'd know I rarely refer to specific genders.'

I went on to talk about Gabby's case, and my involvement in it, mentioning her parents' desire to make a statement.

'What would they know? They were on the other side of the world when this crime was committed.'

'Yes, but Gabby had told Sandra about the ex-boyfriend's stalking. They'd discussed her fear of this man, his behaviour leading up to this crime.'

'I didn't know any of this.'

'Why not talk to them? You can work out what's useful to the case.'

'Fine.'

'And with VOCAL's involvement, and the media interest here and overseas, it'll be such good PR for you boys in blue. Everybody will be watching.'

This man wasn't stupid. He could hear the subtext loud and clear. Stuff up, and everyone will know.

Twenty-three

Towards the end of 1998, with only weeks until my case against DOCS was to be heard, Judith Mundey, Annette Nicholson and I all agreed that as the legal system was a boys' club, we needed a boy on our team. Not just any boy, but a senior counsel, a QC.

'It's short notice, but we've found someone,' Annette told me in her office one morning. 'Bob Toner.'

'You mean Robert Toner?'

Annette looked at me sharply. 'Why?'

'I know him. Sort of, anyway.'

She closed her eyes for a moment and gave a small sigh of resignation. 'How?'

'It was through my appearance on *The Midday Show* about the legal system, around 12 months ago. I wasn't actually in the studio for it; they taped me at Dad's place.'

'So I suppose Robert was there to defend the system.'

I nodded. 'They really put him in the hot seat.'

'Well, we're lucky to get him,' Annette said. 'He's up this way on holidays. He agreed to have a brief meeting here, and then do some background reading on his break.'

When I met Robert the next week, he shook hands with me then tugged at his beard. 'You look familiar.'

'*The Midday Show*, August 1997.'

'Oh, that's right!'

'They really tried to ambush you, didn't they?'

'How did I handle it? I can't recall.'

'You went very well. Put us all in our places,' I said, only slightly tongue-in-cheek. After all, he *was* my QC.

We arranged to have a case conference in Sydney in January, which would hopefully include all the witnesses for the prosecution – some in person, some by phone.

The waiting room in Robert's office was impressive, painted in muted colours and furnished with rich, brown Chesterfield lounges, thick carpet and glossy side tables. Dad, red-faced and ominously subdued, was already there when I arrived with Mum and Bodean. Brian appeared soon after with Coe, who was now 16 and living and working with his dad in Sydney.

It soon became apparent that Brian was the only one enjoying himself, swaying like an elephant in his baggy trousers and joggers, and pleased that everyone was still talking to him. My parents were never openly rude to Brian but it was becoming a real effort to be polite. In any event, Brian was willing to take the stand to endorse my parenting, which contradicted the picture his own family had painted.

I was called into Robert's chambers first, just as John and Shirl arrived. There were the usual law books, leather chairs, polished furniture and autumnal tones, but somehow it was all bigger, richer, shinier – more impressive than Judith's. Over to one side a neat-as-a-pin secretary tapped away at a keyboard, providing a staccato backdrop to our discussion.

Robert's manner was aloof, confident. He kept his face expressionless. No smile or grimace; his mouth seemed to barely move behind the thick bristles of his beard as he questioned me.

He asked about my methods of discipline as a parent: 'So, you hit your children?'

'No, I didn't hit my children. However, I may have smacked.'

'So you did hit Coe when he was naughty?'

'No, I smacked him. But not often. Sometimes on the hand or on the bottom. Never anywhere else.'

'What's the difference between a hit and a smack?'

'I think of a smack as using an open hand. A hit would be using a closed fist.'

'I see.' He paused for a moment and regarded me across the paperwork in front of him. 'I do find it hard to believe you rarely hit your children. Many people would resort to that type of discipline. I mean, when a child is really naughty ...'

'I do remember one time in particular.'

'What were the circumstances?'

I told him about the day Coe, still a pre-schooler, had pinched Brian's matches, which he persisted in leaving around the house. Coe went down the back of the yard with Jodie, the next-door neighbour. I'd caught them, sitting cross-legged, giggling and whispering, hunched together over a pile of dead leaves and dried grass. Coe had a match out. He was holding it between his thumb and finger, ready to strike it on the side of the box. Seconds later and the whole yard would have gone up.

'And you smacked him afterwards?'

'I was constantly asking Brian to put his matches out of harm's way. I'd do my best to pick them up, and reinforce to Coe that he mustn't touch them.'

'How many times did you smack Coe?'

'Never – ever – do – that – again.' I counted each word off on my fingers. 'Five times, on his backside, through thick trackpants.'

We discussed other parenting issues: who worked, who paid the bills, who looked after the children. I did all of them. After this, we moved onto the subject of my drinking.

'I enjoy a drink,' I told him.

'How much would you drink?'

'I'm a social drinker. I like going out with my friends.'

'Have you ever got drunk?'

'No, I've been tipsy.'

'But have you ever been really drunk?'

'I told you, I've been tipsy.'

'What's the difference?'

'I think of drunk as falling down, out of control. I didn't get drunk. I had responsibilities. I had work, my children. I wouldn't have been able to operate if I was falling down drunk.'

'You're trying to tell me you've never been rip-roaring drunk, dancing on the table with a lampshade on your head?'

'No, I like to be in control of my actions, to know what's going on around me. In fact, I was often called upon to deal with difficult customers up at the club. Ones who'd had too much to drink and wouldn't leave quietly. I've even broken up fights.'

Robert raised his eyebrows slightly.

'If I was rip-roaring drunk with a lampshade on my head, I wouldn't have been able to do that sort of thing.'

He asked further questions and made a phone call. 'I've just found out who the judge will be,' he said, replacing the receiver. 'He's very good. We like him.'

'That's something,' I said, before adding, 'strange that it's been scheduled to start on a Friday though.'

He frowned. 'That can't be right. It's been set down for a few days, so it wouldn't start on a Friday. You must be mistaken.' He picked up his desk calendar and scrutinised it for several seconds. 'Hmph! Now that *is* unusual.'

'I'm not surprised,' I said. 'The whole thing seemed fishy from start to finish. It's one more tactic to make it as inconvenient as possible for me, having me pay for all my witnesses' accommodation over the weekend on top of everything else.'

'Let's see if we can call your witnesses for the following week, and then you won't have that expense. But that really is strange.' He frowned again at his calendar before resuming. 'Now, there's a possibility they may want to settle out of court. They're not talking to us yet, not negotiating, but they may as the day draws closer. We believe that if we can get what I suggested, that should do you.'

'If I got millions, it wouldn't make up for the damage they've caused. This is about receiving an apology for something they got wrong. It isn't about money.'

'I'm afraid money is exactly what it's about, whether you like it or not,' he said, unblinking. 'The legal system works well. It's just all you victims wanting justice, but the legal system has nothing to do with justice.'

'It's a shame nobody explained that to me a long time ago.'

'Nothing is guaranteed though,' said Robert. 'By law I have to let you know that if we lose the case you will be facing a huge bill for all costs involved. Tens of thousands of dollars.' He enunciated the amount with particular care. 'Do you understand? Tens of thousands of dollars. Have you got that sort of money?'

'To the first part, I say yes, I do understand. And to the second part my answer is no, but that's not your problem.'

My senior counsel stared at me, clearly unimpressed. 'You might think you know what you're doing, but you're going to be like everyone else in that witness box. You won't be able to answer a straight question. People go on and on. They go here, they go there –' he waved his hand around. 'You're even starting now. When you're asked a question, you must listen to it, and then give just a yes or no answer.'

'But –'

'You're argumentative – and talkative. Just listen.'

So I bit my tongue and listened to his lecture. Robert turned his attention to a pile of documents on my lap. 'What have you got there?'

I took hold of a large wad of stapled papers lying on top of the heap. 'This is the timeline of events you asked me to prepare.' I stretched my arm across the desk and placed it in front of him. If I expected a 'well done', I was to be disappointed.

'Yes,' he huffed, flicking through the information. 'I already have a copy of all this. You've included a lot of unnecessary detail. What's all that other stuff?'

'Documents, reports, records – to verify the events I refer to in the timeline.'

'Such as?'

I leaned over the desk and tugged the timeline towards me, flicking to different examples. Robert was still unimpressed.

'Got that. Got that. That's useless. That's biased. That's irrelevant. Too flowery. Too vague.' On and on he went, ticking off nearly every piece of documentation I'd put together. I did manage to get his attention with one item – one little gem he wasn't expecting.

'I have the draft letter my DOCS case worker wrote for me, to help me put together my original letter of complaint to the Department.'

He stared at me, eyes like saucers. 'You have *what*?'

'I've got a draft copy of my complaint, written by Neil Wilkins.'

'In his handwriting?'

'Yes. Neil was the caseworker who finally got my file from Parkes. It took so long he knew something was wrong. We had a meeting, Neil and I. I wasn't allowed to actually read my file at that stage, but he had it in front of him and he told me it was scandalous. He said, "You need to take this to the top." I didn't know what to do. He sketched out a letter for me and I kept it.'

'Is it the original?' Robert asked.

'Yes, like I said, I kept it.'

He held out his hand. 'Give it to me.'

I handed him the letter.

'This is brilliant,' he muttered. He seized the phone. The next minute he was speaking to Annette Nicholson in Taree.

'Do you realise what I've got in my hand? The original draft letter that a DOCS worker in Taree, a worker on Donna's case, wrote out for her. He actually drafted a letter for her to use in her complaint against the Department. And I've got it, right here in front of me.'

Friday, 5 February dawned hot and humid. Mum, Dad and I met at Robert's chambers in the city.

'DOCS made an offer,' he told me. 'But it's very low. I've rejected it.'

My shoulders slumped. I'd been hoping for a miracle.

'It's a good sign though.' He turned and picked up a large red bag decorated with fancy braid and embroidered initials. 'Remember: try not to veer off the point. Don't go rambling on. And above all, don't argue!'

We stepped out onto Martin Place, with Robert leading the way.

'The walk will do us good,' he said. 'We'll head down Castlereagh Street.'

Dad frowned and looked at him. 'Elizabeth Street'll do us. It's quicker.'

'No, we'll take Castlereagh,' Robert replied firmly.

'I'm telling you it's quicker to go Elizabeth.'

I put a hand on Dad's arm. 'Calm down, Dad. It doesn't matter, as long as we get there.'

Dad wrenched his arm away. 'I was on the trams for years. I've worked on the buses; I've been a courier in the city. I know Sydney like the back of me hand!'

I turned to Robert, who was doing his best to hide his annoyance. 'And you think *I'm* argumentative? In this family, I'm the diplomatic one.'

I don't remember which way we walked in the end, but I do remember it felt like I was a dead man walking. I was steaming in the morning heat, covered against the sun in black trousers and a loose blouse as I couldn't stand any more pressure on my skin: the burns suit was enough. I was raw with nerves, anxious about what lay ahead.

Mum was in her best dress, wide-eyed and pasty, staring ahead as she walked and clutching her handbag in the crook of her arm. If Mum was pale, Dad was the opposite. Crimson-faced and furious, he marched stiffly beside Mum in his old flares and a crisp blue shirt. It wasn't his safari suit, but it wasn't far from it.

I felt sick just looking at them, imagining the defence tearing Mum to shreds and goading Dad to explosion point. It would take very little to demonstrate their image of the incompetent grandmother and the aggressive grandfather.

The foyer of Madison Towers was teeming with people – a mass of billowing gowns and dark suits pushing trolleys stacked with files, tugging suitcases, juggling armloads of folders. The crowd was being sucked into a row of lifts, the doors snapping shut behind them.

I hated lifts. Jammed into a wall of bodies, I was close to hyper-ventilating. Tens of thousands of dollars, I kept thinking.

Eventually we were spewed out into a huge waiting area surrounded by doors leading off into courtrooms and offices. Robert was talking to Judith, small and dark in her wig and gown. I stood with my parents at an enormous window, staring out at the city, and beyond it to Redfern, where we grew up.

Dad was pacing – still fuming and now muttering to Mum, who was doing her best to calm him. But she wasn't doing so well herself. She had gone from white to custard-yellow, and her eyes were glazed; she was prime heart-attack material. I took a deep breath. Just do what you have to do – I chanted my old mantras, over and over. We'll see who can't do this and can't do that. We'll see.

I turned and noticed Robert by my side. 'Come with me, Donna.'

'Mum and Dad too?'

'No, they're right where they are.'

He led me across the vast waiting area to a small office, and offered me a chair. 'Wait here. Something's happening.' Then he left, closing the door behind him.

I checked my watch. We were due in court in less than 15 minutes. If something were happening, it had better hurry up. I sat, still as stone, my hands folded in my lap. I concentrated on the closed door.

In another minute, Robert was back. Judith was with him, grim-faced and silent.

'They want to settle,' he said.

I jerked my head up to meet his eyes. 'What happens now?'

'The amount is not as much as we want. I'm going to reject it. But we'll just sit here for a minute or so – make out we're discussing the offer.'

I buried my head in my hands.

'This is good, Donna,' said Judith.

We sat in silence for a little while, before Robert swept out again, with Judith behind him.

The seconds ticked on. Please God, be with me.

Soon I heard footfalls, the sound of the door opening. I straightened up. Robert was back. 'They're starting to up their bid.'

'Is it enough?' I whispered.

'We need more.' His face was blank. He certainly didn't look hopeful.

Robert left the room again. In less than a minute he reappeared.

'We're nearly there. We'll give it a few more minutes,' he said, taking a seat.

At last, Robert stood up. 'I'm going to tell them we're rejecting their offer,' he said calmly. 'Get yourself ready to go into court. The doors will be opening at any moment.'

I watched him disappear out the door and the skerrick of hope I'd allowed myself to feel drained away in an instant. They were not going to settle; I knew it. Minutes from now I would have to face court. I would be put under the microscope again and, worse than that, I would be forced to witness my parents suffer the same indignity.

I pushed myself to stand, picked up my handbag and took a deep breath. Clutching the back of my chair, I steadied myself as a wave of dizziness swept over me. Come on, Donna. You can do this.

Suddenly my focus was broken. Robert flung the door open and sailed back into the room. I looked at his face. 'What's happened?'

He gave me the gift of a small smile behind his beard. 'They've agreed. We've settled. It's over.'

A short while after my time in the District Court, I underwent more therapy. Retail therapy. I bought a beautifully restored timber home in the heart of Wingham, a box of deluxe golf balls for senior counsel Robert Toner and three stunning crystal bowls: one for Annette Nicholson, one for Judith Mundey and one for myself. Appropriately, the bowl was called 'The Cauldron'.

'It was a witch hunt, after all,' I told Judith when she rang up to thank me. 'So now we three witches each have our own cauldron.'

'It was a good result, Donna. Although I'll always regret one thing.'

'Oh? And what's that?'

'Not having the opportunity to cross-examine Denise Blakemore and Maria Williams. I must say, I was looking forward to that.'

'After all that "undue stress and drama" DOCS inflicted, I'm peeved about something else. I don't really feel my actions made much of a difference to DOCS. They've paid me off without admitting liability, and now they'll continue removing children when they shouldn't, not taking action when they should. I mean, I've never disagreed with their existence, just with their incompetence.'

'Donna, let me assure you of one thing,' said Judith. 'You made a great deal of difference. You rocked that department to its very foundations. It was a moral victory. We need more people like you to come forward and take a stand.'

I wanted to believe Judith, but I had my doubts. 'I hope you're right. I hope I did do some good.'

'These people don't give up unless they have to. If they're confident they can defend a case, why settle? Believe me, you had them on the back foot. What you've achieved is nothing short of astonishing.'

So I had my settlement – a little more than I'd hoped as Robert, Judith and Annette had all been overly generous in their fee structure. But weeks after the case, I was still waiting for an apology. After several newspaper articles had mentioned that I had not heard from Carmel Niland, the Director-General of DOCS, she contacted me to arrange a meeting in Taree.

She presented me with a magnificent bouquet of purple and yellow flowers and a letter of apology on behalf of DOCS, without admissions. She spent some time explaining the 'ins and outs' of departmental procedures, unaware that I was well-versed in the Department's procedures. She stressed the fact that the children were always the Department's main concern.

'However, Donna,' she said, looking me straight in the eye, 'obviously your case was not handled as well as it could have been. And I'm truly, truly sorry for the extra grief and trauma you and your family suffered. Will you accept my apology on behalf of the Department?'

After listening and nodding politely for so long, at this point I began to cry. 'From the beginning, that's all I ever wanted to hear. I'm not a vindictive woman. I understand people make mistakes. All I wanted was for your department to say sorry.' I fished a handkerchief out of my bag. 'I think DOCS is important but, in reality, it failed my children. It failed me as a parent. It failed my family. You need to look more closely at how you go about things so families like mine don't have to suffer needlessly.'

'Let me assure you, our procedures for notification and investigation have been improved. We want to get it right.' She stopped then, and in the ensuing silence regarded me coolly. From another room I could hear muffled voices, laughter, a phone ringing. I dabbed at my eyes again and opened my mouth to speak, but Ms Niland cut me off. 'I must add that *you* need to look more closely at your choice of men.'

As these words slipped smoothly out of her mouth, my tears vanished. Just like that. I spoke slowly. 'I hope you're not insinuating that your department's bungle is somehow my fault, or that I'm responsible for someone else's behaviour.'

Ms Niland's cheeks reddened. 'I didn't mean it like that.'

'I know exactly what you meant.'

We sat in awkward silence for a minute or two before the Director-General stood up. 'I feel like a cup of coffee,' she said brightly, straightening her skirt. 'Would you like me to bring you one as well?'

※

My case against DOCS was finally over, but another major legal battle appeared on the horizon in 1999. And, while I wasn't a player in this one, I intended to be closely involved.

Twenty-four

The trial of Stephen Rae was scheduled to take place in October 1999 at Parramatta District Court. Gabriella Mazzali's ex-boyfriend was listed as pleading not guilty to the charge of attempted murder.

Gabby had returned to the UK the previous year to continue her recovery. Still a sucker for homeless pets, I'd adopted her cat, and Gabby phoned regularly to check up on him. She also needed moral support over Stephen's impending trial. He had sacked his legal team more than once, repeatedly delaying the trial date.

'I'm sick of packing my suitcase and preparing to fly over only to be told yet again that the trial's been delayed. I can't do this anymore, Donna.'

'It's a tactic to wear you down. They want you to give up, Gab, but you're strong. This man is going to be jerking your chain for some time, so you're going to have to change your response. Pack a bag and keep it packed. Leave it under your bed.'

While we waited for the trial date to be set, I supported Gabby long-distance. Anytime she received news, she'd phone and I'd decipher the legal jargon. When it was beyond my understanding, I'd ring Robyn Cotterell-Jones or Howard Brown from VOCAL.

Gabby rang when the trial date had been set. 'My WAS officer contacted me. She said the DPP felt it was unnecessary for me to fly over. I want to be there but they seem to think they can do this without me. How can they say that? I'm the victim!'

'I imagine they'd love it if you weren't there,' I said.

'What do you mean?'

'Well, without you in their faces, they may have a better opportunity to cut a deal with the defence. And let's face it, the defence wouldn't want you anywhere near the courtroom if they could help it. The jury sees you and he's gone. You need to be there.'

'They're telling me they're saving me –'

'Undue stress and trauma?'

'How did you know?'

'That's one of their favourite lines. As a victim of crime, you have every right to attend, and you have a right to a support person. Explain to them that attending the trial is part of your healing process. You need to do this, for your recovery. You also need to do it to keep an eye on them, but we won't mention that.'

Gabby did fly over for the trial, with the DPP covering expenses. By this stage she had become very newsworthy. Involving the media in her case meant her profile had been built up significantly in the papers and on television, and VOCAL's Howard Brown was monitoring the case closely. All the services involved – the investigating officers, her DPP representatives, even her WAS officer – were working together. And Gabby's involvement significantly increased the chances of a good result.

Stephen Rae decided to plead guilty to maliciously causing grievous bodily harm with intent to murder. Gabby did not have to take the stand, due to a last-minute guilty plea. As she did not have this opportunity to be seen and heard by the judge, I helped her prepare a victim's impact statement.

On 23 December 1999, Stephen was sentenced to 19 years and eight months' imprisonment, with a minimum term of 14 years and nine months.

'It doesn't seem fair,' Gabby said later. 'My guy got almost 15 years. Yours got 15 months.'

'Gab, maybe your guy got 15 years *because* mine only got 15 months. In my case the services involved did the minimum. In your case they did the maximum.'

Two years later, I read a mention of what I assumed was Gabby's case in Nicholas Cowdery's book, *Getting Justice Wrong: Myths, Media and Crime*. The same man I'd written to over and over about my case – the Director of Public Prosecutions who'd claimed 'what's done can't be undone' – had detailed the disadvantages of bringing the victim back from the UK for the trial. He mentioned the 'unnecessary burden on the resources of the agencies involved', the 'great cost to the public' and the 'huge pain and discomfort' the victim would suffer.

In 2001, I wrote Mr Cowdery one more letter, drawing his attention to a hearing in the Court of Criminal Appeal on 12 December 2001. Stephen Rae was appealing against the severity of his sentence. I pointed out that this was not only causing the victim further stress and trauma, but it was also a waste of court time and resources, and therefore a financial burden to the community. Perhaps he would like to take an interest and give his personal support to the DPP representative assigned to this hearing?

I had only found out about the appeal by accident. *Reader's Digest* had written a story on Gabby and me but the researcher told me that they couldn't print it because the magazine's legal team had found out Stephen was appealing. I told Gabby and Howard. Howard, obviously surprised, contacted the DPP.

Gabby wasn't able to attend court for the appeal – she had been out here on a holiday but had flown back a few days before it was scheduled. Howard arranged for her to meet with the DPP beforehand.

'This won't be the same team, Gabby,' I warned her. 'You need to get these new people involved. They don't know you from Adam.'

'What will I say?'

'Howard will do the talking. But it's important they meet you, see you, get to know you. If they start to lose interest, peel off your cardigan, hitch up your skirt. Show them your scars. Let them imagine what it might be like to be in your skin.'

Our plan seemed to help. After meeting Gabby, the DPP representative said, 'I try not to get emotionally involved, but when I saw Gabby for the first time, my heart went out to her.'

I attended the hearing in Gabby's place, representing her as a victim of crime and a burns survivor. I sat in the public gallery, next to Howard, pleased at the puzzled looks from the offender in the dock and the judges. Did they mistake me for Gabby? I certainly hoped so. If anyone asked, I had my answer ready: 'Gabriella Mazzali? Oh goodness, no. I'm Donna Carson. Gabby's burns injuries are much more extensive than mine!'

As it turned out, Stephen Rae's appeal was dismissed and the judges gave the defence quite a lecture. Stephen leapt up and began to scream.

Howard leaned over. 'Oh, that'll be good when he comes up for parole. Must make a note of that.'

'So much for his anger management course.'

It was all back-slaps and smiles outside the courtroom. But something still worried me.

'Who's going to keep tabs on this guy? When he appeals again, who's going to inform Gabby?'

'He won't try again,' the DPP representative told me.

'You believe that, do you?' I said. 'We've all just heard how intelligent he is. Do you think he's going to be sitting around in jail twiddling his thumbs?'

There was a general assurance from the group that they would let Gabby know of any further appeals, if they happened, which they doubted.

In 2005, Stephen Rae appealed again. This time, Gabby was informed beforehand by the DPP through her WAS officer. When she told me, I told Howard Brown and the media. The *Daily Telegraph* placed a reporter in the courtroom.

The appeal was unsuccessful.

Postscript

As the world moved into the 21st century, my work with both burn survivors and victims of crime continued. It was a privilege to be invited into the lives of so many courageous Australians: Gloria Stock, a victim of the Kogarah gas explosion; Wingello firefighters Frank and Gale Pritchett; and Wendy van Buuren and her daughter Niki, badly burned in the Canberra bushfires of 2003.

My own protracted burns treatment had thankfully finished. There would be no more reconstructive surgery, physio or speech therapy. For me, the nightmare was finally over.

Emotionally I was healing too. With the settlement of my case against the Department of Community Services those deep-seated feelings of betrayal and injustice had begun to subside. I had new fixations though – doing whatever I could to help our nation's abused. Through volunteer work, magazine and newspaper articles, radio and television interviews and speaking engagements, I was reaching Australians from all walks of life, trying to shed light on the violence that lurked behind so many closed doors. As I see it, life has never been about what you *can't* do. It's what you *can* do that matters.

My hospital wish list now had a sequel. My first wish was for a one-stop shop where victims could access all services and receive the help required. It would have representatives from the Department of Housing, Community Health, Centrelink, Legal Aid and Court Support. A bewildering array of services was scattered throughout our towns, but to expect a traumatised victim to discover it all by themselves was neither ideal nor realistic.

My second wish was simple. I wanted every court to have a victims' safety room, where victims could wait in privacy, away from prying eyes and their offenders.

My third wish concerned women's refuges. Like other important public services, such as hospitals and police stations, women's refuges needed to be well signposted. Secret refuges lying low in suburbia made themselves far more of a target for offenders than emergency accommodation that declared its presence, its purposes and its methods of dealing with trespassers. The police generally avoided taking more extreme cases to refuges anyway, and the majority of women in refuges were hiding from abusers reluctant to bully in a public arena. Refuges that had 'come out' were an effective deterrent to the average abuser.

My final and most idealistic wish was for refuges not to be necessary at all: to remove the offender, not the victim. This already happens in so many spheres – the violent customer in the pub is sent away; the customers having a quiet drink are never made to leave the premises. And in many circumstances, police who attend a domestic violence incident have the power to arrange and enforce temporary removal of the offender. But, unless there's obvious physical assault, the victim often ends up gathering their things together, waking the children and shuffling them off to a strange place while the abuser stays in the family home.

I looked over my wish list. If only I could lay it like an offering at the feet of the nation …

The phone call came in December 2003. It was Bodean's 12th birthday. I had a house full of people, including Coe, who had moved back home. The lounge room was full of noise and laughter and I had to take the phone call in the spare bedroom.

'Donna? It's Warren Pearson from the National Australia Day Council. I've got you on speaker-phone. We have some good news.'

'Oh yes.' I was distracted by Mum's voice on the other side of the door, complaining that I was 'always on the bloody phone'.

'You've won! You've been chosen for Australian of the Year, Local Hero.'

'Yes, I know. Thank you so much. I've already received the award.'

There was laughter down the other end of the line. 'No, Donna. Not the New South Wales Regional. The big one – you've won the *national* title.'

For a moment I couldn't speak. 'You're kidding,' I said at last, tugging at the filigree heart around my neck. It was silver now; the gold had rubbed off years ago.

Mum was at the door. 'Hurry up! You do too much bloody work.'

'I'm sorry, Warren. I've got a house full of people. It's my son's birthday.'

'Okay, but you can't tell anyone. There will be a presentation in Canberra on Australia Day. You'll be attending, all expenses paid, of course. That's when your award will be announced and you'll get a chance to speak to the nation.'

'The nation!'

My wish list. If only I could lay it like an offering at the feet of the nation.

⁂

Taking my seat with my family among Canberra's Australia Day crowd, I gazed up at the stage, thinking about lives saved and lives lost. I was one of the lucky ones.

I was terrified as I moved up to the stage to receive my award from Prime Minister John Howard and made the mistake of looking out to the audience, a sea of wriggling people on the front lawn of Parliament House, stretching all the way back to the War Memorial.

The Prime Minister shook my hand and gave me a kiss on the cheek. I closed my eyes for a moment and stifled a nervous laugh. Did he know where they'd harvested that skin he'd just kissed? Ridiculously, it was all I could think about as I stood next to him, waiting to speak to an audience of millions. I was so out of breath from climbing the stairs and from nerves, I was afraid my voice would give out. I had been given 30 seconds. Half a minute wasn't long enough to impart my wish list to the nation. Terror aside, I wished I had longer. This, for the moment, would have to do.

I suffered burn injuries due to an act of crime called domestic violence. Let it be understood, there is nothing domestic about any type of violence.

Once a school teacher, I am now a volunteer and advocate for VOCAL with Robyn Cotterell-Jones and Burn Survivor Network, funded by KIDS Foundation, with Susie O'Neill – two brilliant organisations that value their volunteers and embrace the knowledge survivors have to give.

I would like to thank the many Australians who never gave up on me. My parents, sister, family, my beautiful sons Bodean and Coe, friends, colleagues, students, the communities of Dubbo, Taree and Wingham, and many dedicated professionals. Their commitment and love gave me life.

It's in their honour I will continue to serve, assisting others on their journey to survive, all the while reminding that it's up to us all to eliminate violence from our homes, schools and communities, joining together against this war of terror that rages in our own backyards.

On behalf of all survivors of crime and other tragedies, and in loving memory of those who did not survive – thank you, Australia.

Acknowledgments

To Debbie – I thank you for your skill, friendship and trust in following a dream. To Deb's family, particularly her son Pete, thanks for sharing her with me.

Many thanks to agent Pippa Masson at Curtis Brown and all at Hardie Grant – Emma Schwarcz, Megan Taylor, Fran Berry and Jenny Macmillan for your patience, Sandy Cull for your design, and Rod Morrison – you spoke with tears in your eyes at our first meeting, you cared for a stranger and that told me everything I needed to know about Hardie Grant and its people.

To my own family, thank you for being there when I needed you the most. To my light, my joy, Coe and Bodean, and my grandson Zane – you make it all worthwhile.

I am indebted to so many who believed in me – many mentioned in this book and so many not. Dear friends John and Shirley Heller, Gabby Mazzali, Mick and Meg Andrews, Mary Muller; colleagues Pam Harris, Nancy Lander, Kate Fowler, Helen and Julie Brown; Emergency Services; Careflight; the medical teams; Dr Zielinski; the media; service providers; survivors and their loved ones. I thank you and wish you – and the heroes I'm yet to meet – continuing strength, courage and spirit.

Donna Carson

To Donna and her family for sharing their past with such generosity and candour, and to various others who helped clarify technicalities and fill in the gaps.

To my agent, Pippa Masson, for making a dream come true.

To the wonderful team at Hardie Grant, particularly Rod Morrison for his warmth and enthusiasm, and editor par excellence, Emma Schwarcz, for her patience and professionalism.

To my mentor, Nick Bleszynski, for perceptive feedback and impromptu counselling, and for championing the cause.

To Barbara Taylor, for the title.

To my son, Pete, for putting up with his distracted and time-poor mother for the past two years, and to his father, Denne, for stepping into the breach again and again.

And to B.A.J. for making me laugh, even when I was determined not to.

Debbie Ritchie